Marie–Dominique CHENU, OP

Vatican II Notebook
A Council Journal
1962–1963

Critical Edition and Introduction
by Alberto Melloni

Translated by Paul Philibert, OP

The original edition in French with the title *Notes quotidiennes au Concile*, Marie-Dominique Chenu, © Les Éditions du Cerf, Paris, France, 1995.

ISBN: 9781925232325 (paperback)
ISBN: 9781925232318 (hardback)
ISBN: 9781925232332 (epub)
ISBN: 9781925232349 (pdf)

The cover photo of Fr Chneu was kindly provided by the Archives of the Dominican Province of France, thank to Fr Jean-Michel Potin, OP and Fr Régis Morelon, OP.

Cover design and Layout/Artwork by Astrid Sengkey
Text Minion Pro Size 11
Published by:

Making a lasting impact
www.atfpress.com

An imprint of the ATF Ltd.
PO Box 504
Hindmarsh, SA, 5007
Australia
ABN 90 116 359 963

Marie–Dominique CHENU, OP

Vatican II Notebook
A Council Journal
1962–1963

Critical Edition and Introduction
by Alberto Melloni

Translated by Paul Philibert, OP

ATF Theology
Adelaide
2015

Signs and Abbreviations

[1]	page number in the notebook manuscript: r° (recto), v° (verso)
[ ]	unreadable words or passages
< >	additions made by Fr Chenu
[ ]	guessing at the meaning
{ }	translator's notations

AS	Acta Synodalia
CESEP	The Redemptorist Library of São Paulo
CRThl	Cahiers de la Revue théologique de Louvain
CLG	Lumen Gentium Center at the University of Louvain–la–Neuve
CUA	Archives of the Catholic University of America, Washington, DC.
DAna	A Nicora Alberigo, Collaborazione al concilio: Diario, Archives of the ISR
DCcl	C Colombo, Diario (Dibattitu, Sottocommissioni), Faculty of Theology for Northern Italy, Milan
DSri	G Siri, Diario conciliare in B Lai, Il papa non eletto (Rome–Bari, 1993)
DTcc	R Tucci, Diario: Concilio Vaticano II, copy in the archives of ISR
DTrm	S Tromp, Diarium secretarii
DZzp	V Zazpe, Diario Conciliár, archives of the Archdiocese of Santa Fé
FGL	Vatican II Collection of the Library of the Theology Faculty of Louvain University
FHä	Häring Collection, Archives CSSR, Rome

FMcG   McGrath Collection, Notre Dame University, Indiana
ISR   Collection of the Instituto per le scienze religiose in Bologna
JCng   Y Congar, Mon journal du Concile (Paris), cited here as:
CgMJC   Congar, My Journal of the Council, translated by Mary John Ronanyne OP and Cecily Boulding OP (Adelaide, ATF, 2012)
JLbd   M Labourdette, "Souvenirs Ire Session," Toulouse
PUG   Archives of the Pontifical Gregorian University
SChn   Archives of Le Saulchoir (Paris), Chenu Collection: Concile Vatican II
Sedb   N Edelby, Souvenirs (Aleppo), Edelby Archives
ST   O Semmelroth, Tagebuch zum II. Vatikanischen Konzil, 1962–1965

{NB: In the notes within the journal, the citations are followed by the original language; references are to the original text.}

Table of Contents

Translator's Remarks

The decision of Alberto Melloni and his colleagues at the *Instituto per le scienze religiose* in Bologna to provide a critical edition of Chenu's *Vatican II Notebook* has offered scholars and general readers a document of great interest and critical significance. Melloni's scholarship weaves Chenu's experiences into a narrative that clearly changed the face of the Catholic Church for good. Melloni provides a stunning contrast of perspectives by comparing Chenu's vigorous initiatives with efforts of the Curia and of some leading Italian cardinals to stifle renewal. How did the forces of renewal win out over the power blocks of the Curia? That remains an enduring question. Chenu's *Notebook* helps to fill in the gaps by describing the climate in which the early struggles of Vatican II emerged.

The French Dominican Marie–Dominique Chenu was never a familiar name in the English–speaking Catholic world. Medievalists and students of St Thomas Aquinas knew him for his remarkable works on twelfth and thirteenth century philosophy and theology. As a scholar and professor, he was habitually inclined to look for theology's influence on the life of the world around him. In this journal he uses an expression that often appears in his writings: *la théologie en acte*—a phrase that is difficult to translate but that means essentially 'theology doing its thing—theology having an influence on what people think and do.' And that practical perspective shaped both his historical scholarship and his more popular pastoral writings.

After completing a doctorate in Rome in 1920 at the University of St Thomas Aquinas (referred to here as the Angelicum), he returned to his Province of France to teach at the Dominican study house known as *Le Saulchoir*, at that time exiled in Belgium. Chenu had brilliance, imagination, and an infectious personality. He was a genius at finding ways to say impossibly difficult things, if not easily, at least unforgettably. In the 1930s *Le Saulchoir* welcomed African seminarians as students, and its professors entered into dialogue with Canon Joseph Cardijn and the chaplains of the Young Christian Workers (a movement that was to have a wide influence in the French-speaking world until the 1960s).

As Le Saulchoir's director after 1932, Chenu shaped and guided a school of theology that promoted intellectual freedom and that took pastoral problems seriously. In 1937 he wrote a small book entitled *Le Saulchoir: A School of Theology* that described in detail the Paris Dominicans' study program in terms that look very much like an early draft of the future Council's *Pastoral Constitution on the Church in the Modern World*. It was not at all acceptable to the Vatican, and in 1942 Chenu's book (published only privately but known by word of mouth) was placed on the church's *Index of Forbidden Books*. Twenty years later, as Vatican II began, Chenu was still considered a dangerous man by the cardinals running the Roman Curia's congregations.

For his part, once exiled by the Vatican from *Le Saulchoir* (then situated in France), Chenu continued his research and writing, published several classic works on medieval theology, and became involved with France's most creative pastoral movements (worker priests, the 'social weeks', the Young Christian Worker movement, and the *Mission de France*). He possessed resilience and inspiration in equal measure.

When Pope John XXIII convoked the Second Vatican Council, a former African seminarian at *Le Saulchoir*, by then a bishop in Madagascar, asked Chenu to assist him at the Council as his personal theologian or *peritus* (expert). The journal here describes how Chenu, although not an official *peritus* of the Council, nonetheless threw himself into his service of his bishop sponsor and—whirlwind of ideas that he was—began to influence the Council fathers through lectures, assistance in drafting their interventions, and lobbying theologians and bishops for important changes and developments in the Council's agenda.

Although never officially a 'Council theologian', Chenu was the most important of the bishops' personal *periti*, in part because of his close connection to Yves Congar (who *was* an official *peritus* of the Council) and in part because he was well known through his writings to almost all of the theologians. Chenu kept modestly in the background and willingly allowed his ideas to have a life of their own in the hands of others who took them up and pursued them. Yet he was forceful in pursuing what he saw as important for the Council's success, such as his initiative for a *Message to the World* and his determined advocacy for placing an Eastern Catholic bishop on the Doctrinal Commission (detailed in the journal). He also persistently nurtured the uncertain beginnings of a schema on the problems of the modern world that would eventually become *Gaudium et Spes*.

Chenu lived to be ninety-five; he died in 1990 at the Priory of Saint-Jacques in Paris. His obituary in *Le Monde* observed that the Church owed him so much for the splendid vitality of his life and influence—more than it was ever willing to acknowledge. His *Vatican II Notebook* allows us to see him at his joyous, creative best.

Alberto Melloni's masterful work as a historiographer turns Chenu's brief notebook into a resource to illuminate crucial background developments of the Council's early days. Through Melloni's exhaustive comparison of complementary texts that confirm, amplify, or critique Chenu's descriptions, he provides us with a wealth of insight into what the experience of the Council felt like, both to major players in its work and to observers interested in the Council but not privy to its machinations. We owe Professor Melloni a deep expression of gratitude for this remarkable tribute to Chenu.

Chenu's journal was published in French in 1995 under the title *Notes quotidiennes au Concile* (Daily Jottings at the Council), but we have given it here the English title *Vatican II Notebook*, since the manuscript comes entirely from a single *cahier*, a notebook, that Chenu kept for his notations day by day for the first two years of the Second Vatican Council.

Paul Philibert, OP
Aquinas Instiutue of Theology
Saint Louis, Missouri

Introduction

Private Journals in the History of Vatican II

Research on the councils of the modern period pays a lot of attention to memoirs and private journals as historical sources.[1] Memoirs and personal journals, first of all, are often fascinating in a literary sense and have a flowing narrative style. Moreover, they characteristically have an 'I' telling the story, continuity in the writing, and faithful attention to the chronology of events. They have great historical–critical importance not only because they record minor facts, secret events, private matters, and confidential reactions that would otherwise be ignored or lost by researchers, but also for their 'literary' quality. What makes them valuable and indispensible for research is that they offer an analysis that emerges from inside the atmosphere of the assembly engaged in the council.

If all of the official documents are needed to reconstruct how decisions were made, so also are newspapers and, among others, reports in the first person that are irreplaceable for the history of a council, especially a 'modern' council that has not been convoked to defend the faith or to promulgate papal decrees.[2]

---

1. I frequently make reference to the Vatican II collections held in Bologna at the *Instituto per le scienze religose* (ISR), at the *Lumen Gentium* Center in Louvain-la-Neuve (CLG), at the Library of the Faculty of Theology of Louvain (FGL), in the archives of the Pontifical Gregorian University (PUG), in the archives of the Catholic University of America in Washington (CUA), and at the Redemptorist Library of São Paulo (CESEP).
2. See HJ Sieben, *Die Konzilsidee des lateinischen Mittelalters* (Paderborn, 1984), as well as *Traktate und Theorien zum Konzil: Vom Beginn des Grossen Schismas bis zum Vorabend der Reformation (1378–1521)* (Frankfurt, 1983); *Die katholische Konzilsidee von der Reformation bis zu Aufklärung* (Paderborn, 1988); *Die katholische Konzilsidee im 19. und 20. Jahrhundert* (Paderborn–Munich–Vien-

Researchers cannot ignore the subjective accounts that are accessible to them as they create a critical reconstruction of what happened. The conviction that this subjective element is needed to assess the complex characteristics of the assembly is now an accepted part of historical research on the councils.

Clearly without the council diary of Cardinal Filâtre we would not have a complete picture of the events at the Council of Constance.[3] Likewise, specialists on the Council of Basel are familiar with the edition of the *Tagebuchaufzeichnungen* [day by day accounts] (printed in Basel in 1904 by G Beckmann, R Wackernagel and G Coggiola) relating to 1431-1438, as well as the (unsigned) journal of Andrea Gatari.[4] We also know the importance of the Ἀπομνημονευματον by Sylverster Syropoulos for studying the Council of Florence from 1438-1439, published in a critical edition by V Laurent (Paris, 1971). In addition, since 1951, G Hoffmann, editor of the series *Concilium Forentinum*, has consecrated part of the fascicle III-II to private journals alongside those written as acts of the notaries. That is where we find the journal of Geminiano Inghirami, already taking part at Constance, and that of Andrea da Santacroce, the consistorial lawyer. But it is above all S Merkle who points out the importance of this source in his Introduction to the first volume of the series *Concilium Tridentinum*, which opens with journals. Merkle does this with an apologetic aim: if the enemies of the Roman Curia should accuse the conciliar acts of bias, thanks to the journals *'vera et integra eius [concilii] historia hauriatur'* [a true and complete history of the council may be drawn up].[5]

This idea opened the way for the publication of the journals of Ercole Severoli, Angelo Massarelli, Ludovico Bondoni de' Branchi Firmani, Onofrio Panvini, Antonio Guidi, Lorenzo Pratani, Girolamo Seripando, Pedro Gonçales de Mendoça, Nicola Psalmei (fragmentary), Giovanni Ficleri, Gabriele Paleotti, Aristolfo Servanti, Filippo Misotti, all the way down to the *Libro originale delle spese* by Antonio Manelli that U Mazzone published in 1985, the last volume in the collection devoted to this literary genre.[6]

---

na–Zurich, 1993).

3. Published in *Acta concilii Constantiniensis*, II (Münster, 1896-1928).
4. Wackernagel translated it himself in 1885; Gatari was perhaps also the author of a chronicle edited by Muratori.
5. CT (*Concilium Tridentinum*) 1/1, XXXIV.
6. Already in his Introduction to volume one, Merkle raised the question of exactly

It is characteristic of the two Vatican Councils that journals as sources of information were left in the shadows when the official acts were published. As late as 1960, at the international meeting on the history of the church held on the occasion of the Eleventh International Congress of Historical Sciences, Roger Aubert complained that the journals concerning Vatican I had not been collected and published.[7] A bit later, U Betti happened to learn of the existence of the 'journal' of the First Vatican Council by Bishop Giulio Arrigoni. As we know, this manuscript, offered to John XXIII as a gift, was handed over to M Maccarrone who published it in 1966. Meanwhile L Dehon's *Diario del Concilio Vatican I*, was published in Rome in 1962. Then J Hennesey showed that private journals could be used as important sources, particularly the journals of Archbishop FN Blanchet of Oregon City,[8] of the Sulpician Superior General H Icard,[9] and of A du Boÿs.[10] Other publications have followed down to the recent publication by G Croce of Vincenzo Tizzani's journal.[11]

THE FORGOTTEN JOURNALS OF VATICAN II

Even though Aubert's pleading seems to have been useful in making known the journals about Vatican I, the journals of Vatican II are still too little used as a source. In my view this justifies and confirms the

---

how to define this literary genre, and he struck from his list some works that are in fact repetitions of other accounts or summaries of the acts without any original material.

7. However, some journals had been published, like that of J Friedrich's *Tagebuch während des Vatikanischen Konzils* (Nordlingen, 1873) that disputed Pius IX's choice to call the council Vatican I.

8. J Hennesey, *The First Council of the Vatican: The American Experience* (New York, 1963), 27.

9. Hennesey, 29.

10. See Hennesey, 46, concerning the *Souvenirs* of this French layman (published in Louvain in 1968 by J. Gadille); he was a confidant of Dupanloup, who also wrote a journal (ibid., 63), *Journal intime de Mgr Dupanloup évêque d'Orléans* (Paris, 1902—edited by L. Branchereau).

11. GM Croce, 'Una fonte importante per la storia del Pontificato di Pio IX e del Concilio Vaticano I: I manoscritti inediti di Vincenzo Tizzani', *Archivum Historiae Pontificiae*, 23 (1985), 217–345; 24 (1986), 372–75; 25 (1987), 263–364 (index at 310). Following this there appeared V Tizzani, *Il Concilio Vaticano I: diario di Vincenzo Tizzani* (1869–70), 2 volumes (Stuttgart, 1991–2).

impression that research on doctrinal analysis of the council's texts is highly developed, while analysis of works by those in the assembly has not really matured.[12] Two different but related phenomena have reinforced this unfortunate tendency.

The first has to do with the publication of the documents of Vatican II undertaken by the Holy See itself—a publishing endeavor for which Paul VI personally guaranteed that privileged place be given to papers from the council and set up distinct archives collected and directed by the *Archivo Segreto Vaticano*. Although they were published just after Roger Aubert's call for the publication of journals in 1960, the *Acta Synodalia* have only included the pure and simple publication of the papers of the General Secretariat, a unique and important documentary source gathered and introduced into the *Archivo du Concilio Vaticano II*.[13] Thanks to the constant and indefatigable work of Vincenzo Carbone, everything coming from Cardinal Felici concerning the aula, including the publication of the council minutes from the Commissions sent to the General Secretary, has now been published.

Today it is clear that the credibility of these sources needs to be re-evaluated since, even with the most scrupulous care, the quality of the historical information is always less satisfactory as more and more papers become accessible that are not the product of those small Roman circles that were closed in on themselves. The new papers provide an echo of the work of an assembly that was multilingual, international, diverse and very large. On the other hand, for a long time the 'objective' criterion adopted by the acts of the council made questionable the need to give proper attention to letters and journals. As a result, we lost track of the evolution of some important events.[14]

---

12. See G Alberigo, 'Criteria ermeneutici per la storia del Vaticano II' in G.Alberigo (editor), *Il Vaticano II fra attese e celebrazione* (Bologna, 1995), 9–26.
13. The conciliar section of the Ex-Secretariat for Christian Unity has recently been added. For the nature of these collections, see V Carbone, 'Genesi e criteri della pubblicazione degli Atti del Concilio Vaticano II', *Archiva Ecclesiae* 34–5 (1991–2), 57–67.
14. Take for example the striking case of the minutes of the Secretariat for Extraordinary Affairs (*de negotiis extra ordinem*), the entity in charge of everything outside the ordinary schedule. In the troubled weeks at the start of the Council, the Secretary of State sought to control what was going on in competition with the Holy Office and with the Secretary General Mgr Felici (who didn't even receive the minutes of this entity). The *Acta Synodalia* clearly denied the existence of

The second phenomenon that explains this critical neglect of sources is linked to the council itself. The publication of journals and memoirs, even during the council sessions and just after the council that tried to shape public opinion,[15] cast a shadow over the more serious journals. Of course, it often happened that the ones that got published were really abridged versions of the journals themselves,[16] perhaps purged of malicious comments, but also stripped of their militant position in the debates. Finally they were not scrupulous in scientifically verifying their sources. There was a forest of books that critically eclipsed the manuscripts. For example, for the first session alone there were several dozen representing very different roles relative to the council. Many journalists for newspapers and magazines all over the world immediately published in 1963 collections of their articles with anecdotes and profiles of persons at the council mixed in. René Laurentin, Xavier Rynne, Raniero La Valle, José L Martin Descalzo, Antoine Wenger, Bonaventura Kloppenburg, Dolcino Favi, and von Galli were the quickest in creating books out of their journalistic work.[17] Some, like Ettore Masina, did little

such minutes, although today eight sets of minutes are found in the papers of Siri in the appendix to Benny Lai, *Il papa non eletto: Giuseppe Siri cardinal di Santa Romana Chiesa* (Rome–Bari, 1993), 348–55.

15. See reflections on this in A. Melloni, 'Lo spettatore influente: Reviste et informazione religiosa nella preparazione del Vaticano II (1959–1962)' in G Alberigo (editor), *Il Vaticano II fra attese e celebrazione*, 119–191.

16. We will have to briefly examine such journals because they too can help us untie the critical knot that we have to open up. Journals can no longer have the affirmative function with regard to the *Acta* of Vatican II that Merkle assigned to them in the historiography of Trent, nor can they be limited to filling in the relation between the Pope and the assembly as for Vatican I. In cognitive terms, the enduring function of the journals (once they have been identified, classified, and if possible edited) is to make researchers aware of the complexity of the factors at play, from the creation of unforeseen partnerships within the assembly and of cooperative actions that fill in gaps, to the formation of a common opinion through a great variety of channels—in brief, they open up the history of the council *as* a council.

17. See R Laurentin, *L'Enjeu du Concile II: Bilan de la première session* (Paris, March 1962—followed by three other volumes until 1965); X Rynne, *Letters from Vatican City: Vatican Council II (First Session): Background and Debates*, volume 1 (London, 1963); JL Martin Descalzo, *Un periodista en el Concilio: 1 Etapa* (Madrid, 1963–1965 [2]); A Wenger, *Vatican II: Première session* (Paris, 1963—followed by three other volumes until 1965); B Kloppenburg, *Concilio Vaticano II: Primera sessão (set.–dez. 1962)* (Petropolis, 1963) (4); D Favi, *Vaticano II: Cro-*

more than prepare a typewritten text.[18] Others were active in several contexts, like Y–M Congar who in his *Vatican II, le council au jour le jour*[19] put forth his views as the journalists did; but in fact Congar is a much respected and informed theologian involved in all the circles where the possibilities and the future of the council were under discussion. Moreover, he was also writing (we will come back to this) a large journal; that begins with his being named as a consulter of the preparatory Theological Commission in 1961.[20] In this case, we have

---

naca della I sessione (Vicenza, 1963) (10) (with an appendix about *De revelatione* by Rahner!). The series of 'Briefen aus Rom' from *Orientierung* appears in M von Galli and B Moosbrugger, *Das Konzil: Chronik der ersten Session—Ein Bild-und Textbuch* (Mainz, 1963); *Das Konzil: Von Johannes XXIII zu Paul VI: Chronik der zweiten Session-Die Pilgerfahrt ins Heilige Land—Zweites Bild-und Textbuch* (Mainz, 1964); *Das Konzil: Dritter Text—und Bildbericht* (Mainz, 1965); *Das Konzil und seine Folge* (Lucerne, 1966). The work of W Kampe, *Das Konzil im Spiegel der Presse*, I (Wurzburg, 1963) is different in its aim of reviewing the offerings of the international press for German readers; the *Centrum informationis catholicum* collects documents in W Seibel and LA Dorn, *Tagebuch des Konzils: Die Arbeit der zweiten Session* (Nüremberg–Eichstätt, 1964) (3). R La Valle began to collect his editorials in *L'Avvenire d'Italia* beginning with the second session (*Il coraggio del concilio* [Brescia, 1964], followed by two volumes in 1965 and 1966 on the third and fourth sessions). The collections published after the end of the Council that often bring together articles from daily papers are less interesting, since they have a perspective that is colored by the Council's success. Examples include *Council Daybook—Vatican II: Session I, Oct. 11 to Dec. 8, 1962; Session 2, Sept. 29 to Dec. 4, 1963*, edited by Floyd Anderson (Washington, 1965); H Fesquet, *Journal du Concile* (Paris, 1966); Ch Reymond and L Richard, *Vatican II au travail: Méthode conciliaire et documents*, translated from the German (Paris, 1965); RM Wiltgen, *The Rhine Flows into the Tiber* (New York, 1967); GF Svidercoschi, *Storia del Concilio* (Milan, 1967); G Vallquist, *Dagbok fran Rom: Journalistminnen fran Vatikankonciliet* (Stockholm, 1964); DA Seeber, *Das II. Vaticanum: Konzil des Überganges* (Freiburg, 1966).

18. There is a copy at ISR.
19. Volume I (Paris, January 1963).
20. For Congar also, however, his accounts in *Le Concile au jour le jour* was his way of putting into circulation ideas that he hoped the Coordinating Commission (the group that would oversee the reorganization of the Council's themes to be taken up in the first half of 1963 between the first and the second session) would take into account. In the same perspective B Häring wrote *Das Konzil im Zeichen der Einheit* (Freiburg, 1963). Just as the journalists did, some of the Council's protagonists waited until after the Council to publish selections of their memoirs; see, for example, the volume by the Secretary General P Felici (*Il lungo cammino del concilio* [Milan, 1967]) or that of Cardinal A Bea (*Der Ökumenismus im Konzil*, Freiburg, 1967).

an echo of the council's proceedings that is less passive than what the bishops characteristically described in their pastoral letters.[21]

The memoirs of the non–Catholic observers present at Vatican II provide yet another very different perspective. In considering only the period of the council itself, many representatives of the churches invited to take part formulated their impressions right away in books: Kurt Viktor Selge, Max Lackmann, George Richard–Molard, Douglas Horton, and Robert McAfee Brown are among those who published such works for which it is difficult to imagine that there was not a private journal as background material.[22]

These two phenomena—the archival instinct for one, and the existence of published journals for the other—partially explain, I think, why actual journals of the council were neglected—journals without which libraries full of commentaries could be written, but not the real history of Vatican II.

A TYPOLOGY OF VATICAN II JOURNALS

Happily for the cause of research, many journals and memoirs related to the council not only still exist (most often in good condition), but they are now well known and accessible either because of the initiative of individual scholars or because of the research of the international group on the history of Vatican II under the direction of G Alberigo and the Institute for Religious Sciences in Bologna.[23] The work of Philippe Levillain, *La Mécanique politique au Vatican II*, that used a confidential summary (or transcription) of Henri de Lubac's

---

21. See the list of available collections in many countries cited in D Menozzi, his 'Introduzione' in *Repertorio delle lettere pastorali dei vescovi dell'Emilia–Romagna in età contemporanea* (Genoa, 1988).

22. See M Lackmann, *Mit evangelischen Augen: Beobachtungen eines Lutheraners auf dem Zweiten Vatikanischen Konzil* (Graz, 1963); G Richard–Molard, *Un pasteur au Concile* (Paris, May 1964); D Horton, *Vatican Diary 1962: A Protestant Observes the First Session of Vatican Council II* (Philadelphia–Boston, 1964); R McAfee Brown, *Observer in Rome: A Protestant Report on the Vatican Council* (New York, 1964); KV Selge, *Evangelischer Bericht vom Konzil: Erste Session* (Göttingen, 1965).

23. See J Famerée, 'Vers une histoire de Vatican II,' *Revue d'histoire ecclésiastique* 89 (1994), 622–42.

journal,[24] belongs in the first category. An analogous procedure (tacit and unacknowledged) was used by Monsignor Gérard Philips (one of the protagonists of Vatican II) who used in his 'Notes to contribute to the history of the *Nota explicative praevia*' one of his own manuscript notebooks composed irregularly between 1963 and 1969.[25]

In the course of advancing the project for a history of Vatican II, thanks to many efforts to find local sources and to a climate of confidentiality that was able to be created, dozens and dozens of journals that have not yet been utilised came to light, and they now allow us to make a preliminary classification.

Personal Journals that Include the Council

Some of the participants at Vatican II were already keeping a journal before the announcement of the council's convocation, and their notebooks are an important critical resource for the history of the council. The range of narrative perspectives on different events allows for a precise evaluation of the point of view, the mentality, or simply the literary connotations of each writer.

The double journal of John XXIII is like that. It is double because it is composed on the one hand of spiritual jottings begun by the young clergyman from Bergamo: during his seminary days in Rome he entitled it *The Journal of a Soul.*[26] On the other hand it was made up of irregular and occasional notes concerning his daily encounters between 1904 and 1925, but then becoming regular and daily when they treat the matters that Roncalli had to deal with between 1935 and 1963.[27] These notes, often only descriptive and limited to an

---

24. Today in the keeping of the friends of Henri de Lubac in Paris and possibly held as a copy by the same researcher who used it tacitly as a source in Ph Levillain, *Le Mécanique politique de Vatican II: La majorité et l'unanimité dans un Concile* (Paris, 1975).
25. This journal is contained in two handwritten notebooks kept by the Philips family: Cahier XI (30 f⁰ numbered in pencil), April 8, 1963–June 2, 1963; Cahier XII (66 fᵒ): 14 November 1963–20 June 1969. Mgr Leo Declerck in Bruges and Jan Grootaers in Brussels have a photocopy of mediocre quality that is not available to the public.
26. AG Roncalli–John XXIII, *Il Giornale dell'Anima*, critical edition with notes by Alberto Melloni (Bologna ISR, 1987), 802.
27. The original is found in the papers of Paul VI at ASV; there is a copy at AR–ISR.

account of conversations during the day (possibly as a help for his diplomatic work), nonetheless furnish precious clues as to the climate of something like the Council where every encounter—even with the pope—became briefer and more 'invisible' from the point of view of documentation.

Notes like those of Roncalli have parallels with other council participants. Domenico Tardini wrote similar notations with a caustic sense of humor in a journal that treats what he wrote during the war and pages dealing with John XXIII's decision to convoke a Council.[28] Loris F Capovilla, personal secretary of the Pope and his assistant, also kept a daily notebook.[29] Finally, we find a particular kind of journal—also a source concerning the council's preparation—kept by Roberto Tucci, SJ, one of the rare persons for whom John XXIII felt both esteem and trust. Tucci collected the remarks that the Pope made to him. These notes converge with others, first in the *Cronache* signed G Caprile, then in a dossier of memoirs that form a block of evidence that is very valuable for the history of the pontificate as well as for the history of Vatican II.[30]

Some local bishops and theologians also kept journals treating the preparations for the Council.[31] In Italy, this was the case of Ermenigildo Florit, an important cardinal and a member of the Theological Commission. His notes are useful in reconstituting the details and the atmosphere of this key preparatory organ.[32] Domenico Bertetto, a Salesian theologian, consulter for the Preparatory Commission, kept a journal of spiritual thoughts in which there are occasional allusions to the council.[33] In Catalonia, Cardinal Albareda left to the Monastery

28. John XXIII had spoken to Tardini about it in an audience of 27 January 1959; Mgr Felici made an allusion to it in a conference (see *Osservatore Romano*, 30 September 1962); the text of the agenda was edited by Mgr Samore on 7 July 1964, in a conference held at the Circolo di Roma (see *Osservatore Romano*, 16 July 1964). For the journal entries for 1933–36, see C. Casula, Domenico Tardini (1888–1961), *L'azione della Santa Sede nella crisi fra le due guerre* (Rome, 1988), 291–390.
29. Held by the author in Camaitino, Berganza.
30. A copy is held by ISR.
31. This information was brought out by MT Fattori, 'Fonti italiane per la storia del Vaticano II', in *Revista di storia della chiesa in Italia*, 49 (1995/1): 1–23.
32. E Florit, 'Diario', (Florence—Archives of the archdiocese).
33. In the archives of the Salesian Faculty of Theology in Rome; I am grateful to

of Montserrat his journal that covers with bland detachment Vatican II and its preparation, but it is augmented by a 'parallel' journal done by his secretary, Fr Alexander Olivar.[34]

Let's not forget either the diplomatic journals of a classic type that contain some interesting references to the Council.[35] In this regard, the journal of the Italian ambassador to the Holy See, Bartolomeo Mignone, is important because it has interesting information about the moments leading up to the Council and it contains moreover confidential remarks from the Pope.[36]

The Council also figures in memoirs—some published—that do not focus on the Council as such. The souvenirs of Christophe Dumont, published in 1967, devote some space to the Council. Other published memoirs include those of Hubert Jedin, Suenens, Henri

---

Professors Stella and Semeraro for pointing this out to me.

34. In the Archives of Montserrat, Barcelona; see H Raguer, *Fuentes para la historia del Vaticano II: España*; J Grootaers and C Soetens (editors), *Sources locales de Vatican II: Symposium Leuven–Louvain-la-Neuve 23-X-1989*, 89.

35. Another example is a journal of the Spanish Ambassador, F Gomez de Llano; furthermore, see the principal characters in GF Pompei, *Un ambasciatore in Vaticano: Diario 1969-77* (Bologna, 1995).

36. *Concerning the Council*: Mgr Felici doesn't speak foreign languages. [The Pope said that] he doesn't know them. He was suggested to him. He tells the story of the Italian Secretary General of Vatican I who had to be replaced by an Austrian (he was the only one who supported the Pope). *Concerning the great number of experts at the Council,* he says that he was advised to let them come because there would be ample means to keep them from speaking. But on the contrary, the Pope wanted complete freedom of discussion; '*Quaerite primum regnum Dei et haec omnia*'-the theme of the address on 11 October [;] should I change it? [...] Among the difficulties at the Council, the greatest is that between the old partisans of the status quo, as if the world had not changed, and the young who want to change everything as if the world began with them [...] Some wanted to exclude the great number of experts, but the Pope said, 'No, on the contrary...' Edited by A Melloni, 'Governi e diplomazie all'annuncio del Vaticano II' in M Lamberigts and Cl Soetens (editors), *À la veille du concile Vatican II: 'Vota' et réactions en Europe et dans le catholicisme oriental* (Louvain, 1992), 214-257. The journal of Mignone is being edited by G Miccoli and GG Migone.

de Lubac, and Visser't Hooft.[37] It is likely that among these published accounts a journal in the strict sense was source material.[38]

Journals About the Preparation

Alongside journals and memoirs that considered the conciliar events, there are those that started with the preparation of the Council and which continue, with differing regularity, during Vatican II itself.

Professors at the Gregorian University, some of whom played an almost controlling role in the preparations, wrote notebooks about daily events that give the sense of the context of the commissions' structures. Sebastian Tromp, SJ, secretary of the Preparatory Theological Commission and of the Doctrinal Commission of the Council, wrote about facts and impressions in a sober Latin text.[39] His *Diarium secretarii* is a kind of verbal picture dominated by his scrupulous wish to account for what was going on at every moment. That type of committed and conscientious account of the preparatory work was not limited to this Dutch ecclesiologist. We know that there was a journal kept by Fr Hurth, another theologian from the Gregorian University, as well as the *Journal Jarlot*—and we need to add other theologians, both Roman and not, to the list.

For example, the rare non–Roman theologians involved in the preparatory work took notes *pro memoria*: from the USA, Joseph Fenton,[40] John F Dearden,[41] George Tavard, AA;[42] from Innsbruck,

---

37. See CJ Dumont *(Chemin faisant vers l'unité)*. *L'Église catholique romaine et le movement oecuménique: Souvenirs d'un pionnier (1925–1965)* (Paris, ds. 1967, Istina); H Jedin, *Lebensbericht*, edited by K Repgen (Mainz, 1984); H de Lubac, *Mémoire à l'occasion de mes écrits* (Namur, 1989); LJ Suenens, *Souvenirs et espérances* (Paris, 1991); WA Visser't Hooft, *Memoirs* (London, 1973). See also *Dialogue avec le patriarche Athénagoras*, edited by O Clément (Paris, 1969).
38. There is a manuscript in Aix-la-Chapelle by Heribert Schauf who was first a consultor for the Preparatory Theological Commission, then a *peritus* at the Council, but its literary genre is not yet clear nor its extent; but it certainly is concerned with the Council.
39. Kept in the archives of the PUG.
40. CUA: Joseph Komonchak is working on this journal.
41. His papers, gathered in Detroit, are now held by the Cushwa Center at Notre Dame University.
42. Tavard held on to his papers himself at Marquette University (Milwaukee).

there is the journal of the Jesuit liturgist Joseph A Jungmann;[43] and in Barcelona, there is the journal of Bonet i Muixi, member of the preparatory Liturgical Commission and then, during the Council, editor of a rather well known circular describing the Council's activities and debates.[44]

The Dominican Y–M Congar opens his journal at the moment of his nomination as a consulter for the preparatory Theological Commission, giving a broad retrospective look at its preparation. Y–M Congar did not have a particular institutional audience in mind. By formation as well as by culture he knew that he was writing something for the future. He is therefore precise in what he writes, often rechecking and correcting his text. He completes his text with explanatory notes and scrupulous additions that are clearly not meant for some immediate re–use by the author, but are for the sake of the future and of readers in times to come.[45]

These are certainly not the only journals treating the Council's preparation. There are indications and hints of several others that have not yet surfaced. This allows us to imagine from a heuristic perspective that it is not wrong to imagine until proved otherwise that there might be a journal for each person involved in the preparation.

Journals of the Council

If during the preparatory period so many people involved in that work took time to take notes, the opening of the council 'impressed' an even greater number of journalists, theologians, and council fathers with the need to keep a journal. From East and West, from North and South, religious and diocesan priests, ambassadors, journalists, pastors or bishops—many took up keeping a journal[46] with no

---

43. A copy of the transcription made by R Pacik is held at the ISR.
44. At the Benedictine Nuns' Monastery in Barcelona; F Vergès, chaplain to the nuns, is keeping it.
45. ASch has the original, and there are copies at CLG and at ISR: Cardinal Congar himself confirmed in several conversations that his journal could be published in its entirety after the year 2000; moreover, he gave a copy of it to ISR with the understanding that it could be used in partial citations for the project of the history of Vatican II.
46. MT Fattori's systematic exploration of Italian diocesan archives has had remarkable results: the diocesan archives in Iglesias have the journal of Giovanni Piras–

other ambition or role than that of simple members of the conciliar assembly or witnesses to the event.

'Pro memoria' Documents

Journals of the *pro memoria sua* type are reflections of the impressions and concerns of an individual type, for example: the bishop of Prienne, Jacques Le Cordier; the auxiliary bishop of Namur, Jean Baptiste Musty[47]; the Spaniard Josep Pont i Gol,[48] the Salvatorian Giovanni Gazza, prelate *nullius* of the Abaeté do Tocantins in Brazil[49]; the bishop of Lucca, Enrico Bartoletti[50]; all the way to the extraordinary bishop of Belém do Para who kept his journal in the form of cartoons.[51]

Some give their notes more a tone of the collective memory of a group or of a particular milieu. That is the case with the journal of Nephytos Edelby that reflects what the Melkite Church lived through at Vatican II[52]; or the journal of Vicente Zazpe,[53] the bishop of Rafaela, a key figure in a complex and litigious group from Argentina. It is

tru, those in Modena the journal of Mario Bergonzini, those of the Friary of Saint Francis in Gubbio the journal of Vittorio Maria Constantini, the bishop of Sessa Aurunca. Fattori (*Per una mappa*) provides information about the current state of these finds. Several researchers have alluded to a journal of Liénart in Lille that they haven't yet seen; the same for Emilio Guano (held in Irribarreu), and for O Rousseau.

47. JB Musty, 'Notes sur le concile oecuménique Vatican II', Louvain-la-Neuve, CLG.

48. Bishop of Segorbe–Castillon de la Plana, whose journal was placed in the archives of the monastery of Montserrat by A Deig, the bishop of Solsona; J Famerée stresses its importance: 'Instruments et perspectives pour une histoire du Concile Vatican II' in M Lamberigts and C Soetens (editors) *À la veille du concile Vatican II: 'Vota' et réactions en Europe et dans le catholicisme oriental*, 263.

49. He holds on to the journal himself in Parma; see LJ Barauna, 'Fondo Vaticano II en Brasil' in JO Beozzo, *Cristianismo e Iglesias de América latina en visperas del Vaticano II* (San José, Costa Rica, 1992), 41 n.16.

50. 'Agenda', held at Viareggio by his former secretary; M Toschi told me about this.

51. Alberto Gaudencio Ramos; kept in the CSSR Library (São Paulo). A journal through letters of Adelmo Machado, archbishop of Marció–Algoas (Brazil), has been published (Adelmo Machado, *Vivendo o Concilio*, edited by MH de Melo Santa).

52. Riccardo Cannelli is working on editing it (to appear in an Italian translation, Cinisello B., 1995).

53. Copy at ISR; Loris Zanatta is working on it.

true as well for the journal of the bishop of Kabgayi in Ruanda, André Perraudin, who was active among the missionaries at the council.[54] The journal of Helder Camara, that he addressed to his diocesan collaborators in Brazil, is a genuine journal in epistolary form: the frequency of the entries and their precise details make it clear that this is not a collection of letters, but a document destined to be collected as a memorial to be read as a whole.[55]

The Leaders

The journals of the key leaders of the conciliar entities naturally have their personal qualities, but they delve directly into the activities of those entities and the major decisions that the conciliar assembly arrived at.

I think of the journal of Julius Döpfner, archbishop of Munich and a member of the group of moderators. His manuscript notes, while in general dry and concise, not only bring color to the events, but above all furnish indispensible details that clarify crucial moments at Vatican II.[56] I think also of the epistolary journal of Giacomo Lercaro, also in the circle of moderators,[57] who each day informed the young people who lived with him in Bologna—the *cinni*—of the developments and the tensions within the assembly.[58]

Similarly valuable is the journal of the Canadian Cardinal Paul–Émile Léger, another important figure on the Coordinating Committee and in the conciliar assembly.[59]

---

54. A Perraudin, 'Deuxième concile du Vatican: Note personnelles', CLG.
55. LC Marques has taken on the work of a critical edition of Camara. Likewise, Antonio Santin, the bishop of Trieste, sent letters to his diocesan weekly *Vita Nuova* and these have been collected as 'Atmosfera e impressioni di mons. Antonio Santin vescovo–arcivescovo di Trieste e Capodistria', Diocesan Archives of Trieste.
56. G Alberigo is using this journal and shows its importance in 'Concilio acefalo? L'evoluzione degli organi direttivi del concilio Vaticano II' in *Il Vaticano II fra attese e celebrazione*, 193–238.
57. There is some kind of journal by Suenens which won't be made public before the cardinal's death; concerning the papers of Agagianian that are in the Armenian College in Rome, we don't have precise details.
58. G Lercaro, *Lettere dal concilio 1962–1965*, edited by G Battelli (Bologna, 1980).
59. See P Lafontaine, *Inventaire des archives conciliaires du Fonds Paul–Émile Léger* (Montreal, 1995).

On the other hand, we don't know anything about the journal of the Secretary General of the Council, Pericle Felici; it is held, some say, by Vincenzo Fagiolo, his close collaborator from the time of the preparatory phase.

With regard to the great bishops, the recent discovery of the council journal of Cardinal Urbani is highly significant for studying the participation of the Italians and their interactions at the Council.[60]

The archbishop of Mainz, Volk, is a leader *sui generis*. His notebooks, still being put into form, will give us important information about the circle of theologians that he set up and organised around himself.[61]

The journals of important members of the Council's minority are already edited, at least partially; for example: the journal of Alfredo Ottaviani, Secretary of the Holy Office, has already been used for some postconciliar studies.[62] Recently the notes, particularly emotional but only irregularly kept, of Cardinal Siri have been edited.[63] He was the leader of the Italian episcopate and a member of the crucial secretariat for affairs *extra ordinem*.[64]

The Theologians

The relationships and contacts that shaped the work of the commissions behind the scene are easier to understand thanks to the journals of theologians. Among these, the journals of Congar (already mentioned) and of Otto Semmelroth, an influential Jesuit from Frankfurt, are distinctive for the richness and extent of the information they contain. They took notes every day about all the personal encounters, meetings, and editing sessions that they were involved in or that they heard about.[65]

---

60. The Urbani family has a copy in Venice; G Turbanti is making a transcription of it.
61. Mainz: Archives of the archdiocese.
62. E Cavaterra, *Il prefetto del Sant'Offizio* (Milan, 1990).
63. Recently published by Lai, *Il papa non eletto*.
64. This source is fundamental for following not only the ideas of an important Italian cardinal, but also the activities of this secretariat. Stephan Wyszynski, the primate of Poland, is also a member: his journal—limited to the parts concerning his contacts with John XXIII—has been edited; see S Wyszynski, 'Byl Czlowik oslany od Boga, a Jan mu bylo na imie', in B Bejze, B Dziwosza and W Ziolka (editors), *Jan XXIII i jego dzielo: Praca zbiorowa* (Warsaw, 1972), 41–156.
65. Semmelroth's journal is in Cologne at the archives of the Jesuit Province of West

Even rather brief journals—Michel Labourdette, OP, stopped after the first session;[66] Marie-Dominique Chenu, OP, before the end of the second session—clear up some essential moments of the Council's unfolding. In general, theologians had a greater mobility and were more active than the bishops, and their manuscripts allow us to reconstruct not only what happened at the Council, but also the critical work of the conciliar commissions and private working groups.

With regard to the 'Belgian team,' we have now the notes of Albert Prignon, Rector of the Belgian College in Rome[67] and of the important *periti* Gustave Thils[68] and Charles Moeller.[69] Moeller's rich 'notebooks' include not only conciliar events, but in a more general way his own work as a theologian and ecumenist. There is the journal of Jacques Dupont, the exegete who was also the attentive and diligent corrector of scriptural references in the schemas on ecclesiology.[70] And finally the journal of Bernard Olivier, OP, that concerns only the second and fourth sessions.[71]

For the American context, this role is filled by the journals of James H Griffiths[72] and of Joseph Fenton (already mentioned). Of a different type, the memoirs of Schema XIII, written by Achille Glorieux at the end of the council and duplicated, are the result of the transcription of his personal notes.[73] Fr Umberto Betti, OFM, a consulter for the preparation and a *peritus* at the council, also kept a journal now available *per fragmenta* {in bits and pieces}. Carlo Colombo, a theologian trusted by Cardinal Montini, later Pope Paul VI, kept eleven notebooks of observations about the council debates

---

Germany. Aloys Grillmeier has a copy of it and has given a microfilm of it to ISR for use in its work.

66. 'Souvenirs', archives of the Dominicans of Toulouse, 23 f° ms r, made available by É Fouilloux.

67. A Prignon, 'Notes manuscrites', Louvain-la-Neuve (CLG), indexed in the volumes of inventory CRThL 24, 11.

68. G Thils, 'Carnet bleu', Louvain-la-Neuve (CLG, CRThL 21, 125).

69. Louvain-la-Neuve (CLG, CRThL 21, 73–6).

70. CLG, inventory edited by E Louchez, CRThL; the journal only begins with this monk exegete's arrival in Rome in November 1962.

71. Also kept at CLG.

72. Archives of the Archdiocese of New York; the journal may be consulted through the copy held by Joseph Komonchak at CUA.

73. A copy at FGL.

and four notebooks of observations made about the commissions or subcommissions. They were not meant to be a journal, but they recount the climate of the milieu all the same.[74] Among liturgists, beside the pages of those who kept a journal about the preparations, there is a journal by a Spanish Benedictine named Franquesa.[75] It is not difficult to understand the importance that the journal of the Redemptorist Bernard Häring would have. It is still in his hands although available for use by researchers. Unfortunately it is written in a personal stenographic script that cannot be decoded without the help of the author himself.

The Laity

Lay people—and not only those like Rosemary Goldie who was a lay auditor at Vatican II—kept significant journals.[76]

For example, Angelina Nicora Alberigo, from the Bologna group of supporters of the conciliar activity of Cardinal Lercaro (of which Dossetti was a participant and its leader), kept a journal of the Council based on second–hand information (but nowhere else to be found) about important moments and the orientations of one of the 'dispensaries' of Vatican II.[77] Alceu Amoroso Lima wrote his journal to his daughter (a nun in a Brazilian convent) in the form of letters (not yet edited).

The independent journalist Jan Grootaers also kept accounts of his extended conversations in his notebooks.[78] Giancarlo Zizola, a highly respected Vaticanista, kept a journal, especially for the fourth session, that is much more than just preliminary sketches for his articles in the Italian daily *Il Giorno*.

---

74. Archives of the Faculty of Theology of Northern Italy in Milan; they were put in order by AP Adorni.
75. A copy is at ISR.
76. R. Goldie's bibliography gives such precise remembrances and circumstantial details that it makes one think that she kept a personal journal. H Raguer tells me that there is a journal by Bonet i Marrugat being held in Barcelona.
77. In the Alberigo family, a copy of extracts about the Council at ISR. Concerning the 'Bolognese dispensary', see G Alberigo, 'Introduzione' in G Lercaro, *Per la forza dello Spirito: Discorsi conciliari* (Bologna, 1984), 9–52.
78. He is keeping them himself, but they will be given to Louvain at the author's death. G Zizola also has his own journal for the fourth session.

THE CHARACTER AND FUNCTION OF JOURNALS:

TEST CASE—OCTOBER 11, 1962

The wealth of all this material can be better appreciated by moving away from an abstract evaluation of the types of sources and into an effective comparison of the diverse approaches and perceptions of a particular event.

The day that the Council opened provides a good test case. The agenda for the day is brief, since it was completed dedicated to the opening ceremony and to the Pope's opening address. No one could then imagine what was about to happen at the assembly's first general congregation in the aula.

The journals focus on different aspects of the ceremony, including spiritual reflections, observations about the atmosphere, and statements about anxieties and concerns.

Front and center was the problem of the Pope's address, very moving and very liberating by comparison with what had been expected even a few weeks before. Apparently, however, it had little influence on the unfolding of the Council. In his personal notebook, John XXIII emphasised his spiritual attitude:

> Today marks the solemn opening of the Ecumenical Council. The news is in all the newspapers and in Rome in the jubilant heart of everyone. I thank the Lord that he did not judge me unworthy of the honor of opening in his name this dawning of great graces for his holy Church. It was his will that the first spark that set this event in motion during the past three years came out of my heart and my mouth. I was prepared to be detached from the joy of this dawn. With the same calm spirit I repeat *fiat voluntas tua* that I may remain in this primary post of service for all the time and in all the circumstances of my humble life, knowing that I shall have to stop at some point and let the initiative, the pursuit, and the achievement [of the Council] pass on to my successor. *Fiat voluntas tua, sicut in coelo et in terra.*[79]

---

79. '*Questa giornata segna l'apertura solenne del Concilio Ecumenico. La cronaca è su tutti i giornali, e per Roma è nei cuori esultanti di tutti. Ringrazio il Signore*

He was aware, however, of new elements in his address, because he confided to his secretary Capovilla, who put this in his journal, that the pope often glanced to the right to see the reaction of Cardinal Ottaviani.[80] Details like this were not noticed by many.

But others details were noticed. It is symptomatic that Joseph Jungmann, a key figure in the liturgical movement, analysed the ceremony rigorously, taking it apart, observing it in silence, and giving more weight to a genuflection after the chanting of the Litanies than to the significance of the event itself:

> The opening did not please me. Still without an identity card, I had to make my way into the Vatican with my decree of appointment, without any instructions about the hour or the place. Wherever I asked for help, the answer was always '*Non so*' (I don't know)! At last, after an hour of vainly wandering around, I reached the basilica and I was politely led by an *assignator* to the place reserved for the experts, where, however, almost none of these were found (it was the wrong side of the galleries). Still there I was able to see the entry procession of the bishops and I could hear everything well. As to the liturgical action, it was carried out correctly: good church music, excellent sound systems, but as a whole, it was in the style of Leo XIII. They haven't learned anything from the *statio orbis* in Munich. Then a solemn high Mass without the distribution of communion. Instead of integrating the ceremonies of the opening

---

che mi abbia fatto non indegno dell'onore di aprire in nome suo questo inizio di grandi grazie per la sua Chiesa santa. Egli dispose che la prima scintilla che preparò durante tre anni questo avvenimento uscisse dalla mia bacco e dal mio cuore. Ero disposto a rinunziare anche alla gioia di questo inizio. Con la stessa calma ripeto il fiat voluntas tua circa il mantenermi in questo primo posto di servizio per tutto il tempo e per tutte le circonstanze della mia umile vita et sentirmi arrestato in qualunque momento perchè questo impegno di procedere, di continuare e di finire passi al mio successore. Fiat voluntas tua, sicut in coelo et in terra.' AR–ISR; edited by LF Capovilla in fascicles each year. Compare with the text in *The Journal of a Soul*, dated November 11, but unquestionably it should be October 11. See AG Roncalli–Giovanni XXIII, *Il Giornale dell'Anima*, 762-764.

80. See Melloni, 'Giovanni XXIII e l'avvio del Vaticano II' in É Fouilloux (editor), *Vatican II commence... Approches francophones* (Louvain, 1993), 75.

(the gospel proclaimed in several languages, the Pope's address, the *professio fidei*, prayers of intercession...), all these things were done as appendages without any order. A *flectamus genua* followed the litany! The unlovely prayer to the Holy Spirit, *Adsumus* (as I was able to tell Bugnini, it comes from Pseudo-Isidore), was said at least by only one person and not by the whole assembly. But that would surely have pleased most of those present. Perhaps the idea was to make clear the *terminus a quo* {point of departure—to be left behind} in matters liturgical.[81]

Another *peritus*, Domenico Bertetto, already involved in the preparations, was content to make some purely spiritual reflections (perhaps done even before the ceremony):

Active participation in the Council: with the apostolic prayer *cum Maria Matre Jesu*. With my commitment to the good of the church. With supernatural charity along with all the members of the C.M. With the suffering and the cross that God sends me and that I will accept with faith and love in union with Jesus and Mary, always remaining peaceful under the light yoke of divine goodness.[82]

---

81. 'Angenehm war für mich die Eröffnung nicht: Noch ohne Ausweis mußte ich mich meinem Ernennungsdekret in den Vatikan durchschlagen; ohne Angabe wo und wann. Wo immer man fragte, immer nur: Non so! Schließlich bin ich nach einer Stunde vergeblichen Umherirrens in die Basilika gekommen und dort von einem assignatos höflich zu den posti riservati für periti geführt worden, wo aber fast niemand von diesen zu finden war (falsche Seite auf den Galerien). Immerhin konnte ich hier den Einzug der Bischöfe gut sehen und alles sehr gut hören. Als liturgischer Akt zwar sauber durchgeführt: gute Kirchenmusik, vorzügliche akustische Einrichtungen; aber als Geamtkonzeption: Stil Leo XIII. Von der statio orbis in München hat man nichts gelernt. Also Hochamt ohne Kommunionspendung. Anstatt die Eröffnungsakte einzubauen (mehrsprachiges Evangelium, Papstansprache, professio fidei, Fürbitten...) kamen alle diese Dinge als Anhängsel ohne Ordnung. Ein Flectamus genua folgte nach der Litanei! Das an den Hl. Geist gerichtete unschöne Gebet Adsumus (wie ich Bugnini mitteilen konnte, stammt es von Pseudo-Isidor) wurde wenigstens nicht von allen zusammen, sondern von einem einzelnen gebetet. – Aber den meisten wird es ja gefallen haben. Veilleicht sollte so der terminus a quo der liturgischen Dinge anschaulich gemacht werden.' {Transl: statio orbis refers to the 1960 Eucharistic Congress in Munich.}
82. 'Partecipazione attiva al Concilio: Con la preghiera apostolica cum Maria Matre

Many bishops who wrote after the end of the morning's ceremony were struck by the rhetoric and the emotion of the ceremonial (as Jungmann imagined they would be). Enrico Bartoletti was one of these, and in his journal the Pope's opening address and his later words to the crowds 'under the moonlight' are of the same sort:

> Monday, Oct. 11 1962, the Maternity of Mary. *Solemn Opening of the Council.* At 8:30 AM, starting from the Vatican museum's Sala dei Lapidi, the bishops' procession began. We entered St Peter's—*this* is what the church looks like: it is truly an Epiphany of the ecclesial mystery. Everything is unfolding like a great liturgy. The Mystery of the Church is at work, at the height of its visibility. Nothing too external or secular here. The modern age has made a clean sweep of all the secular baroque elements in which the past delighted. That is already a good sign. The prayer 'Here we are, Lord, gathered in your name' underscores the religious meaning of our assembly and reminds everyone of his own responsibility and his own weakness. The pope's profession of faith, made alone in front of the entire Church, is astonishing! Faith is our true bond, and it is by this faith that we serve [...] God's holy church. The Pope—what a gift of God to his church!—spoke simply and clearly. His optimism, his confidence in this new age, his faith in the church seem to be so rooted in his spirit that it would be difficult for them to be drowned out by the voices of the Council. This is the line to take. Either well or poorly, the Council will emerge with certainty. Very beautiful words of the pope to the crowd gathered in St Peter's Square for the evening's torchlight procession: 'Fatherhood and brotherhood are equally gifts from God.' This man speaks to people as if they were really his children and his brothers gathered in his house. Whatever its future labors and conclusions, the

---

Jesu. Con la fedeltà ai miei impegni a bene della Chiesa. Con la carità soprannaturela con tutti i membri del C.M. Con la sofferenza e la croce che Dio mi manda e che accetterò con fede e amore in unione con Gesù e Maria, sempre sereno sotto il soave governo della bontà divina.'

Council has already borne fruit. It has forced humanity to consider the mystery of the church in its true light. So many ideas are circulating and so many questions are being asked that they cannot fail to break through the general indifference and secularism. God knows how to speak when he wishes to those who wait for him or seek him.[83]

Cardinal Lercaro of Bologna in his 'Letters' to the young people with whom he lived and to whom he wrote an epistolary journal, was more fascinated than disappointed by the ceremony:

The Council opened this morning. I am not going to describe the very solemn ceremony for you, since I suspect that you watched it on TV. Moreover, it would be difficult for me and too long to describe the series of rituals that unfolded. Instead I will share some of my thoughts with you. First of all, I never felt so immersed in the Church of God as I did today: the presence of

---

83. '*Lunedì 11 ott. 1962, Maternità di Maria. Solenne aperture del Concilio. Alle 8,30 dai Musei Vaticani, Sala delle Lapidi, comincia la sfilata dei Vescovi. Entriamo in S. Pietro: ecco la Chiesa: veramente questa è una Epifania del Mistero Ecclesiale. Tutto si svolge davvero come in una grande liturgia. Il Mistero della Chiesa è operante, al suo massimo di visibilità. Non vi è davvero nulla di troppo esteriore o profane. I tempi moderni hanno fatto piazza pulita di tutto il barocchismo profane, di cui si compiaceva il passato. È già buon segno. La preghiera "Eccoci, Signore, uniti nel tuo nome" sottolinea il senso religioso della nostra adunanza e ricorda ad ognuno il peso della propria responsabilità e della propria debolezza. La professione di fede fatta dal Papa da solo, dinanzi a tutta la Chiesa, è una cosa stupenda! È la fede il nostro vero vinculo: ed è quella fede che tutti serviamo [...] la Santa Chiesa di Dio. Il Papa—che dono di Dio per la sua Chiesa!—ha parlato con semplicità e chiarezza. Il suo ottimismo, la sua fiducia nei tempi nuovi, la sua fede nella Chiesa appaiono cosa tanto radicata nel suo animo, che ben difficilmente potranno essere soverchiate dalle voci del Concilio. Quella è la linea. O bene, o male, verrà fuori sicuramente. Bellissime la parole del Papa alla folla riunita in <piazza> S. Pietro alla sera per la fiaccolata: "Paternità e fraternità sono ugualmente dono di Dio." Quest'uomo parla alla gente come fossero davvero figli e frateli suoi, raccolti in casa sua. Qualunque siano i lavori e le conculsioni future il Concilio ha già dato i suoi frutti. Ha imposto alla considerazione degli uomini il mistero della Chiesa nella sua vera luce. Circolano tante idee e corrono tanti interrogativi, che non possono non rompere l'indifferentismo e il laicismo generale. Dio sa parlare, quando vuole, agli uomini che l'attendono e lo cercano.*' E Bartoletti (Bishop of Lucca), 'Quaderno', kept by his secretary, with a copy at ISR.

the Pope, of all or almost all of the Sacred College, of bishops from the whole world, around the altar that stood in the center and on which the Sacrifice was celebrated and then the gospel was enthroned; the gaze of the entire world was fixed on what was happening, as was clear from the delegations from so many nations and the presence of the separated churches . . . All this made me feel the vitality of the church, both its unity and its diversity, its humanity and its divinity; and it created within me, who felt myself a member of it invested with special functions and powers, a deep feeling of joy and gratitude to the Lord. In the council hall I found myself sitting between Cardinal Wyszynski (who was loudly applauded all across the courtyard and the object of the crowd's sympathy) and Cardinal McIntyre; in front of me I had Cardinals Spellman, Ruffini, and Caggiano (Buenos Aires); a short distance away were President Segni with his entourage and Prince Albert of Belgium; almost directly opposite I saw the abbot and a monk from the Calvinist monastery of Taizé in Switzerland [*sic*] (we listened to the abbot on TV on the third program about the Council). All these were visible signs of the church's effective presence in the world. I really felt how necessary it is that the Holy Spirit should guide this undertaking from which everyone is expecting so much. But the prayers of this immense assembly along with the prayers of people all over the world guarantees that the Spirit of the Lord will be with us as we work. All of you, follow us with your prayers and . . . be good! I hug you and bless you.[84]

---

84. '*Dunque stamane ci fu l'apertura del Concilio; non sto a descrivervi la cerimonia veramente solenne, perché penso che l'avrete seguita per la T.V.; e poi sarebbe per me piuttosto difficile et, certo, lungo ripetervi il seguito dei riti svoltisi. Vi dirò invece alcuni pensieri miei. E, primo, che certo non mi sono mai sentito così immerso nella Chiesa di Dio come oggi: le presenza del Papa, di tutti, o quasi, il S. Collegio, dei Vescovi di tutto il mondo, intorno all'altare che stava al centro e sul quale prima si celebrò il Sacrificio, poi si collocò in trono il Vangelo; lo sguardo del mondo intero fisso sull'avvenimento, come si rendeva evidente dalla presenza delle delegazioni di tante Nazioni e dalla presenza delle Chiese separate...; tutto questo faceva sentire la*

This triumphalistic splendor didn't delight everybody. Cardinal Florit, the archbishop of Florence referred to it almost in passing in his notes for the day:

> I celebrated early in the Chapel of the Sisters of the Villa Orsini. I went to the Vatican for the Ecumenical Council Vatican II—an historic and glorious day. A spectacle like this has never before been seen in this glorious basilica. The mystery of the church was made apparent in a visible way as never before. The mustard seed of the gospel parable appeared like a great tree. And perhaps in a few years it will become a gigantic tree. *Christus vincit!* Late at night I visited Rev Msgr Paschini.[85]

The Argentine bishop of Rafaela, Vicente Zazpe, was more impressed by the diversity of the assembly than by anything else:

> Mass at 5:45 at the hotel, then dressed for the opening of the council. We left by bus. We entered through the Vatican museum. Impossible to describe: all these bishops—blacks, chinese, whites, Germans, languages, different robes. We marched in ranks of six across. Hall, corridor. The procession was spectacular . . . The

---

vitalità della Chiesa, la sua unità e varietà insieme; la sua umanità e divinità; e in me, che me ne sentivo membro investito di funzioni e di poteri qualificati, creava un senso profondo di gioia e di riconoscenza al Signore. Mi trovaro a sedere nell'aula conciliare tra il Card. Wishinsky (applauditissimo lungo tutto il corteo e oggetto di simpatia della folla) e il Card. McIntyre; avevo davanti i Cardinali Spellman, Ruffini et Caggiano (Buenos Ayres); poco distante erano il Presidente Segni col suo seguito e il Principe Alberto del Belgio; quasi di fronte vedevo l'abate e un monaco del Monastero Calvinista di Taizé nella Svizzera (abbiamo sentito l'abate alla T.V. nella 3 trasmissione sul Concilio): erano tutti questi segni visibili della presenza efficiente della Chiesa nel mondo. Davvero sentivo il bisogno che lo Spirito Santo guidi questa impresa da cui tutti attendano tanto; ma la preghiera ripetuta della immense assemblea, seguita dalla preghiera di tante anime nel mondo tutto dava garanzia che lo spirito del Signore sarà con noi in questo lavoro. Voi seguiteci tutti con la preghiera vostra e...state buoni! Vi abbraccio e vi benedico.'

85. 'Celebro di buon'ora nella Cappella delle Suore di V. Orsini. Me reco in Vaticano per il Concilio Ecumenico Vaticano II. Giornata storica e gloriosa. Uno spettacolo simile mai avvenuto nella gradiosa Basilica. Il mistero della Chiesa Cattolica si è sensibilizzato forse come non mai. Il granello di senapa della parabola evangelica è apparso come non mai un grande albero. E diventerà forse a non lungo andar d'anni un albero gigantesco. Christus vincat! In tarda serata visito il rev. mons. Paschini.'

cardinals were at the end [...] then the *sedia gestatoria*
with John XXIII: little old man, almost squashed—he
blessed, deeply moved . . . I saw [?], Fulton, [?], Spellman.
I was next to the auxiliary bishop of the Vicar of Israel.
. . . In the afternoon I studied the schemas. I met Don
Santos who brought me letters and Tamayo Reyes. M
Tato also told me that I had letters. At night we went
to see the torchlight procession with M Tato, Viola [?],
Aramburu, Cafferata and another Uraguayan. We met
M Carreras. He gave me letters from Guillermo, Perette
[?], etc, etc.[86]

Cardinal Wyszynski made notes in his journal, 'Rzym–Otwarcie
Soboru Watykanskiego II,' of the progress of the ceremony and
its atmosphere, including the spirit of veneration, the inaccurate
pronunciations, and the odd seating arrangements that placed him
between the American primate and the cardinal of Soviet Armenia,
and ironic comments about his own thinness which 'embarrassed
someone who comes from a materialistic regime,' and acts of devotion
to Mary, Queen of Poland:

Today, the Feast of the Maternity of the Blessed Virgin
Mary, the Holy Father John XXIII opened the Second
Vatican Council. At 8:30 we came together at St Peter's
Basilica in the Sala dei Paramenti and waited for the
pope. Almost all the cardinals were already there. I
spoke with them, moving from one to another. Many of
them wanted me to know of their interest in the church
in Poland. The Pope arrived half an hour later, having
had trouble getting there. The procession was formed

---

86. '*Misa a las 5.45 en el Hotel y vestimenta para la apertura del Concilio. Nos llevaron
en autobus. Entramos al Museo Vaticano. Imposible describir: todos los Obispos.
Negros, chinos, blancos, alemanes, idiomas, habitos diferentes. Atravesamos en fials
de 6. Salon, corridor. El desfile era espectacular. [...] Al fin los Cardenales [...] silla
gestatoria con Juan XXIII: viejito, como aplastado benedicía emocionado [...] Le vi
a [?] Fulton, [?], Spellmann. Estuve junto al Obsipo auxiliar del Vicario de Israel.
[...] Por la tarde estudié los esquemas. Me encontré con don Santos que me trajo
cartas y Tamayo Reis. M. Tato me anunció cartas también. Por la noche fuímos a
ver la procesión de antorchas con m. Tato, Viola [?], Aramburu, Cafferata y otro
uruguayo. Nos encontramos con m. Carreras. Me dieron las cartas de Guillermo,
Perette [?], etc.*'

according to a list: my place was next to Cardinal Lercaro of Bologna, a short man. The procession moved toward the Bronze Door. The Holy Father walked; he was praying. He has a remarkable talent for concentration in the midst of the great noise around him. It is clear that everything has been carefully organised. Through the windows of the Scuola Regia, you could see the bishops filing into the basilica. Then we found ourselves in St Peter's Square. I was always faced with Italians whistling 'Lyssinski,' when they mean 'Wyszynski.' Their whistling was coupled with applause and calls to 'look here' for photographs. 'How thin he is!'—remarks like that are annoying for someone who has come from a materialistic country. They say, 'The Primate is always smiling,' and I reply, 'That's because I represent the church in Poland where the church is the source of joy and hope.' Most willingly I confide the glory of my country to the Queen of Poland—Our Lady of Jasna Gora. As we enter the basilica, the archbishops and bishops have already taken their places on the high grandstands that fill the main nave. It's impressive. We slowly approach the Confession of Saint Peter. I find my place easily, near me right in the first row.

At my side there is President Segni and the royal delegation; in front of me, Cardinal Spellman; behind me, Cardinal Agagianian. Just like that, in a very small space *extrema tanguntur* {very different worlds touch one another}. A cardinal who passes me on his way to go up higher stops and, before I realise it and can stop him, he kisses my hand twice, repeating: 'I kiss the hands of heroic Poland.' Everything happens with calm, despite the huge crowd. In the stands placed in front of the great columns I see many special delegations and the diplomatic corps. The Holy See's place is right in front of the main altar. They intoned the *Veni Creator* and then the Mass was celebrated by Cardinal Tisserant.

Then there was the ceremony of obedience of all the cardinals to the Pope, of two bishops, and of two religious superior generals. Then prayers sung in Latin and the gospel sung in Latin and in oriental languages. The prayers of the Eastern Church are long, but beautiful. When the chants are finished, the Holy Father gave his address with a strong, vibrant voice. Nobody mentioned his fatigue. The public celebration ended, and the Holy Father and the cardinals are going back to the Vatican. I run into Cardinal Carinci, who tells me that during Vatican I he was eight years old—probably the last of that period. I get back home near 2.00 pm. Tonight I will write to my nation a letter about the Council.[87]

---

87. *'Dzisiaj, w uroczystość Macierzyństwa Najświętszej Maryi Panny. Ojciec Święty Jan XXIII otwiera Sobór Watykański II. O godzinie 8.30 zbieramy się w Bazylice Świętego Piotra, w Sali Paramentów, oczekując na Papieża. Są już niemal wszyscy kardynałowie. Rozmawiam z kardynałami, co chwila zmieniajac rozmówcę, gdyż wielu stara się okazać mi swoje zainteresowanie Kościołem w Polsce. Papież przychodzi z półgodzinnym opóźnieniem, co jest wskazane choćby z uwagi na wielkie trudności dyslokacji. Ustala się wśród kardynałow porządek według listy. Łatwo znajduję swoje miejsce, gdyż trzymam się kard. Lercaro z Bolonii, człowieka małego wzrostu. Wyrusza pochód kardynałow w kierunku Portone di Bronzo. Ojciec Święty idzie peiszo i modli się. Ten człowiek ma przedziwny talent skupiania się wśród największego rozgwaru tego świata. Przyznać trzeba, że wszystko odbywa się niesłychanie sprawnie.Przez okna Scuola Regia widać juz szereg biskupów wchodzących do Bazyliki. Znajdujemy się na placu Świętego Piotra. Jestem zawsze narażony na to włoskie sykanie "Łyssiski"—co ma oznaczać "Wyszynski". Tym sykaniom towarzyszą oklaski i prośby "o twarz" do fotografii. "Che magro"—takie uwagi pod moim adresem zawstydzają człowieka, przybywającego z kraju o ustroju materialistycznym. "Prymas jest zawsze pogodny"—mówią. "Bo reprezentuję Kościół Polsce, a Kościół to źródło pogody i nadziei"—odpowiadam. Nie jest mi trudno oddawać chwałę Polski w ręce Królowej Polski, Pani Jasnogórskiej. Wchodzimy do Bazyliki, arcybiskupi i biskupi są już na swoich miejscach—na wysokich trybunach, które wypełniają całą długość nawy głównej. Widok imponujacy. Powoli zbliżamy się do Konfesji Świętego Piotra. Łatwo znajduje swoje miejsce, w szeregu pierwszym do Konfesi Świętego Piotra. Tuż obok siedzi, na miejscu wydzielonym, prezydent Segni i misja królewska. Przede mną—kard. Spellman, a nade mną—kard. Agagianian, a więc, na małym odcinku "extrema tanguntur". Jakiś kardynał, wchodzący wyżej, zatrzymuje się przy mnie i zanim zdołałem się zorientować i przeszkodzić, całuje moją rękę, dwukrotnie z naciskiem powtarzajac: "Całuję ręce bohaterskiej Polski." Przebieg uroczystości jest normalny i spokojny pomimo mnóstwa obecnych. Wiele miejsc na trybunach, ustawionych przy potężnych filarach podtrzymujących kopułę, zajmują misje specjalne i korpus dyplomatyczny. Ojciec Święty zajmuje miejsce przed wielkim ołtarzem Konfesji Świętego Piotra. Odśpiewano Veni Creator, po czym mscę święta celebruje kard.*

The Polish cardinal saw himself representing the church and his nation, but he didn't limit his notes to that. At least at the beginning, his solitude as primate, apart from the other Polish bishops, is symptomatic. There is another bishop who, by contrast, writes a truly 'synodal' {collegial} journal, Neophytos Edelby, the Archbishop of Aleppo in Syria. His 'Remembrances of the Second Ecumenical Council of the Vatican' are effectively a collective memoir of the Melkite Church at Vatican II. From this perspective, his concerns about ritual questions at the start of the council make sense principally in a context of ecclesiology:

> This is the day of the solemn opening of the Council. I can't describe the whole ceremony, but I'll remark on what matters to us. At 7.30, we gathered in the large Sala dei Lapidi in the Vatican palace to take part in the procession. Only our Patriarch did not participate in this solemn session. (He watched it on television.)
>
> There were 2,500 bishops and superior generals. I was surprised to see that almost every council father brought a *socius* {assistant} to help him carry his things. With that, I could have brought my full pontifical regalia. I decided however only to wear the epitrachilion and the omophorion, and I didn't regret it.
>
> Our vestments made us stand out among all the others, and I found it relatively less hard with these less solemn vestments to put up with a ceremony that lasted more than 5 hours. We decided to walk together as a group, but we couldn't find one another in these huge galleries. As a result, we joined the procession in two groups of

---

Tisserant. *Odbywa się ceremonia obejiencji wszystkich kardynałow oraz po dwóch arcybiskupów, biskupów i przełożonych zakonnych. Następują modlitwy w języku łacińskim i śpiew Ewangelii po łacinie i w językach wschodnich. Modlitwy Kóscioła wschodniego długie, lecz piękne. Po tych modlitwach Ojciec Święty wygłasza alokucję głosem żywym i mocnym, tak że nie zauważa się żadnego zmęczenia. Kończy się uroczystość publiczna, po której Ojciec Święty i kardynałowie udaja się do Watykáńu. Spotykam abpa Carinci, który mówi o sobie, że w czasów. Wracamy do domu na godzinę 14.00. Wieczorem piszę list z Soboru Watykańskiego II do narodu.'* Published in *Jan XXIII i jego dzieto*, 98–9.

6 bishops, separated by several hundred Latin bishops. We were however in the ranks of the archbishops. The procession lasted almost an hour, from 8.30 to 9.30. At St Peter's they didn't have time to give each bishop his place. So we were together on the same side and in the same row. So the Melkite Church was represented by a group that could easily be recognised in the midst of these thousands of white miters. In the ranks of the Patriarchs, there was the Coptic Patriarch, the Maronite Patr, the Latin Patr of Jerusalem, the Chaldean Patr and the Armenian Patr. As the seat of our Patriarch was empty, they asked the 4 last Oriental Patriarchs to move up and they brought in the retired Patriarch of the East Indies to take the sixth seat. The bench reserved for the Patriarchs was only differentiated from the rest of the hierarchy by a green drape hung in front of the prie-dieu and the back of the chair. It was the first bench of those reserved for the hierarchy. But it was decidedly inferior to the places reserved for the cardinals both as to location and decoration. Despite all our efforts, it was impossible to get Rome to give the Patriarchs the rank that had been given them by the first Ecumenical Councils. But we don't give up hoping for that some day.

People noticed the absence of our Patriarch. Those aware of such things figured out that his being sick was not the only reason for his absence. The Mass *de Sancto Spiritu* was sung by Card. Tisserant, dean of the Sacred College. After that came the Profession of Faith, said first by the Pope and then repeated in the name of all the council fathers by Archbishop Pericle Felici, General Secretary of the Council. <Then there was the ceremony of the 'obedience.' One by one, the cardinals came to kiss the pope's hand. The Patriarchs did exactly as they had done. Two archbishops and two bishops, representing their confreres, came and kissed the pope's right knee. Then two superior generals came and kissed his foot.> Next they did a brief office in Latin for the beginning of the Council. Then there was the singing of an 'oriental supplication' (Ektenia) from the Byzantine rite. The pope presided at that and read his part in Greek. Three Byzantine bishops celebrated with him: Bishop Hakim, who read the first prayer in Arabic; Bishop Katkoff, who chanted a Slavonic Ecphonia, and Bishop Gad who ended in Greek. Two deacons said litanies in Greek. One of them also read the gospel in Greek. This was an abbreviated Ektenia, since the ceremony had already taken 5 hours, but the chants were a success and the Greek ceremony pleased everyone—a fortunate innovation due to the Pope's deep love for the East. This long ceremony terminated with a long address by the Pope in Latin. The Pope said some beautiful things. But it was in Latin and many of the council fathers have difficulty understanding it; moreover, everyone was tired. Some of the bishops were already asleep. The others were obviously exhausted. People couldn't stand any more when the time came for the procession out of the basilica. It was already 2.00 pm. But after all it was beautiful, both grand and moving. For the first time in history, 2,500 bishops came together for a council. At Vatican I, there were only 700, and at the first council of Nicea in 325 A.D. there were 328!

Observers from non–Catholic churches were there, welcomed and given good places. We don't yet know their names. I only saw the Brothers of Taizé piously recollected and praying with all their hearts. It was very touching to see so many [Protestant] pastors praying, taking part in their common responsibility for people all over the world. [Almost] all the [Latin] Catholics bishops from behind the Iron Curtain were able to come to the council. The Russian Orthodox Church announced last night that it is sending two representatives. There was also, in the first row, the President of the Republic of Italy, the Prince of Liège, and representatives from 85 countries. At the end of the ceremony, they gave out printed notebooks with the names of those that are slated to be voted in as members of the conciliar commissions.

Since the commissions are very important, I spent the afternoon preparing lists. They say that exceptional measures for security had been taken for the ceremony this morning. Three thousand Italian secret agents were on alert in the basilica and its surrounds, without counting the Vatican police and troops. Before the entry of the council fathers, the basilica was checked out from top to bottom. They even looked in the organ pipes. Happily nothing unpleasant occurred. Even the Communist Party stated that it joyfully welcomes the Council, since it hopes that it will bring about a strengthening of bonds of friendship and peace among nations. At night a torchlight procession was organised in St Peter's Square, calling to mind the procession of the faithful at Ephesus on Oct. 11, 431, to celebrate the proclamation of Mary's divine motherhood. The Pope spoke to the crowd and then sent them away saying, 'Go on home. It's time to go to bed. Bring to all your family the Pope's "Good Night."'

If the ritual pomp fascinated some, it turned as many others off. The auxiliary bishop of Namur, JB Musty, wrote in his 'Notes on the Ecumenical Council Vatican II' his disappointment about the liturgy's insensitivity that morning:

October 11: opening session. Grandiose. Lack of liturgical participation. Everything in polyphony, including the Creed. No distribution of Holy Communion. Still it was impressive. Conversed with Bishop van Bekkam *zigt de progressistsch? 't hiet oun aardig tii doen, maas de wereld hunked er naar* {said to be progressive? Not a bad thing if the world were}.

The English bishop Butler caustically underlined the contradiction between the spirit of the gospel and the liturgy's rites:

I thought of Jesus of Nazareth and his attitude to the Jewish institutional religion; then, appropriately, they began to sing the *Magnificat—exaltavit humiles.*[88]

---

88. *'Rose about 5.10 and said Mass 5.45, Br Giles serving. We left here in a 'brake*

The Dominican theologian Labourdette, in his unmethodical 'Souvenirs of the First Session' found himself perplexed and critical of the ceremony, which he observed with his Dominican colleague Fr Gagnebet:

[sic] *Archabb Beuron, Ab. Maredsous, Ab. Rio di Janiero, Ab di Monte Vergine & self about 7.30, carrying rochettes, white copes and mitres. Some rain, I think in the morning, but as we went along the sun began to shine. Lot of traffic. We walked up a ramp into what I take to have been the Julian ambulacrum (Gallery of Stone) inside the Vatican Museum, where we put on our vestments. This was a long slow walk, crowd going up, some going down. We then processed down again, to the crowded Piazza, where singing began, and up the center towards the Church. Swiss guards and lots of zouaves (I suppose about, and much splendor). I thought of "Jesus of Nazareth" and his attitude to the Jewish institutional religion; then, appropriately, they began to sing the* Magnificat—*exaltavit humiles. The Church was arranged with facing tiers of rising seats with stuffed leather, each apparently with a folding desk front and a chained biro. At first we Abbots were taken to excellent seats low down and nearest to the altar. But it seems some flunkey decided that these would be needed for more exalted persons (as indeed I think they were), and we were taken back to what seemed like a press gallery with movable chairs and little view. One got a bit warm in one's vestments. The loud speakers relayed the singing, and at last the clapping of the crowd, and the Pope came past our place on the* Sedia gestatoria *about 9.45 (the procession had started shortly after the assigned time, 8.30). People clapped in the Church as he passed (but the cries of Papa were only when he was outside, it seemed.) The Pope intoned the* Veni Creator, *which was sung alternately with a choir that was beautiful (to hear). The Mass of the Holy Ghost followed, sung by Card. Tisserant, and the Pope gave the closing blessing; he seemed to be in good voice throughout. I didn't see the "obedience" being given. It was followed by the Pope's reciting the long Creed, then by someone else and finally by us all together. Meanwhile some documents had been distributed containing this Creed* inter alia, *and we each signed the Creed which was handed to the* notatores locorum. *Then the Pope recited a good prayer, which was followed by Litanies. Next the Gospel from the last verses of St. Matthew was sung as at Pontifical Mass. It was followed by* Supplicatio Orientalis *in Greek (including a Gospel which was however possibly not the same one?) in rather lovely music and a pronunciation which heavily stressed the accents and hurried the other syllables including those naturally long—e.g. diphthongs. Then the Pope preached a long sermon which I didnt* [sic] *pick up much of—presumably it will be published. After a Plenary Indulgence, he left in the* Sedia gestatoria, *and we ahead.* [We] *took off our vestments there and then (about 1.20 or so), and found our way to the waiting car. When our pary* [sic] *has assembled we came back, and I began lunch (in a calefactory?) about 2.50. It was followed by coffee and I escaped about 3 p.m. and smoked a pipe and read, before mental prayer and Mattins.'* (Archives of Downside Abbey, Bath.)

Solemn opening at St Peter's. At 7.15 {am}, Fr Gagnebet and I went to the Vatican by taxi. It was raining. (Lelette was getting up an hour later, and by then it was clear.) We got to St. Peter's by going through the museum. We had to look for our seats. At last: on the left, closest to the Confession of the Apostles, almost right above the cardinals, facing the bronze statue of St Peter (vested in pontifical vestments). An unforgettable spectacle. Religiously the ceremony was grand and striking, despite some mistakes; for example, chanting the Creed in polyphony rather than having the bishops chant it. And what a perfect occasion it might have been for a *concelebration*!

Fr Semmelroth ignored the address and gave a larger place in his journal to the work of preparation with his colleagues:

So today is the opening of the Council. Yesterday afternoon and early this morning it was raining so hard that it looked like it would be a problem for the opening solemnities. But like a sign from God, a little bit before everything started, the sun came out and the weather turned lovely. On television I watched the bishops' procession into the Council and continued down to the Mass; then later, the obedience. It was really spectacular, and we can only hope that it was also more than that. Unfortunately I did not listen to the pope's address. It should have been good and a significant indication of the spirit of the Council's work. Tomorrow I will certainly read it. In the afternoon I went to St Peter's. I had hoped to get into the basilica. Theoretically that was possible, but the throng of the crowds was so great that I gave up trying to get in. I went first to see Fr Grillmeier who lives in the {Jesuit} Curia; I also met Fr Hirschmann there. I found my short conversation with Fr Daniélou very interesting. Next I went to see Bishop Volk, who gave me some technical information that was significant for the moment. The German bishops agree on a list of bishops who ought to be voted for by the

German side for the commissions. Bishop Volk, as I had
hoped, is going to come onto the commission on the
faith. That is even more important because he remains
on Bea's commission. Fr Hirchmann seems to function
a lot like a manager. In returning by bus, I got caught
in Roman traffic. By comparison, Frankfurt is golden.
It took me about three quarters of an hour to go from
the Risorgimento Square to the Germanicum. I even did
the last bit on foot, because that was faster than the bus.
I can't describe the madness of these cars that dare one
another to pass at every corner without any help from
the police. In general, traffic in the city is unbelievable.
The Council's opening has obviously brought a lot of
pilgrims. And I hear a lot of Germans also.[89]

---

89. '*Dies ist nun der Tag des Eröffnung des Konzils. Gerstern Nachmittag und auch
heute früh hat es heftig geregnet, sodaß es sehr bedenklich für die Eröffnungsfeier-
lichkeit aussah. Aber wie ein Zeichen Gottes kam dann kurz vor den Beginn die
Sonne, und es wurde schönes Wetter. Die Prozession der Bischöfe in das Konzil bis
zur [sic] Messe und nachher wieder die Obödienz habe ich im Fernsehen ange-
schaut. Es war doch ein erhebendes Schauspiel, von den man nur hoffen kann, daß
es nict nur ein solches sein wird. Leider habe ich die Ansprache des Papstes nicht
mitbekommen. Sie soll sehr gut gewesen sein und recht bedeutsam für den Tenor
der Konzilsarbeit. Morgen wird man sie ja lesen können. Nachmittags bin ich dann
nach St. Peter. Ich hatte gehofft, man könne in die Basilika hinein. Das war theore-
tisch auch möglich, aber der Andrag der Massen war so groß, daß ich es augegeben
habe, Einlaß zu finden. Ich ging zunächst zu P. Grillmeier, der in der Kurie wohnt,
wo ich auch P. Hirschmann traf. Ein kurzes Gespräch mit P. Daniélou war mir recht
interessant. Dann war ich bei Bischof Volk, der mir einiges über die technischen
Dinge sagte, die bisher von Bedeutung sind. Die deutschen Bischöfen haben sich
auf eine Liste der Bischöfe geeinigt, die von deutscher Seite in die Kommissionen
gelost werden sollen. Es wird wohl Bischof Volk, was ich gehofft hatte, in die Fides–
Kommission kommen. Das halte ich für wichtiger, als daß er im Bea–Sekretariat
bleibt. Ziemlich viel scheint P. Hirschmann als Manager zu wirken. Bei der Rück-
fährt mit dem Bus habe ich den römischen Verkehr in eine Weise erlebt, gegen die
Verhältnisse in Frankfurt gold sind. Ich habe ca dreiviertel Stunde gebraucht, um
von der Piazza del Risorgimento zum Germanicum zu kommen. Das letzte Stück
bin ich zu Fuß gegangen, weil es so schneller ging. Ein solches Gewüll von Autos,
die sich an der Kreuzugen ohne polizeiliche Hilfe durchlavieren müssen, kann man
sich nicht vorstellen. Es ist überhaupt ein unglaublicher Betrieb in der Stadt. Die
Eröffnung des Konzils hat offensichtlich viele Pilger herbeigezogen. Man hört auch
viele deutsche Leute.*'

Fr Congar doesn't report on the Pope's opening address either because, as he says in *My Journal of the Council*, he was not willing to just observe and note his dissatisfaction with the triumphalistic [*pharaonique*] character of the ceremony. He actually left St Peter's:

> I have just come back from the opening ceremony. Left here at 7 am with Fr Camelot. We entered by the Bronze Door and the great staircase, then in front of the Pauline Chapel, we wandered by mistake into the places reserved for the bishops (saw Mgr Guerry, who is entirely in favor of the idea of a Message to the World); we were ejected from there by a huge gendarme in a bearskin hat, like an ogre in a puppet show: one would hardly know how to dream up such a complete bogeyman. We wandered about in search of somewhere where we would be admitted. We encountered Fr Salverri, Mgr Schmaus, Mgr Fenton and some other American prelates who were talking rather loudly, Mgr Colombo, Fr Tascon, etc. In the end, we were admitted to a tribune, on condition that we eventually moved back from the front rows in favor of the Council Fathers (they would be the Superiors of Congregations). I tried to absorb the *genius loci* [spirit of the place]. St Peter's was made for this kind of thing. There is an enchanting display of colors, in which gold and red predominate. The nave is entirely filled with 2,500 tiered seats: in front of the Altar of the Confession, and actually on the Confession, stood the papal throne: *Petrus ipse* [Peter himself]. On the right–hand side, the statue of St Peter dressed as though Boniface VIII; right beside it, like a barrel, the ambo for the speakers. The nearest places, draped in red, are for the cardinals; the others, draped in green, for the archbishops and bishops, stretching as far as the eye can see. The tribunes are draped in red velvet and tapestries. It all gleams, shines, sings under the spotlights. Solemnity, but with a rather cold air about it all. A decorative scheme inspired, as it were, by the theatre of the Baroque. Between the tribunes, the huge statues of the founders of Orders in the niches. I could

only identify St Ignatius of Loyola, throwing impiety to the ground. I wish these statues could speak! What would they say? I imagine what they might say as men of God, consumed by the fire of the Gospel.

At 8.35 am, we heard over the loudspeakers the far-away sound of a sort of military march. Then the *Credo* was sung. I have come here *IN ORDER TO PRAY*, to pray WITH, to pray IN. I did in fact pray a lot. However, in order to pass the time, a choir sang in succession anything and everything. The best known chants: *Credo, Magnificat, Adoro Te, Salve Regina, Veni Sancte Spiritus, Inviolata, Benedictus* . . . To begin with, one sang with them, but then got tired.

The most curious pushed to the front and stood up on the chairs. We were overwhelmed by young clerics of all colors. I refused to give way to this unrestrained and ill-mannered behavior, with the result that I was pushed to the back of the tribune and did not even see the Pope. Little by little, but very slowly, the bishops came in, in cope and mitre, from the lower end of their tribunes. They seemed dead with fatigue and overcome with heat. They removed their mitres and mopped their foreheads. The superiors of the Congregations arrived and took up their seats in the front rows of the tribunes. Hoary ecclesiastical heads, their appearance etched by the regularity of their pious exercises and their prudent and edifying behavior. Some were trembling and seemed ready to collapse. Others were fine and strong.

My God, who have brought me here by ways that I did not choose, I offer myself to you to be, if you will, the instrument of your Gospel in this event in the life of the Church, which I love, but I would like it to be less 'Renaissance'! less Constantinian . . .

We heard clapping in St Peter's Square. The Pope must be coming. He must have come in. I saw nothing, behind six or seven rows of cassocks, standing up on chairs. From time to time there was clapping in the Basilica, but shouting and no words.

The *Veni Creator* was sung, alternately with the Sistine Choir, which is nothing but an opera chorus. DELENDA [to be suppressed]. The Pope sang the versicles and the prayers in a firm voice.

The Mass began, sung entirely by the Sistine Choir: a few bits of Gregorian (?) and some polyphony. The liturgical movement has not yet reached the Roman Curia. This immense assembly says nothing, sings nothing. It is said that the Jews are people of hearing, the Greeks of sight. There is nothing here except for the eye and the musical ear: no liturgy of the Word. No spiritual word. I know that in a few minutes a Bible will be placed on a throne in order to preside over the Council. BUT WILL IT SPEAK? Will it be listened to? Will there be a moment for the Word of God?

After the epistle, I left the tribune. In any case, I could not take any more. And then I was overcome by this seigneurial, Renaissance set-up. I paused for a moment beneath our tribune. From directly behind the bishops and above their tiers of seats one could see the whole of the immense white assembly of copes and mitres, in which Eastern bishops stood out on account of their multi-colored costumes and headgear. Five or ten minutes later I was ejected by a gendarme in a bearskin hat.

I tried to get out of the basilica. It was not easy. The unused side aisles and the ends of the transepts were crammed with crowds of young clerics moving around, endeavoring to squeeze in somewhere where they could SEE. All people want is to SEE.

I got out through the Vatican. In St Peter's Square, under the colonnades, crowds of people. The loudspeakers were transmitting the rest of the Mass. From the Square and from the street I thus heard the Preface, the Sanctus, the Pater Noster and the Agnus Dei. I returned, exhausted, by bus to the Angelicum. After about half an hour during which my hand was unable to hold a pen, I wrote these notes.

I unfortunately saw too little of the wonderful sight of the senate of bishops in session. I only saw them for the five or ten minutes during which I was able to stand in the doorway leading downwards, and above the tiers of bishops. The whole Church was there, embodied in its pastors. But I regret that a style of celebration was employed that was so alien to the reality of things. What would it have been if those 2,500 voices had together sung at least the *Credo*, if not all the chants of the Mass, instead of that elegant crooning by paid professionals? I returned with an immensely stronger desire: 1) to be evangelical, to aim at being a *homo plene evangelicus* [human being fully dedicated to the Gospel]; 2) to WORK. THAT produces results. THAT remains. That will prepare, for the next Council, a state of things where what is missing today will be taken for granted.

Afternoon. Fr De la Brosse, who saw it all on TV (until 12.30 pm), told me that it was splendid, very well photographed, transmitted and explained. And to think that with Telstar the whole world could see it all, at the very moment at which things were happening . . . ! (No: the direct link was restricted to Europe only.)

I thought more about this morning's ceremony. Its pomp implies two things: in addition to the fact, not only inevitable, but normal and good, that there must be order, solemnity, and beauty; that it is impossible to have an inauguration involving more than 3,000 people without organising some kind of display, a certain ceremonial. That is entirely good and noble. Over and above this state of things, I see how Eastern the Church is. The Reformation was not at all such at its birth: it may win members in the East, but it was not in any way or to any degree Eastern in its creators, in its origins, in its native and formative shape. On top of that, I see the weight, that has never been renounced, of the period when the Church behaved as a feudal lord, when it had temporal power, when popes and bishops were lords who had a court, gave patronage to artists and sought a pomp equal to that of the Caesars. That, the Church has never repudiated in Rome. To emerge from the Constantinian era has never been part of its programme. Poor Pius IX, who understood nothing about the movement of history, who buried French Catholicism in a sterile attitude of opposition, of conservatism, of Restorationist sentiment...was called by God to listen to the lesson of events, those masters which he gives us with his own hands, and to free the Church from the wretched logic of the 'Donation of Constantine', and convert it to an evangelical attitude which would have enabled it to be less OF the world and more FOR the world. He did exactly the opposite. A catastrophic man who did not know what ECCLESIA was nor yet what Tradition was; he oriented the Church to be always OF the world and not yet FOR the world, which nevertheless stood in need of it.

And Pius IX still reigns. Boniface VIII still reigns; he has been superimposed on Simon Peter, the humble fisher of men!

As they left this morning's ceremony, each of the bishops was given a folder containing the voting papers for them to elect sixteen bishops from among themselves for each of the ten Commissions; a booklet containing a complete and fully up-to-date list of the bishops of the Church; a list, for each Commission, and in the format of the voting paper, of the bishops who were already members of the various Preparatory Commissions. It amounted to an invitation to elect these . . .

Yet, a certain continuity between the work of the Council and that of the Preparatory Commissions is desirable. But it is also desirable to do now something both different and better than what has been prepared: something pastoral, less scholastic. Nearly all the bishops that I have spoken to and whose opinion I have been told about, deemed the four dogmatic *schemata* much too academic and philosophical. A Council, they say, does not need to argue by syllogisms, to speak to the principle of sufficient reason, etc.

Basically, scholasticism has penetrated the government of the Roman Curia. The Preparatory Commissions reflected this state of affairs, both because they wanted to produce a *summa* of papal addresses and utterances, and also because most of them (at any rate almost all those who drafted the schemata) were made up of professors in the Roman colleges. But scholasticism hardly has a place in the pastoral government of dioceses, and it is this that now has the floor. {CgMJC, 11 October 1962}

On the other hand, Cardinal Giuseppe Siri, archbishop of Genoa and president of the Italian episcopal conference, was one of those who—after a long rather literary note in his journal—showed that he found disturbing things in the Pope's address. This is expressed in ecclesiastical euphemisms, stating that he feared that what the Pope said might be put to bad use, but, in an historical perspective, this is nonetheless significant:

The weather turned out favorable and the opening ceremony was able to go forward with the procession through the square. There were not too many people, probably because they zealously blocked off many of the streets. The ceremony was very solemn and I think it impressed people. On entering St. Peter's I felt that I needed to prepare myself spiritually, to make myself docile before God, to humble myself—I who am a sinner—to be childlike, to have charity for everyone in spite of zeal. In reality, I fear that love of the Church may make me oppose someone who could be more effective.

[I sought to work through all that as I slowly ascended
the stairs of the great temple toward my place in the
procession.]

I paid attention to very few or none of the others since it
seemed that my duty was to pray a lot. I simply glimpsed
by chance some personalities: Prince Albert of Liège,
Mgr Castelli, Mgr Botto and, in leaving, Mgr Pardini. I
didn't understand very much of what the pope said, but
concerning the little I heard, I found it a good occasion
to make a great mental act of obedience. From what I
could see and from what my secretaries said, it was badly
disorganised. Before the ceremony we waited a long
time in the sacristy, where there were chairs for thirty-
some cardinals. But we were about eighty. I gave up my
chair to let Cardinal Lercaro sit down. When they finally
brought more chairs, I finally found myself between
Cardinal Confalonieri and Cardinal Rugambwa, along
with Cardinal Döpfner. Speaking as a member of the
Commission for Extraordinary Affairs (that's why he
also spoke to Döpner), His Emin. Confalonieri took
the occasion to tell me with deep interest that he was
working to prepare for the council 'a text—two short
pages addressed to the world.' Döpfner agreed, saying
that Cardinal Frings had already proposed this in the
Central Commission (that's true) and that he approved.
I would have liked to ask him what could be said to
the world (!) in two short pages, but I judged it better
not to continue the conversation. The incident shows
that some people do not have a very elevated idea of
an ecumenical council, which pains me. We ought not
look to the world in order to offer it some agreeable
feelings, but only to our Lord. Let's hope that the solemn
enthronement of the Holy Gospels during the ceremony
will have suggested appropriate thinking. What touched
me the most was the Pope's profession of faith. When I
made my own profession with the others, I felt choked
up because I was so moved by the power of this gesture.
I greeted and hugged Cardinal Ruffini, telling him that

he should be a central figure for the council. He asked
me to support him. To go see him tonight if I can. But
Cardinal Ruffini was not at home. I visited Mgr Peruzzo,
the bishop of Agrigento at Saints John and Paul, one
of our best bishops. We were concerned with the
election of the members of the conciliar commissions.
How will the 2,000–3,000 council fathers be guided
on unfamiliar subjects? It would be logical to think of
having spokespersons for the groups. Perhaps tomorrow
it will be clearer how to resolve this matter. Mgr Peruzzo
was able to speak with Fr Balić who is in contact with
many Franciscan bishops staying at the Via Merulana,
etc. Tonight I read the Pope's address critically so as
to be able to align my thinking with that of the Vicar
of Christ. On two points I fear that people can use his
words badly. Probably that's what kept me from sleeping
for a long time.[90]

---

90. *'Il tempo si é abbastanza ristabilito e la cerimonia di apertura ha potuto così svolgersi col corteo in piazza. Non c'era troppo gente, probabilmente perché con molto zelo avevano fatto molti blocchi stradali. La cerimonia è stata solenne veramente e credo abbia impressionato assai. Entrando in S. Pietro mi pareva di dover fare una grande preparazione spirituale, farmi piccolo davanti a Dio, umiliarmi peccatore, essere come un bambino, avere carità per tutti ad onta dello zelo. In realtà temo che l'amore alla Chiesa mi porti a scagliarmi contro qualcuno che potrebbe agire meglio. [Ho cercato di fare tutto questo mentre lentamente salivo i gradini del gran tempio al mio posto nel corteo.] Ho guardato poco o nulla perché mi pareva essere mio dovere pregare assai. Ho scorto solo per caso qualcuno: il principe Alberto di Belgio. Mons. Castelli, Mons. Botto e uscendo Mons. Pardini. Ho capito poco del discorso del Papa: in quel poco ho subito avuto modo di fare un grande atto di obbedienza mentale. Credo ci sia stata abbondante disorganizzazione a quel che ho visto e a quello che ho sentito dei miei segretari. Prima della cerimonia abbiamo lungamente atteso nella sala dei paramenti, dove c'erano seggi per una trentina di Cardinali, mentre dovevamo essere ottanta circa. Per questo io ho lasciato il mio posto per far sedere il card. Lercaro. Così, quando hanno portato altre sedie, sono andato a finire tra il card. Confalonieri e il card. Rugumbwa con davanti il card. Döpfner. L'Em.mo Confalonieri ne ha approfittato per dirme con molta enfasi che bisognava permettere (ne parlava come commissione extra ordinem e pertanto appellava anche a Döpfner) al concilio "un testo, due paginette, al mondo". Gli ho detto che non mi pareva ci fosse il tempo per farlo... Ha riposte che vi voleva poco a "buttarle giù". Döpfner assentiva, dicendo che il card. Frings l'aveva già proposto in Commissione central (era vero) ed anche Lui assentiva. Io avrei volute chiedere che cosa dire al mondo (!) nelle due paginette. Ma ho giudicato meglio non con-*

In the journals of some 'minor' bishops, such as the missionary Perraudin, we see on the contrary how the novelty of the opening allocution was welcomed:

> Thursday, October 11. (48th anniversary of my baptism.) Solemn opening of the Council by HH Pope John XXIII. What is impressive here is the presence in Rome, gathered around the Vicar of Christ, of the universal Church—living, diverse, filled with good will but open to important reforms. I don't think that the magnificent solemnity of the ceremonies was what was needed—rather more simplicity. The major currents are beginning to bubble up among the conciliar fathers. People speak freely and with lots of hope. People prayed deeply—but the liturgy was not sufficiently communal, too much theatre or a concert. The Church has to get rid of some anachronisms and be more clearly poor in its Head, more evangelical. I think of our poor people [at home] who don't even have a chapel for Sunday prayer, while here in Rome there is a superfluity of buildings and luxury even in the Church. The Church of the Missions must speak up. The Catholic Church needs to 'catholicise' itself. The missionary collegiality of bishops

---

tinuare il discorso. Esso dimostra che taluni non hanno una idea molto elevate di un concilio ecumenico e questo mi fa pena. Noi non dobbiamo guardare al mondo per offrirgli qualche emozione gradita, ma solo a Nostro Signore. Speriamo che la solenne esposizione del Santo Vangelo fatta durante la Cerimonia abbia suggerito appropriati pensieri. La cosa che più mi ha commosso fu la Professio Fidei del Papa. Quando con gli altri feci la mia un nodo mi serrò alla gola, tanto sentii l'atto. Ho salutato e abbracciato il card. Ruffini, gli ho dette di essere lui un fulcro del concilio. Mi chiese di sostenerlo. Stasera se posse andrò da lui. Il cardinal Ruffini non era in casa. Ho visitato ai SS. Giovanni e Paolo mons. Peruzzo, Arcivescovo di Agrigento, uno dei Vescovi migliori. Ci se è preoccupati per la elezione dei Membri delle Commissioni Conciliari. Infatti come seranno orientati i Padri (2000–3000 = circa soggetti non conosciuti? Sarebbe logico pensera a trattative di gruppi. Forse domani si farà più chiaro sul modo di risolvere la questione. Lui, Mons. Peruzzo, avrebbe parlato con P. Balić, che ha voce presso i molti Vescovi francescani, ospiti di Via Merulana, etc. Questa sera ho analizzato bene il discorso del Papa per poter uniformare il mio modo di pensare a quello del Vicario di Cristo. Di due punti ho timore qualcuno possa usare male. Forse è questo che me impedisce di dormire per del tempo.'

has to 'become a reality'. It is still much too theoretical or in any case too timid in reality.[91]

Although not in Rome, the Louvain theologian Ch Moeller made notes in his 'Notebooks' about things that seemed promising in the Pope's address:

> Council on TV—Pope John tired, anxious, serious. His kindness written on his face. A spirit of profound grace visible in his entire person—the brief oriental part of the ceremony made the universality of the Church concrete. But it must be admitted that the structures are indeed 'Latin of the Latins'—The patriarchs, for example, are placed after the cardinals. A choice heavy with consequences—the Pope's address: excellent in its openness: explanation of the truth rather than condemnation; see the good aspect of the modern world (against the birds of ill omen) rather than only the bad— Very remarkable commentary by F Colleye.

Yet another dimension can be seen after October 11 in the journal of Giovanni Urbani, in some ways so 'Italian' in its literary style of underlining some aspects of the ceremony and by its mixing of the Council in with matters in the Italian Church. We see a network of exchange of information among the bishops, and we note the confusion concerning the duration of the work of the council:

> October 11—an extraordinary, historic day. Even the weather became fine following a rainstorm, and when we went in procession, the sun was shining. At 8 am in the Sala Borgia for vestments, then we waited for the Pope in the papal vesting hall. As usual, all the seats are full; at the last minute they remedied the situation by bringing in more chairs. The Pope arrived around 9 o'clock. He was calm. He vested—then we went into the Pauline chapel for the chant *Ave Maris Stella*—then the procession—as always the royal stairs are impressive. There are many people in the square, but not an enormous amount.

---

91. A Perraudin, 'Deuxième Concile du Vatican: Notes personnelles' (CLG); he was the bishop of Kabgayi in Rwanda.

By the time I entered the basilica, all the bishops were in their places. It's a beautiful sight, but I'm afraid that for the sessions the rectangular format will make those near the door feel outside the assembly. The service is beautiful but a bit too long—something shorter would have been to everyone's spiritual advantage. The Gospel was given a solemn enthronement. The Pope's profession of faith was a moving moment. Above all the gathering of the entire 'teaching church' makes this a historic event. I thought of St Peter when he got to Rome, impelled by a divine inspiration, and of his martyrdom, and of this extraordinary triumph. A long address from the Pope concluded the ceremony—a talk marked by optimism and a very broad vision of the world. In the afternoon, a phone call from Capovilla—at 5 pm Mgr Bortignon tells me of the uncertainty about the voting. Same idea from Mgr Santi, who talks to me about the oriental churches.

At 5.30 pm a long conversation with Cardini about the catechism and about Catholic Action. At 7 pm on the balcony of the Majordomo to see the torchlight procession and to hear the Pope give a brief talk from his balcony. Well-chosen words—only the hint that he hopes to be finished by Christmas in view of another gathering left us puzzled. An extraordinary day.[92]

---

92. '11 Ottobre—*Giornata stupenda, storica. Anche il tempo, dopo una prima onda di pioggia s'è messo sereno: quando si esce in processione c'è il sele. Alle 8 somo in Sala Borgia per i paramenti, poi attendiano nella sala dei paramenti di Papa. Come sempre i posti a sodere sono i soliti; quindi si rimedia all'ultimo momento con sedie. Il Papa arriva verso le nove. È sereno. Si veste—si passa nella Capp. Paolina per il canto dell'Ave Maris Stella—poi il corte—come sempre è imponeto per la scala regia. In Piazza c'è abbastanza gente, ma non molta. Quando entro in Basilica i Vescovi sono tutti al'loro posti? Fanno un bel vedere, ma temo che per le sedute la forma rettangolare tenga i più vicini alla porta quasi estranei all'assemblea. La funzione è bella, ma un po'troppo lunga—si poteva abbreviare con vantaggi spirituali di tutti. // Il Vangelo meritava una più solenne intronizzazione. Momento commovente la professio fidei del Papa. È sopratutto la presenza della Chiesa docente al completo che rende storica l'assemblea. Peaso a S. Pietro quando giungeva a Roma, spintovi da divino impulse, al suo martirio e a questo stupendo trionfo. Un lungo discorso del Papa conclude la cerimonia: discourse venato di ottimismo pur nella*

After the opening ceremony another new departure for Vatican II shows up in the newspapers, where the whirlwind and the contacts with the press shake up the 'starchy' reserve at the beginning.[93] A case in point is the fiery Brazilian Helder Camara who wrote to his spiritual 'family' his first letter–journal on 13–14 October.[94] The same

---

visione arupia del mondo. Al pommeriggio telefonata entusiasta di Capovilla—alle 17 mons. Bortignon mi informa della incertezze circa le votazioni. Cosi pensa S.E. Mons. Santi, che mi parla anche delle Chiese Orientali. Alle 17.30 lungo colloquio con Cardini circa il Catechismo e l'Azione Cattolica. Alle 19 in Loggia del Maggiordomo per vedere la fiaocolata e ascoltare il Papa che tiene breve discorso dal balcone. Felici parole: solo il cenno che spera per Natale sia finito al massmo per nuovo incontro lascia perplessi. Giornata stupenda.'

93. The journal of J Dupont is an example: for his papers about the Council, see the inventory produced by E Leuchez.

94. The first journal–letter of Helder Camara, *A querida familia do S. Joaquim*, dated 13–14 October, speaks already of the rapidity of the bishops' change of attitude and mood: 'It is easy to send my impressions of the Council's solemn ceremonies, but it is difficult, especially in these first days, to sum up my impressions of the spirit of the Council—its tendencies, its perspectives, and its goals. As to the solemnities, I sent some things that can give you an idea of the opening of Vatican II. I call special attention to the Holy Father's address, the very beautiful prayer spoken at the end of the Mass (*Adoremus, Domine Sancte Spiritus*) and the prayer of the Eastern Bishops. / As to the Council as seen from inside—and with caution from someone who recognizes how impossible it is to judge—here are some observations (subject to revision): 1) *The Council is going to be very difficult.* The Sacred Congregations imagined that it would be easy to think for the bishops and decide for them. For example, the schema [...] seemed to *many* bishops from all over the world to be out of touch with what the Pope stated as the spirit of the Council. Today, when the task was to elect sixteen bishops for each of the ten commissions of the Council, the episcopate gave a first demonstration of its choice: it refused to vote precipitously or to accept a list that was imposed. It was decided that the different episcopal conferences should indicate names and that together they would seek to agree on them. / That means that the bishops are going to choose their own representatives. And this is the beginning of the beginning. Probably Latin will not be accepted as the official language since many bishops don't understand it, especially the way it is spoken by the French and the Germans. Next will come the battles over changing the sche-

thing goes for the telegraphed notes of Döpfner, beginning with 12

---

mas. 2) *The developed world and the underdeveloped world.* Just as at the United Nations, we have at the Council the presence of both the developed world and the underdeveloped world. Asia and Africa are still far from Latin America. We understand one another at a distance, looking toward coming closer together. / We have in common a desire to universalize the Church's vision; and to prevent the problems of continents so foreign and so distant being treated according to European norms. There are genuine concerns about our numbers and the significance of our interventions. The Council would be worth the effort just for this kind of dialogue. / 3) *Progressives and integrists.* Among the Europeans (and for the great centers of Latin America), the debate is between progressives and integrists. / There are disturbing symbols: in the middle of the twentieth century using Latin as the official language of the Council of a living Church that wants to understand and be understood, to be present and to be active… Lighting up the Castel Sant'Angelo and other Roman monuments (to charm the tourists) is like the torches of the Council of Ephesus. 4) *The European rhythm of life and the Brasilian rhythm.* The Brasilans are anxious about the rhythm of work: a meeting every two or three days…/ What is terrible is that December will be here without the Council having made much progress. Many bishops won't be able to remain. Very few will be able to return. As for me, since Providence brought me here, I have a well established plan: ––to get involved in the Council (preparing with my brother bishops the themes that need to be treated. For example, the bishops and the episcopal college. After a theological presentation, pastoral conclusions:/ the bishops and the Sacred Congregations / the bishops and the apostolic nuncios / the bishops and religious / the episcopal college and the college of cardinals / titular bishops); ––to make contact with bishops from all over the world (systematic contacts, create friendships, firm up linkages); ––to study (I will send on my ideas); ––to prepare myself spiritually. The Feast of Our Lady of Fatima has passed and I have not been able to meet the Holy Father. But I haven't given up on the idea. I have three suggestions for him: ––prayer for unity, a meeting during the Council of the bishops from the Third World, and a concelebration for closing the first session (one single Mass celebrated by the Pope and all the council fathers, consecrating the same host and the same wine, giving in this way a concrete expression of the Church's unity). We don't know anything yet about the date of the close of the first session. They talk about December 8. At the *Domus Mariae* (via Aurelia 481, Rome, Italy) we Brasilian bishops have a privileged situation. There are more than 50 altars for celebrating holy Mass. The house is run by a secular institute that reminds me of Begonda. We are praying to God who alone stirs up love of the Church (far from our personal vanities and dangerous regional interests). May we return with a more supernatural spirit (deeper in faith, hope, and charity!). Up to now I don't know anything about myself. The nuncio is going to come here to the *Domus Mariae* on days without meetings beginning Monday, the 15th. I intend to ask him for news (if there is any). Happily I am totally *in manus Domini* [in the Lord's hands]… I won't mention names here, but I don't forget any of you in my prayers (which are longer), nor in my Mass. Nostalgia and the cold will only get worse as we get closer to December…'
'*É fácil mandar impressões sobre as solenidades do Concílio. É difícil, especialmente*

October by mentioning his meeting with Küng; on his page dealing

---

nos primeiros dias, fixar impressões sobre o espírito do Concílio: suas tendências, suas perspectivas, seus rumos. Quanto às solenidades, enviei algum material capaz de dar uma idéia do que foi a abertura do Vaticano II. Chamo, especialmente, a atenção para: o discurso do santo padre; a oração belíssima rezada após a missa (Adoremus, Domine Sancte Spiritus) e a prece dos orientais. / Quanto ao Concílio por dentro—salvo engano de quem reconhece a impossibilidade de julgar—aqui estão algumas observações, sujeitas à revisão: 1) o Concílio vai ser dificílimo. As Sagradas congregações pensavam que seria fácil pensar pelos bispos e decidir por eles. Acontece por exemplo que o esquema da parte [...] parece, a muitos bispos do mundo inteiro, em dissonância com que o papa anuncia como espírito do Concílio. Hoje, quando s tratou de eleger 16 bispos para cada uma das 10 comissões do Concílio, o episcopado deu uma primeira amostra de su decisão: recusou-se a votar apressadamente ou a aceitar listas impostas. Ficou decidido que as diversas Conferências episcopais indicariam nomes e, em conjunto, se procuraria chegar a um acordo. / Quer dizer que os bispos vão escolher os seus representates. E isto é começo do começo. Provavelmente o latim será derrubado como lingua oficial: grande número de bispos não consegue entender, sobretudo o latim falado por franceses e alemães... Virão depois as batalhas essenciais pela alteração dos esquemas. 2) mundo desenvolvido e mundo subdesenvolvido. Tal como nas Nações Unidas, temos no Concílio a presença do mundo desenvolvido e do subdesenvolvido. A Ásia e a África ainda não estão muito próximas da América Latina. Entendemo-nos à distância, enquanto não vem a aproximação. / Temos em comum o desejo de universalizar a visão da Igreja; a decisão de evitar que problemas de continentes tão distantes e diferentes sejam tratados com medidas européias. Há verdadeiros sustos com o nosso número e com o sentido de noassas intervenções. Só este diálogo já valeria o Concílio. 3) progressismo e integrismo. Entre os europeus (com reflexos em centros maiores da América Latina) o embate é entre progressismo e integrismo. / Há símbolos que assustam: em pleno século XX, o latim como lingua oficial do Concílio de uma Igreja viva que quer entender e ser entendida, estar presente e atuar... A iluminação do castelo Sant'Angelo e de outros monumentos romanos feita (para encanto dos turistas) a tochas como no Concílio de Éfeso. 4) ritmo europeu e ritmo...brasileiro. Os brasileiros estão preocupados com o ritmo dos trabalhos: reuniões de 2 em 2 dias, de 3 em 3... / O terrível é que chegará dezembro com bem pouco avanço. Muitos bispos não poderão demorar. Bem poucos poderão voltar... Quanto a mim, já que a Providência me trouxe, já estou com programa organizado: --de mergulho no Concílio (preparação, em conjunto com bispos irmãos, de temas a apresentar. Por exemplo, sobre os bispos e colégio episcopal. Depois de uma palavra teológica, conclusões pastorais: / Os bispos e as Sagradas congregações / Os bispos e os núncios apostólicos / Os bispos e os religiosos / Colégio episcopal e colégio cardinalício / Bispos titulares). -de contato com bispos do mundo inteiro (contatos sistemáticos, criando amizades, estabelecendo laços); --de estudo (mandarei indicações): --de aprimoramento espiritual. Passou o dia de N. Sra. de Fátima e não me pude avistar com o santo padre. Mas não desisti da idéia. Tenho 3 sugestões a apresentar: --a prece pela unidade; --reunião, durante o Concílio, de bispos do mundo subdesenvolvido; --concelebração como fecho da 1ª fase da Concílio. (A

with the 13th, a longer entry, after noting the thrust of the interventions of Liénart and Frings in the aula, he lists the participants at a meeting in the afternoon in the Via Dell'Anima at which Döpfner, Liénart, Frings, Alfrink and Suenens took part.[95]

CHENU'S JOURNAL

If everything said thus far and the sampling of journals appear convincing and true, then the historiography of Vatican II cannot fail to pay careful attention to the editing and publication of these journals. Editing the journal of Marie–Dominique Chenu, which all these considerations were meant to introduce, hopes to contribute to this phase of the research.

The journal of Fr Chenu, in certain ways, is both typical and of modest length. It is not an immense, analytical, and highly detailed journal like some others. It doesn't go any further than the end of the second session of the Council, but it gets stuck on 12 November 1963. It does not explain the implications of his rank only among the private experts (*periti privati*),[96] but it doesn't hide the subtle and

---

mesma missa celebrada pelo papa e por todos os padres conciliares, consagrando a mesma hóstia e o mesmo vinho, dando una idéia tangível da unidade da Igreja). Nada sabemos ainda quanto à data de término da 1ª fase. Fala-se em dia 8 de dezembro. Em Domus Mariae (Via Aurelia, 481 – Roma – Itália) os bispos brasileiro temos hospedagem privilegiada. Há mais de 50 altares para a celebração da santa misa. A casa é dirigida por um instituto secular que lembra o da Begonda. – Peçam a Deus que só nos mova o amor à santa Igreja – (longe de nós vaidades pessoais ou regionalismos perigosos). Que o nosso desejo único seja corresponder aos planos divinos, às esperanças dos fiéis e às necessidades do mundo... Peçam que nehum de nós desperdice 2 meses na cidade eterna. Que estes dias marquem nossa vida. Que voltemos mais sobrenaturais (avançados na fé, na esperança e na caridade!). Até agora nada soube sobre mim. O senhor núncio, a partir de 2ª feira (15) vai passer os dias sem sessão aqui, na Domus Mariae. Pretendo pedir-lhe novidades. Se é que existem. Felizmente, continuo em absolute in manus Domini... Não cito nomes: mas a ninguém esqueço nas vigílias (que estão mais longas), nem na santa misa. As saudades e o frio só farão aumentar até dezembro...'

95. F° 1–2, ms., given to me by K Wittstadt.
96. His engagement as a *peritus* is due to the bonds created at the Saulchoir in Belgium between the Dominicans and the Missionaries of La Salette. Among Fr Chenu's students was a future bishop of Madagascar, Rolland, who in 1962 asked his former professor to assist him as his expert at the Council. Chenu agreed,

insurmountable ostracism that engulfs the author of *Une école de théologie*. He doesn't cover the intersession during which he worked on writing texts for Schema XIII and also worked at writing the pastoral letter of the bishops of Madagascar. He was not connected to a structured archives, and his notes don't exhaust—far from it— his participation and his own theological contributions to the whole work of Vatican II. [97]

On the other hand, the characters and the substance in Chenu's journal are never bland. This is clear from Chenu's account and commentary noted for the opening day of the Council that has been analysed in the parallel sources that preceded. Fr Chenu was not able to get into the aula and so he did not face the challenge of the opening ceremony that scandalised a man like Y–M Congar who had patiently put up with vexations no less serious during the preparations. Fr Chenu remained seated on the base of a column outside in St Peter's Square. Then finally he waited for the press account and skimmed the Pope's address once more.

The press is one of the original protagonists of his journal: a source of information on the Council itself in the case of October 11, then many other times concerning events outside the aula, outside the Council, and sometimes (as with the political and diplomatic scene) outside ecclesial contexts.

Side by side with the press, the other protagonist in his journal is conversation—almost always vibrant and engaging—with a whole crowd of people. Chenu was not involved in the preparations for the Council, nor was he one of the theologians taken practically 'hostage' in the preparatory commissions. For him, the Council was a moment of freedom based on the experience of rediscovering the Gospel's capacity to speak to the present day.

His journal reflects this spirit and this perspective when he reports on his relations with qualified theologians, but especially with those

---

and his acceptance, announced to the clergy on Holy Thursday, was applauded by them all…

97. Draft documents are held in the archives of Le Saulchoir. In general, see G Alberigo, *Un Concile à la dimension du monde: M.-D. Chenu à Vatican II d'après son Journal*, and G Turbanti, 'Le Rôle de M.-D. Chenu dans l'élaboration de *Gaudium et Spes*' in *Actes du colloque M.-D. Chenu: Moyen Âge et modernité* (Paris, 1995).

who address and welcome the gospel's ferment in the world—the dramatic challenge of contemporary modernity.

Fundamentally according to his journal Fr Chenu has only two occasions when he is in contact with professional theologians (and also with those who have been reconciled and re-engaged). The first has to do with his message to the world, for which he leaned on Fr Congar and on a method that developed at Vatican II to get things done—meetings, drafts, lobbying bishops, then more meetings, etc. It works because it works on consensus, builds it and makes it grow in creative ways, to the point that, as hours and days go by, more than one person recognises as his own work what passes from hand to hand. The attitude of Garonne, when he received the proposition for the message to the world, was that this was something 'already being talked about'; this illustrates how the Council learned to foster consensus. Fr Chenu knew that he had a strong claim to initiating the idea of the message—and perhaps he underestimated how this initiative created the climate of the Council. But he didn't flaunt that or let that become important, he didn't even make his claim on the initative beyond a certain point: he didn't even keep his first draft of the text (which can be found in the appendices of Congar's Journal). He put up with changes that he thought diminished his project, but he was satisfied with the thing in and of itself. In any case, he did not use his initiative to try to get a role in the group of council experts, which did not really attract him and perhaps would have marginalised him.

This was a spirit of mildness that was neither arrogant nor disdainful, but real. When he met with the group around Volk about replacing the schemas of November 1962—his only other occasion of effective contact with the theologians of the majority—his participation was strangely passive. Although fully conscious of the need to put the Council on another trajectory than the dead end that the preparatory schemas had created, Fr Chenu was not someone at home with compromise, which the structure of the assembly suggested or imposed. He almost never saw the great weavers of Vatican II (Philips, Colombo); he had no experience of Ratzinger and he was aware of some awkward declarations or indiscretions made by Küng. And the things that he discussed with the theologians were especially opinions and information about condemnations, humiliations, suspicions and censures about which unfortunately he remained an expert.

The only 'theological' document that he kept in his dossier is one by Dossetti, published here as a note in the journal (see pp 99–101); the only document that he copied into his notebook was the observations on the liturgy that Martimort contributed to the fascicles of *Études et documents* of the French episcopal conference. The only theologians with whom he had a new and durable relationship of trust in 1962 and 1963 were those who dealt with information—first, the director of *Civiltà Cattolica*, Fr Roberto Tucci, and then Fr Wiltgen.

He sought out other theologians and other contexts—that of the Church of the poor, of underdevelopment and of famine, and of social and ecclesiastical reform. Fr Chenu forgot names, eg, Pastore's name on Nov. 29, 1962 and that of Vittorio Peri, an important expert in the Christian Orient. He describes his experiences with young people. His interests will also bring him quickly into contact with persons who will play key roles in future council debates but who will interest him only with respect to their awareness of the challenge of the contemporary world and its new protagonists.

This is neither blindness nor naïveté. Fr Chenu is not self-interested at the Council nor is he fickle. Among the few letters kept in his dossier of the Council is his letter of 3 January 1963, to Mgr Ancel in which brings up again the idea of a secretariat similar to the hugely successful Secretariat for Christian Unity of Cardinal Bea, but devoted to penetrating and open research on the great questions challenging humanity.[98] The persistence of these themes

---

98. 'Your Excellency, Let me share with you the deep emotion—both intellectual and heartfelt—that I felt in participating recently in a private conversation with M. François Perroux, professor in the Collège de France. He is a leading thinker in Economics, a discipline that provides the real human context for evangelization today. This dialogue with Perroux had been instigated by the directors of the university parish who are preparing the annual Easter Study Days (to be at Montpellier in 1963) on the theme of *poverty*, a theme proposed this year for all the teams of Christians in public education. This is a difficult topic, given that the goal is to do more than be moralistic or romantic. I was struck by Perroux's analysis: with an economist's pragmatism he perceives the realistic demands of the Gospel's message. Poverty is not only just one good example: it is an essential dimension of the community of Christians in the world—such as it is emerging. However, as the world is shaping up in countries on the way to development (two-thirds of humanity today), the present economy makes the Christian message institutionally incomprehensible for people. To consent to the dynamics of this economy is already to consent to the defeat of evangelization (leaving salvation only as a

and orientations, characteristic of Chenu's research and study in an already long life, will become explicit in his journal during the two periods of the Council that it covers. The focus will be on two themes that are linked from the start in Chenu's thinking and culture.[99]

One of these is Africa. Chenu owed his active participation in the Council to Mgr Rolland's request, and his journal shows deep investment in the needs and problems about which his former student, by then the Bishop of Madagascar, put him to work.[100] Perhaps in a way different from H de Lubac, for Chenu the fact that he was the expert for an African bishop was the expression of a marginalisation that the French bishops forced on him; but it was also a choice he

---

choice for individuals on the margins of a pagan society). I am overwhelmed by this analysis. Coming from the mouth of Perroux, this is not just a rhetorical statement, but a conclusion derived from rigorous analysis. I thought then of you and of the project for which you and some other council fathers are the protagonists. So I have felt more deeply the apostolic urgency as well as the difficulty of giving this idea a clear conceptual and institutional expression. In parallel with this, your last letter that told me that this project has been blocked, saddened me deeply. Since nothing has been committed for this topic, there is a great risk that the Council will start up again in September without this question being raised in an effective way. In that case, nothing will happen. 1) Since there is no official "secretariat" for this, couldn't we undertake work on the four areas already discussed: worldwide imbalance for underdeveloped countries, poverty, demographic expansion, and war and peace? Although this work would not be official, it could be organized and organic all the same. Couldn't Cardinal Suenens, who had participated in this project, continue to sponsor it? He is well situated in the conciliar structures to give it credibility. Then texts could be sent to the secretariats of the various episcopal conferences. 2) Couldn't we imagine getting help from qualified *lay* experts to assist and strengthen this work—not as members of a commission (since that hasn't been granted), but as 'experts' available to the call from a president. Since the *subject matter* of these gospel injunctions (poverty, justice, peace) is secular [*réalité terrestre*], we should let those who know these areas (people like Perroux, Veronese…) bring their analysis and their witness in a way that churchmen are unable to do from their own expertise. Further, it belongs to the laity to take positions on questions of economics, social policy, and politics. Your Excellency: Don't both to reply to this letter. I only wanted to pass on to you the advice of a qualified economist to raise the question of poverty. Please receive this note as a sign of my respectful and fervent spirit of communion with you.'

99. One example is Chenu's attentive enthusiasm for the work done in tandem by Zoa and Greco to organize the African episcopate.

100.See M Rolland, 'Le P. Chenu, théologien au Concile', in *L'Hommage différé au P. Chenu* (Paris), 247–256.

made for his deep feeling of conviction about the catholicity of the Church in its concrete pluralistic expressions. That explains why in the two sessions covered by the journal we find him at conferences for the African bishops and then for the bishops of Latin America. In both he found signs of promising growth.

The second of his key interests is the Eastern Church. It had not been planned for Fr Chenu to be a counselor to the Eastern bishops (above all the Melkites and Maronites, with a distinction between them that grew as the Council unfolded). But he discovered during the Council that their solicitude for tradition and for the *intellectus fidei* {understanding of the faith} agreed with his own idea of the Council as a renewal and more adequate expression of thinking about the faith and proclaiming it.

There is nothing more in his journal on the Church and the World, on the signs of the times, or on work; but perhaps there is a key there that is needed to grasp the role of Fr Chenu in the schemas of the Council.

The atmosphere of the Council and the way Chenu lived within it are summed up just after the approval of the Message to the World in the letter that he wrote to his Provincial who was possibly startled by learning of the key role played by Chenu and Congar in initiating this event. Fr. Chenu sent his superior an account of the Council that is also a description of his participation, his involvement, and the inner commitment that the effervescence of the assembly prompted in his Christian soul:

> The newspapers have filled you in well enough (*La Croix*, Fesquet's articles in *Le Monde*, the long chronicles in *ICI*) on the start–up of the Council and of its first activities. In addition, the notes of Fr Congar, for example, lay out the shape of the deep problems that lie before it. What else can I tell you? Here are a few anecdotes from my little corner of the world. First of all, my 'place' in all of this . . . As you know, a former student at the Saulchoir (1931–1937), Fr Rolland, a La Sallette priest, became the Bishop of Antsirabé (Madagascar); he asked me to assist him at the Council. He did so in terms that would be touching for many of you {in Paris} by speaking of his moving gratitude for your fraternal fidelity to your black companions at the Saulchoir. I have been welcomed at

the Generalate of La Sallette here in Rome with great
generosity and care, which is good not only for my
physical health but also for my spirits. Clearly I am most
of all committed to helping the bishops of Madagascar
get oriented to their work. I have also found Fr de Lubac
here as theologian for the archbishop of Fianarantsoa.
You'll talk about that unexpected detail for a long time!
From the start, I have gotten the happy impression that
people's geographical isolation and their local concerns
are giving way to a deep sense of solidarity in terms of
the general problems which we all have. Very quickly
this solidarity showed itself in active contacts with other
African groups, both French and English–speaking
(and even Portuguese) and is helping to create working
groups. When the Archbishop of Dakar spoke up in the
assembly on the liturgy, he said that he was speaking
in the name of 250 bishops of Black Africa—a good
example in the midst of the anarchical speeches just
before him. This same phenomenon is occurring for
'episcopal conferences' from different regions (a good
forty of them in the world), but clearly with less ease
and effectiveness. This rather impressive 'consensus'
works at the level of pastoral sensibilities but doesn't
easily move into doctrinal or institutional statements.
That presupposes a technical analysis that many {of
the bishops} aren't ready for. So here is a beautiful
case study not only for sociological reflection, but for
the observation and the interplay of different levels of
theological '*loci*' {sources}. It will be a test of the pastoral
inspiration set out for the Council by the Pope. By the
way, the bishops are hard at work. They have invited
theologians to give them talks. Fr Congar spoke the
other day to the French bishops on Tradition, drawing
trenchant conclusions about the preparatory schemas.
He will give this same course to the African bishops. He
is involved in many other activities of great significance.
None of this happens without lots of meetings where
(it is understood) the Holy Spirit is at work through
secondary causes (even tertiary!). After all that, I need

a good hour of prayer to get back in touch with the First Cause.

This *recollectio* {summary account} by Fr Chenu and his frank disenchantment in describing the conciliar atmosphere can serve as a key to reading the following pages. Look at them in terms of the demands of historical method mentioned at the beginning and see them as a better contextualisation of his participation in the Council as someone 'exiled' from the commissions, but a participation nonetheless deep and fruitful—one that will be able to link up with other sources and other experiences to contribute to a more systematic reconstruction of the Council.

Alberto Melloni

MARIE-DOMINIQUE CHENU, OP

VATICAN II NOTEBOOK

A Journal of Vatican II

1962–1963

[1 r°] Vatican II Notebook

[11 October—8 December 1962], First Session.

[3 r°] *8 September*

I have had the idea of keeping some notes like a 'journal' during the Council, but I wondered if I would really manage to do it . . . Today, even before getting to Rome, I am beginning *ex abrupto* {quite suddenly}. This morning several letters arrived that suddenly put me in contact with tensions that have existed in the church for a long time[1] and that are already becoming evident in the preparations for the Council.

---

1. Fr Chenu had written about this to Karl Rahner on September 4, 1962: 'Reverend and dear Father, called in confidence by a bishop to help him as his theologian in the work of the Council, I have become somewhat acquainted with the preparatory *Schemata*. The first two 'constitutions' coming out of the Theological Commission (Cardinal Ottaviani) caused me distress and regret. I am daring to share this with you.—The bulk of these texts are inspired by and written in a strictly 'intellectualising' (in the bad sense of the word) perspective, that is, they give scholastic analyses and critiques a dominance over the Word of God. Proclaiming the Good News to the world, which ought to be primary and clear, remains only implicit in them.—Consequently a rigid stream of abstract and theoretical statements prevails, although the Council has stirred up hope for a pastoral approach equal to the problems posed by the evangelisation of a world that is new.—The two constitutions that I mention seem to be unaware of this new world; they only denounce errors, intra–theological errors, with no reference to the dramatic questions that people, Christian or not, are raising in response to a mutation of the human condition, both exterior and interior, that history has never seen before.—Thus these texts condemn theological 'opinions'

--A letter from Mgr Marty (Rheims) telling me, in reply to my note to him, that he shares my opinion and that he has 'replied with firmness already insisting on the pastoral and missionary thrust {of the Council}'. Fr Frisque is his theologian.[2]

--A letter from Mgr Glorieux, the theologian of Cardinal Liénart, to whom I had sent my reflections, concerns, and criticisms.[3] 'What

---

widespread in the Church at the cost of the transcendence of the faith and of the freedom needed for research on the *intellectus fidei* (*eg* of human origins, of original sin). Sad and vicious petty-mindedness! The Council is becoming an action of intellectual police behind the closed walls of the School.—The decisions of the Council need to be opened up by a clear declaration in the style of the Gospel: in the prophetic perspectives of both the Old and the New Testaments the plan of salvation in Christ's Incarnation and in the mystical Body of the Church should be proclaimed. [This is a] declaration addressed to humanity, whose grandeur and distress, despite defeats and mistakes, still aspire to the light of the Gospel and the presence of the Creator God—[a goal] that atheists aren't able to recognise under the conceptual and cultic expressions in which they are presented today. 'Missionary Church': a declaration proclaiming the fraternal unity of all people beyond frontiers, race and governments—with a refusal of violence, in love of peace—the test of the Kingdom of God. So let the Community of Christians publicly share the hope that all people have, so as to guide it to its supreme goal. I share my disappointment and my hope with you. May your influence help to give this Council its true character and its right purposes. Accept, reverend and dear Father, my fraternal good wishes and my deep respect', see A Duval, 'Le message au monde' in E Fouilloux (editor) 1962, *Vatican II commence...Approches francophones* (Louvain, 1993), 110.

2. The bishop had received from P Lebret a project for a message from the Council: for that, see D Pelletier, *Aux origines du tiers-mondisme catholique—De l'utopie communautaire au développement harmonisé: Économie et humanisme et le Père Lebret (1944-1966)* (Lyons, 1992), th 930-32. Frisque, from the Society of Helpers of the Missions of Père Lebbe, had written several times in *Église vivante* on the relation between the missions and ecclesiology.

3. These are the 'General Observations on the writing of the first two schemas', held by the SChn and dated September 1962: 'Reading through these texts gives one the impression of intellectualising statements rather than a message about the Word of God as salvation for the people. Of course the Word of God contains an essential teaching about *truths* that intelligence ought to "define" in opposition to threatening errors. But this rigorous necessity shouldn't cover up the primary richness of the Scriptures that seems to be presented here as an authoritative argument to support a thesis, when in fact the "thesis" is a secondary formulation to guarantee the divine message. These days when the biblical movement strives to give its full original richness to the Scriptures, not only in clerical studies but also in apostolic witness and in Christian spirituality, the proposed schemas seem not to have benefitted from this development; they maintain the *tone* of the

frightens me is the theme of the first project.[4] I would really regret it if it were brought to consideration by the Council, for I wonder what effect it will have on people both inside and outside, and on all the observers who are certainly expecting something other than a repetition of authoritarian statements along with severe condemnations. For my part, I would earnestly hope that something other could be substituted for it.'

---

decrees of Vatican I. Certainly the Church must define, but first it has to fulfill the function of transmission and witness to the Word of God. It was in this clear perspective that H[is] H[oliness] John XXIII convoked the Council and has on several occasions defined its spirit. A typical case of this displacement can be found in the second schema, chapter I, where the beautiful texts of Scripture on human knowledge of the truth—as [humans are] images of God, disciples of Christ, and witnesses of the Spirit—end up becoming arguments to support a metaphysical thesis about the first principles of reason. It is easier to understand what's wrong with this problematic prioritising [*dénivellation*] when you consider the Council in terms of those it means to address—people of our time living in a world where the Church has to rediscover its primarily *missionary* function in order to bring the Word of God to them. The Church today presents itself to 'those who are far off': one out of four persons today is Chinese, one out of three lives in a Communist regime, our technical civilisation favors atheism. Many Christians, although separated from the Church, are nonetheless faithful to the Gospel. In my hopefulness I believe that all of them are hearers who can be touched by the Good News. But they don't have any fundamental curiosity for theoretical formulations, as necessary as these may be for the latter education of their faith. In mission territory, we have to distinguish (so we can eventually unite them) the kerygmatic proclamation and the didactic instruction—the saving initiative of God and the theological *didascalia* {teaching}. The *object* of the faith as an expression of the Word of God includes an intimate relationship with the Father and the Son in the Spirit: it is formally in this way a saving and justifying truth. This in no way denies the need for theological definition, but it does preserve its original quality as *doctrina sacra* {sacred doctrine} (S Thomas, *Summa*, q 1). It would be vitally desirable that the writing of these constitutions, without losing the rigor of definition, should have at least in the opening paragraph of each chapter the *evangelical, pastoral* and *missionary* accent that ought to be that of the Council itself.'

4. The volume with the first series of schemas prepared for conciliar debate from the Subcommission on Amendments of the Central Preparatory Commission and sent to the bishops during the summer began with the *De deposito*—for all this, see J Komonchak in *History of Vatican II*, volume I (Maryknoll, NY and Leuven, 1995), 305–311.

--A letter from Père Congar, Mgr Weber's theologian[5], who shares with me news that he received from Fr de Lubac. Fr Lyonnet has to stop teaching at the Biblical Institute. However, [3 v°] since the paper that gave the notification gave no further precise details, the Jesuit General is keeping him not only in place, but also maintaining him as dean.[6] Fr K Rahner is obliged to submit all his writings to the Holy Office. He declared in consequence that he doesn't want a fight with the Holy Office, and so he is giving up publishing anything. The cardinal of Vienna will be taking him to the Council as his theologian,[7] and several bishops have written directly to the Pope to complain about this measure against Rahner. Finally Fr de Lubac is worried about his own work on Teilhard. He wrote some remarks about the article in the *Oss[ervatore] Rom[ano]* that commented on the monitum against Teilhard.[8]

On this same day, a brief item in *Le Monde* (8 September) points out the resistance of Roman prelates to the participation of non-Catholic observers. The first translation of John XXIII's *motu proprio* (about rules for the Council) said: 'Observers will not be able to come either to public sessions or to the general congregations except in particular cases indicated by the council of presidents.' A

---

5. Fr Chenu had a copy of a report in Latin five pages long, written by Fr Congar for Mgr Weber on 4 September1962, about the first schemas (SChn).

6. On 1 September 1961, Fr Zerwick and Fr Lyonnet had been suspended from teaching at the Biblical Institute [in Rome] following a *monitum* [warning] from the Holy Office that incorporated furious attacks against the exegesis [of the Institute] in the *Settimana del clero, Divinitas* and other publications by F Sapadafora, A Romeo, and Cardinal E Ruffini. This attack against the prestigious Jesuit institute began after Zerwick spoke at the Third Congress of Professors of Holy Scripture in North Italy (in Padua, September 1959). It was denounced [*stigmatisé*] by the Rector, E Vogt, in a mimeographed paper intitled *Pro memoria sugli attacchi contro il Pontificio Instituto biblico* (Rome, 1961); see the texts in A Tafi, *Mezzo secolo a servizio della chiesa*, ABI (Treviso, 1985), and G Fogarty, *American Biblical Scholarship: From the Early Republic to Vatican II* (San Francisco, 1989), 261–310.

7. See H Vorgrimler, *Karl Rahner verstehen: Eine Entführung in sein Leben und Denken* (Freiburg–im–Breisgau, 1985), 172–78.

8. The remarks in question can be found in H de Lubac, *Mémoire sur l'occasion de mes écrits: deuxième édition revue et augmentée* (Namur, 1992), 327–35. On the theological climate, see E Fouilloux, 'Théologiens romains et Vatican II (1959–1962)', in *Cristianesimo nella storia*, 15 (1994): 373–394.

correction was published the next day by the AFP: 'Contrary to the
first information given out, it now appears that the observers from
the separated churches will be able to come to both public sessions
and to the general congregations of the Council except in special
cases indicated by the council of presidents.'[9]

[4 r°] *10–25 september*

It occurred to me that an initial declaration from the Council—a
'message' to all people, Christian or not, proclaiming the aims and
the inspiration of the assembly with a missionary perspective and
attentive to the problems of today's world, would be a good response
to everyone's sympathetic interest—people would be disconcerted [if
the Council] started immediately with theoretical deliberations and
denunciations of erroneous tendencies.[10] This is very much in the

---

9. See G Alberigo, 'Dinamiche e procedure nel Vaticano II: Verso la revisione del
   Regolamento del Concilio (1962–1963)', in *Cristianesimo nella storia*, 13 (1992):
   115–164 and 'Ekklesiologie im Werden: Bemerkungen zum 'Pastoralkonzil' und
   zu den Beobachtern des II. Vatikanums', in *Ökumenische Rundschau*, 40 (1991):
   109–128.
10. On this topic, see Duval, 'Le Message...', 105–119; After 8 September 1962,
    Elchinger knew about a proposal {for a message}, and he encourages it in his
    letter to Fr Chenu on the same day: 'Your observations confirm my determination
    to promote a doctrinal Message for today's world. Don't hesitate to send me
    the various ideas that you find yourself writing about' (SChn). {Chenu's} note
    contained 'Observations on the doctrinal Schemata: 1) They are all focused on
    errors to denounce rather than on a positive proclamation of the faith with a
    view to discern possible *values* ('obediential potencies') that are fermenting
    within the problems and hopes of the world today. For that reason they have
    a negative quality instead of presenting Christ's message and the economy of
    salvation in its fullness and with its synthetic power. 2) They are too much
    wrapped up in scholastic disputes, proposing or rejecting 'opinions' that are
    freely discussed among theologians... and in combating isolated local errors, for
    which interventions from the ordinary magisterium would suffice rather than a
    solemn conciliar declaration. It's important to respect the different 'levels' within
    theological *loci* {sources}. 3) They are completely attuned to the problematics
    {perspectives} of western theology. They ignore the perspective of the theology
    of the Eastern Fathers, whose riches are a magnificent part of the Tradition. {That
    is another kind of} *intellectus fidei* {understanding of the faith} that {will} prevent
    us from treating as absolutes certain positions of Latin theology. For example:
    creation, original sin. 4) Serious insufficiency of scriptural *emphasis*. Moreover,
    by way of premature judgments, {they} close down legitimate and beneficial

style of the frequent addresses of John XXIII, especially his message of September 11.[11] It is hard to avoid the impression given by the dogmatic schemas that there are two parallel ideas of the Council: the Pope's inspiration, on the one hand, and the activities of the doctrinaire members of the theological commission, on the other.[12]

---

ongoing research by exegetes. 5) {They} are composed inside a 'climate' of an established Christendom, *without any missionary perspective* (= presentation of the gospel message to new peoples, and to the two billion non–Christians); without a window upon the developing world, without any answers to the questions and anxieties of our times according to the Gospel. 6) In (family and conjugal) morality, {they} give in to moralism rather than emphasise positive and specifically Christian values (for example, concerning conjugal love, Eph 5).'

11. Found in *Discorsi messaggi colloqui di SS Giovanni XXIII*, IV (Vatican City, 1963), 519–28; for the importance of the involvement of the cardinal of Malines–Brussels in the Message and also for the schema presented to the Pope in July, see LJ Suenens, *Souvenirs et espérances* (Paris, 1991), 65–80, and 'Aux origines du concile Vatican II', in *Nouvelle revue théologique*, 107 (1985): 3–21.

12. See the note of Fr Chenu from 15 September 1962 (SChn): '*On the writing of the first two Schemata.* The first two dogmatic constitutions, whatever their truth value and their appropriateness, are not cast in the perspectives and the spirit of the Council such as HH John XXIII has insistently described them. It's not only a question of editorial procedures; the way the questions are posed does not correspond to the world we're living in, nor to a balanced statement of the truths in question, in terms of the proclamation of the Word of God and the presence of the Church in the world. Certainly Revelation and fidelity to the deposit of the faith require a doctrinal formulation and a refutation of errors; that is the precise job of the Magisterium. But this *Magisterium* and its intellectual functioning should not be in the forefront to such a degree that witness to Christ by the Church is left entirely implicit. The word *witness* itself belongs to the substance of the Gospel whether it is a question of Christ or of the Church, for the community or for the individual faithful. The magisterium is at the service of the authenticity of this witness. / Today people certainly have an urgent need to have their errors corrected. They need to be 'taught'. But this teaching should arise definitely and visibly out of the witness of Christ and his Church. This is what people expect, even non–Christians. This witness, attuned to [*homogène du*] the mystery, is at the same time the efficacious *sign* of the truth. At a time when two–thirds of humanity don't hear the Word of God; when our new civilisation, that attracts and unites people, creates values and needs heretofore unknown; it is urgent that the Word of God should be delivered in all its original evangelical intensity— and not only in that secondary state constituted by theoretical statements and the theological discussion of opinions. [But] it is with *that* kind of discussion that the schemata of the two constitutions are preoccupied at length and in a scholastic fashion. Great pastoral work isn't done by applying prefabricated 'definitions'; it is direct and primary, emanating from the Gospel, even when the magisterium of the Church directs the work and guarantees its authenticity.

I told Fr Congar about this idea. He is very favorable and spontaneously shared the idea with people he's in touch with.[13]

Further, the Magisterium can't be reduced to the work of a particular dicastery; it is the functional charism of the entire episcopacy gathered around the Roman Pontiff as the primary and authentic witness to the faith. From the primacy of this witness that is the soul of all pastoral action, it is very significant that the Church is, according to the Gospel, the Church of the poor. This is not a topic for moral exhortation, but a property of the Church's nature. This in no way diminishes the societal and authoritative character of the Church, but it does remind us of the Church's purpose. Sadly, as I see it, these two constitutions in no way evoke—neither doctrinally nor in spirit—the missionary awakening that for twenty years has brought the Church to rediscover its profound nature in service of Christ's mission. [It is] a missionary Church among new peoples who have entered into the economic and political community of the world; it is a missionary Church in the new strata of a scientific and technological civilisation. The two constitutions remain completely within the perspective of the nineteenth century's doctrinal concerns in the liberal western society of 1870, adding to the texts of Vatican I only their application to contemporary deviations. And that is not done without distorting the texts. What we need, however, are not editorial accommodations [of Vatican I]; it is the very ground [*sol*] for the declarations that has to be renewed so that the needed proclamations against menacing errors can draw directly from the power of the gospel message, solemnly recalled, in the present context of people's actual needs.'

13. JCng = Yves Congar, *My Journal of the Council*, translated by Mary John Ronayne OP and Mary Cecily Boulding OP (Adelaide, SA, 2012), 81 [Hereafter cited as CngMJC]: 16 or 17 September 1962 'I received from Fr Chenu the draft of a preliminary declaration. It seemed to me there and then that this initiative was INSPIRED, that it was *THIS* that was NEEDED! Though I did find Fr Chenu's text a little sociological, too human. Of course it is a message addressed to humankind. But I would have liked there to have been a stronger reference to the fact of Jesus Christ and the offer of the Covenant. Also, I wanted to support Fr Chenu's initiative effectively. So I sent his text with a note of my own, to Cardinals Liénart, Alfrink, König, Döpfner, and Montini; also to Frings and Suenens; to the archbishops of Rheims and Durban (Hurley); to Mgr Charue, Mgr Weber, Mgr Gjattas (Coptic bishop of Thebes), and to Mgr Volk. [Attached are the replies from the archbishop of Utrecht from 25.9.62, from Cardinal Gilroy from 17.10, and from the bishop of Namur, from Cardinal König, from Cardinal Döpfner, and from Cardinal Suenens from 26.9]. I received a very favourable reply from several of them, especially from Cardinals Liénart, Alfrink and Döpfner. I wrote to tell Fr Chenu what they had said. Cardinal Liénart's reply suggested that it would be good to preare A TEXT. Fr Chenu had drafted one in French which I corrected and added to as regards the paragraph concerning ecumenism, which was a little too short as originally drafted. I typed this text and sent it on to Küng, so that he could translate it into German.' Fr Congar added to his manuscript the Latin version and the German translation.

Favorable responses from: Mgr Marty, Villot, Garrone ('project already considered'),[14] Léger (talk to the Pope about it first by way of a qualified messenger),[15] Lefebvre (Rabat), Elchinger, Charue (Belgian bishops are favorable), Montini (a kind reply, nothing more), Cardinal Liénart is very favorable and is willing to take charge of presenting the project[16]: he asks for a prepared text written in Latin. That's what I'm doing.[17]

September 27

A letter from Fr Congar.[18] He saw Küng. Pessimistic. Wants to refuse [4 vº] treating the dogmatic schemas that have been presented. To

---

14. Fr Chenu had sent to the archbishop of Toulouse his observations on the first two doctrinal schemas (*De deposito* and *De fontibus*) that confirmed the idea of the message; Garrone wrote back on 19 September 1962: 'The declaration has already been effectively wished for and asked for, and there is every reason to believe that it will happen in the way you wish. As to the first two schemas, your comments are very helpful for me to reinforce the requests already formulated.' Garrone wrote to Chenu again on 15 October 1962, to give him his 'hearty' support for the new version of the message as an addition to the Pope's opening address. The '*already*' alluded to in Fr Chenu's journal might refer to propositions already proposed in the discussion of the Central Preparatory Commission, to which Siri makes reference in speaking to Frings on the morning of the opening of the Council (see DSri, 11 October 1962). For the activities of the preparatory commission, see A Indelicato, *Difendere la dottrina o annunciare l'evangelo: Il dibattito nelle Commissione centrale preparatoria del Vaticano II* (Genoa, 1992).
15. Mgr Léger writing to Fr Chenu (21 September 1962): 'It is very clear that such an initiative has to be carried out with great prudence and, in my humble opinion, ought to be presented to His Holiness personally. I don't have to insist upon the qualities of tact and prudence that this message must have in order to achieve the goal proposed for it by those promoting it' (SChn); Chenu did not take up Léger's proposal to be the messenger.
16. Text found in Duval, 'Le Message...', 111.
17. This is the text c) in the chronology of Duval, 'Le message...', 109, n 8: a) The idea of Congar–Chenu to Rahner on 4 September 1962 (copy in JCng 80); b) First proposal [. . .] Paris, 15 September 1962: M–D Chenu then paraphrased [this] in *L'Église dans le monde de ce temps* (Paris, 1967), 192–3; c–d) Texts in French and Latin sent by Chenu to Congar on Sepetmber 26; d) after the letter of Congar to Chenu proposing the insertion of the ecumenical theme, a Latin text; e) New Latin text (copy in JCng 80); A French text (copy in the Chenu dossier); g) German text translated by Küng (JCng 80); h) the Roman text; i) The text taken from *Témoignage chrétien* of 12 October 1962 (b).
18. See Duval, 'Le Messsage . . ', 110, n 9.

do that, he asks that things begin with pastoral and practical topics: liturgy, reunion. Thinking about a group statement from theologians asking the bishops for this: Küng, Rahner, Congar would be the first to sign.[19]

October 4

Arrived in Rome last night. This morning, a letter from Fr Congar telling me of Cardinal Doepfner's very vigorous favorable response to the project of an initial declaration.[20]

Item, reply from Cardinal Suenens in full agreement; he said that he 'recently gave the Holy Father, in my name and in the name of a group (of Belgian? bishops, cf Mgr Charue's letter), an almost identical proposal'[21] (26 September).

---

19. See JCng ms 80–81/ds 65 = CngMJC 81–2: 'Küng telephoned me on the morning of 27 September asking to see me. He came to Tübingen for this purpose that same day. He, together with several other German theologians, especially Möller from Tübingen, feels that the four dogmatic *schemata* are not good: they must not be amended but rejected. Even if amended, they would remain substantially what they are. As they stand, they present a school theology, that of the Roman schools. For the public, and even in practice for the average clergy, these Constitutions will be regarded as definitions of faith. This will result in further hardening in a direction that offers no real possibility of dialogue with the thinking of the men and women of today. According to Küng, in order to make it easier for them to be rejected, it will be necessary to prevent these dogmatic *schemata* from being THE FIRST to be presented, because they would then be in danger of being tackled in adverse conditions, in a hurry. Hence the need to ensure that the Council begins by tackling schemas dealing with more practical matters. We mulled over ways in which this might be brought about. It seems to me that we can only appeal to the BISHOPS. Küng and I together drew up a text in this sense, of which he sent me a copy in Latin two days later. [...] Here is what I received from Küng on 29 September.'

20. Fr Chenu was residing on the Janiculum in the house of the Missionaries of Notre-Dame de La Salette. Their Superior General, A Dutil, extended the invitation to him on 29 August 1962, insofar as he was the *peritus* for a bishop of their congregation. CngMJC 82: 'I received the LATIN text from Fr Chenu. I at once sent it Cardinals Liénart, Suenens, Döpfner and Alfrink, who, in their replies, had shown themselves most favourable to the idea'; 2 October 1962: 'I saw Mgr Weber and brought him Chenu's two texts (Latin and French). He told me that, in conjunction with Mgr Elchinger, he had sent direct to Cardinal Cicognagi a request for a step of the kind indicated by Fr Chenu. Something of this kind MUST be done!'

21. This letter is not in SChn; but perhaps Suenens was referring to a plea addressed

October 8

Went to the Vatican to take the oath required of bishops' proxies [*procureur*]. In fact, despite my reluctance, Mgr Rolland insisted that I should become not only his own theological assistant, but also the proxy for Mgr Girouard, the bishop of Morondava, who can't come because of ill health. This matter was settled by telephone calls and telegraphs with Mgr G[irouard].[22]

At the Vatican I met Fr Daniélou, the theologian for Mgr Veuillot.[23] He made a severe attack on the doctrinal schemas: they are preoccupied with quarrels among schools of thought, and lack any evangelical perspective or any sense of current needs.

He said that the preparatory Commission [*préparative—sic*] for Missions [5 rº]wrote a text that is more juridical than apostolic and that there must be vigorous 'missionary' interventions.[24]

October 9

A meeting this morning with seven of the bishops from Madagascar at the Trinitarians in San Crisogone (where several of them reside,

---

to the Pope by several cardinals: for that, see G Routhier, 'Les Réactions du cardinal Léger à la préparation de Vatican II', in *Revue d'histoire de l'Église en France,* 80 (1994): 81–301.

22. Claude Rolland, priest of the Congregation of La Salette and bishop of the Madagascar diocese of Antsirabé had asked for assistance from Fr Chenu who had been his former teacher in the Belgian studium of Le Saulchoir. On 2 April 1962, he wrote: 'I was in the group of 'blacks' [who] made up the missionary seminarians of La Salette during the years 1930–1938. I saw you [again] at Evreux [near Paris] in 1960. [...] The Council is approaching and I hardly have time to prepare for it. I don't know any more than what the newspapers are saying about what we will have to deal with. So that I might participate judiciously, I decided to ask your assistance as my theological consultant for the whole duration of the Council.' Fr Chenu's letter of acceptance, not preserved, must have been rapid because it was confirmed on 24 April 1962 by Claude Rolland, who set up a first meeting in Paris for 7 July 1962. Paul Girouard, also from La Salette, was bishop of a diocese in Madagascar since 1956: the procuration did not work out despite the norms of CIC 224 §2.

23. Auxiliary bishop of Paris.

24. See G Butturini, 'Missioni e concilio: La storia, i testi et i criteri della commissione preparatoria' in *Verso il concilio Vaticano II (1960–1962): Passaggi e problem della preparazione conciliare,* edited by G Alberigo and A Melloni (Genoa, 1993), 397–423.

beginning with two Trinitarian bishops, one Italian and one Spanish).[25] Among them are the archbishop of Tananarive and the retired archbishop of Fianarantsoa (French).[26] This is my first contact. [They are] very autonomous vis-à-vis continental Black Africa.

Two problems came up: how to go about choosing in the elections to the Commissions (ten Commissions with twenty-four members each, of whom sixteen are elected by the fathers, eight named by the Pope).

What to think about the proposal to resituate the African churches under the Consistorial Congregation by taking them out from under Propaganda? This was simply brought up, without any precise details.

Fr Greco, SJ, a former Madagascar missionary, chosen as liaison—a difficult chore given the dispersion of bishops in different residences. Next meeting on Friday.[27]

---

25. They are Francesco Vollaro, bishop of Ambatondrazaka, and Angelo Martinez, bishop of Tsiroanomandidy. According to the list of addresses published by the *Peregrinatio Romana* during the Council, these bishops were staying at the Order's generalate and met at San Crisogone at the invitation of the secretariat that Fr Chenu mentions a few lines further down.
26. XFJ Thoyer, seventy-eight year old Jesuit; he will be replaced by Gilbert Ramanantoamina.
27. That is, 12 October. It has not yet been possible to locate the minutes of these meetings that will last throughout the Council. Greco's work as liaison is indefatigable, see DTcc 11 November 1962: ' Visit from Fr Greco (Madagascar), a Jesuit who works for the secretariat for African bishops. He wanted the names of Italian bishops with whom it would be useful for the Africans to be in contact. [Together we thought of Siri.] He told me that they wanted to invite Cardinal Siri with Mgr Castelli and put before them the problem of conscience not to impose on everybody rigid norms unsuited to solve their formidable pastoral problems. To the names of Montini, [Siri] and Lercaro, he added Carraro [agreed!], Guano and Tinivella. [...] I added Amici, Florit, Bartoletti, Confalioneri, Marella and perhaps also Nicodemo. He explained to me how the secretariat for the African bishops is working.' '*Visita del P Greco (Madagascar), gesuita che lavora per il Segretariato dei vescovi africani. Voleva conoscere nomi di vescovi italiani con i quali sarebbe utile che gli africani avessero contatti. [Abbiamo insieme puntato su Siri.] Mi ha detto che desideravano invitare il Cardinale Siri con mons. Castelli e metterli di fronte al problema di coscienza di non imporre a tutti rigide norme che non sono atte a risolvere i loro tremendi problemi pastorali. Ai nomi di Montini e [Siri] Lercaro, ha aggiunto Carraro [d'accordo!], Guano et Tinivella. [...] Io ho aggiunto Amici, Florit, Bartoletti, Confalonieri, Marella e forse anche Nicodemo. Mi ha spiegato come lavora il segretariato dell'episcopato africano*' (cf *Documenti*, n 15). On 17 November 1962, Zoa intervened in the name of the 266 bishops of the panafrican secretariat. See Cl Prudhomme, 'Les évêques d'Afrique noire

After noon, I was invited to meet Cardinal Léger who had received the text for the proposed message.[28] He approves completely, especially since it goes along with suggestions[29] that he made to the Pope before the papal message given on 11 September.[30] The problem will be getting this into the agenda. It will have to go through the cardinals' Commission on Extraordinary Affairs (which I thought was the normal procedure [5 v°]). He proposes to bring it up with Cardinal Suenens who is a member of that Commission.[31]

He spoke to me with excitement about his disappointment with the doctrinal schemas: speculative theses that only repeat Vatican I and don't consider the needs and possibilities of our time. We aren't any longer at the time of the doctrinal liberalism of 1860, nor of anti-ecclesiastical socialism. We aren't in a ghetto either. We can't be content to throw stones at the communists (telling me of something that John XXIII said to him). The Americans are still at the Council of Trent. 'Myself', he said, 'I have become compromised—my opponents call me "the furious cardinal".'

He kept me to talk about Canadian matters and the profound change there in the last two years. The opposition of the *Cité chrétienne*, who refused to welcome him. Integralists, tattle-tales [délateurs][32].

---

anciennement française et le Concile' in *Vatican II commence*, 163–188.

28. In documents kept by the Canadian cardinal and carrying the reference *483–485* in P. Lafontaine, *Inventaire des archives conciliaires du Fonds Paul-Émile Léger* (Montréal, 1995).

29. *Propositions*, corrected.

30. Suenens, *Souvenirs...*, 79.

31. This was the group put in charge of dealing with questions that arose outside the work of the regular agenda; the group, under the leadership of the Secretary of State Cicognani, included Bea, Confalonieri, Döpfner, Meyer, Montini, Ottaviani, Siri, Suenens, and, after 18 October, Wyszynski.

32. *Cité catholique* was a movement of the conservative right that included Marcel Clément. He had denounced Léger to the Holy Office, and Léger had appealed to the Pope on 18 October 1962 (see Archives Léger, Controverses). See also M Lachance, *Le Prince de l'Église, le cardinal Léger* (Montreal, 1982). On 21 October 1962, he had been received by the Pope, who wrote in his notebook: 'A festive day, but incessantly busy. Reception of the new minister from Peru for the presentation of his credentials; Cardinal Léger, archbishop of Montreal in Canada, whom I'll have to encourage concerning his difficulties coming from France and from the Holy Office through the famous new group *Via, Veritas et Vita*, who have a misplaced zeal.' 'Giornata festiva pur sempre occupata. Accolsi il nuovo Ministro del Perù per la presentazione delle credenziali: il Cardinal Léger

October 11

Solemn opening.

While waiting for the ceremony to end, a hour-long conversation with Fr Philippe Godard, OSB, Tioumliline, theologian for Mgr Lefebvre, archbishop of Rabat. They are both strongly opposed to the substance and the spirit of the schemas.[33]

In the newspaper, there is a more precise description of the Pope's address. His lively protest to the pessimists' attachment to the past was evident as was his disapproval of discussions about doctrines that merely repeat the past. Rather doctrines need to be restated so as to correspond to the needs of today.[34]

[6 r°] *October 12*

A meeting of the Madagascar bishops this morning to agree about the elections. There are sixteen of them. Fr de Lubac is there as the theologian for the arch[bishop] of Fianarantsoa.[35]

He gave me news about the recent interventions of the H[oly] Office. The Rahner affair is over: faced with clear support from the German bishops, the H[oly] Off[ice] pulled back; so as not to lose

---

arciv. di Montreal in Canada che me piacque incoraggiare fra i suoi fastidi venutigli dalla Francia e dal S.O. per il famoso e nuovo gruppo di Via, veritas et vita di infelice applicazione.'

33. This conversation took place outside the basilica; Chenu was not allowed inside. He himself recalls: 'the opening of the Council: I was seated on the base of a pillar in the colonnade of Bernini in St Peter's Square' (see *Un théologien en liberté: J. Duquesne interroge le père Chenu* [Paris, 1975], 176).

34. See A Melloni, 'L'allocuzione *Gaudet Mater Ecclesia* (11 ottobre 1962), Sinossi critica dell'allocuzione', in *Fede Tradizione Profezia: Studi su Giovanni XXIII e sul Vaticano II* (Brescia, 1984), 223–283. Fr Chenu addressed this problem a few years later: 'It is not a question of making a distinction between an unchanging "substance" and variable exterior "forms"... This is about the interior: through fidelity to my faith I perceive the truth of the Mystery that is both identical and always new (alive today)—I perceive the Mystery in its very "substance", and not just in the changing adaptation of its formulation. [This is] demanding, subtle, and delicate, following a model of continuity and measured by the unity of a living being' ('Ce qui change et ce qui demeure', in *L'Église vers l'avenir* [Paris, 1969], 87–91: the citation here is on page 91 [A XIV 340]).

35. Despite the bias characteristic of a memoir: see H de Lubac, *Entretien autour de Vatican II: Souvenirs et réflexions* (Paris, 1985).

face, they did not reverse their judgment, but they delegated the power of *imprimatur* to Cardinals König and Döpfner, the defenders of Fr Rahner[36]!

As to Fr de Lubac, he received a very affectionate letter from his Fr General.[37] He also told me that in a meeting of the preparatory doctrinal Comm[ission], a proposed text was presented that began by saying '*Secundum unanimem consensum Patrum . . .*' [according to the unanimous consensus of the Fathers]. One of the participating theologians spoke up: Never did any of the Fathers talk about this problem. So the secretary took out that phrase, but left the text itself unchanged.[38]

He also told me that only one contemporary theologian was cited in the schema—an unknown Canadian who some time ago wrote an article praising a Roman text.[39]

At the end of our meeting, Mgr Sartre gave us the results of the deliberations of the bishops from French–speaking continental Africa who met this morning at San Anselmo.[40] They all asked how they could go about electing 160 members without knowing one another at all.[41]

---

36. See Vorgrimler, 115–117.
37. JB Janssens: the letter is one of those from either 28 June or 27 August mentioned by de Lubac in *Entretien . . .*, 106–7, 326 and 335.
38. See R Burigana, 'Progetto dogmatico del Vaticano II: la commissione teologica preparatoria (1960–1962)', in *Verso il concilio Vaticano II*, 141–206.
39. In reference to the schema *De deposito fidei*, chapter 11, n 9, which cites A Hacault, *La Satisfaction du Christ Jésus à la lumière de l'encyclique 'Humani Generis'*, (Montreal, 1960).
40. Victor Sartre was the bishop of Beroe in the Camerouns.
41. On the last page [35 rº] of Fr Chenu's manuscript is attached a list for the elections at the beginning [of the minutes] of the Secretariat for the French bishops from 12 October 1962, which flows into the larger list from the Central European group. To the mimeographed text Fr Chenu added by hand the titles of the commissions: 'The bishops of France, following their meeting of 12 October, chose for the different commissions the following bishops: *Commission n 1 <Doctrinal>:* Mgr Garrone, archbishop of Toulouse; Mgr Ancel, auxiliary bishop of Lyons, Superior General of the Prado; Mgr Weber, archbishop–bishop of Strasbourg—*Commission n 2 <Bishops>:* Mgr Veuillot, coadjutor archbishop of Paris; Mgr Villot, coadjutor archbishop of Lyons; Mgr Guerry, archbishop of Cambrai—*Commission 3 <Diocesan Clergy>:* Mgr Collin, bishop of Digne; Mgr Raymondos, titular bishop of Chariopolis; Mgr Rupp, bishop of Monaco. —*Commission 4 <Sacraments> [Sacraments Religious]:* Mgr Peuch, bishop of Carcasonne; Mgr Lallier, archbishop of Marseille; Mgr Guyot, bishop of

October 13

At 9.00 am, a general assembly at S[aint] Peter's for the elections. The session finished in twenty minutes: following the invitation to convene and directions given by Mgr Felici, an intervention by Cardinal Liénart requested a delay (applause); it was seconded by Cardinal Frings in the name of the [6 v°] German Card[inals] (applause). After a brief discussion among the council presidents, the elections were postponed until Tuesday 16 October (applause). The bishops' unanimous and spontaneous expression of freedom to break out of the 'regimentation' [*règlement*] caused a sensation among the bishops themselves and everyone around them.[42]

This evening at a private meeting by invitation of Fr Moubarac,[43] pastors Schutz and Thurian (Taizé) who are at the Council as observers, told me of their deep spiritual satisfaction in seeing this phenomenon of the Church gathered in Council.[44]

Mgr Khoury, the Metropolitan of Tyre, was also present at this private gathering. I knew him as a student at the Sorbonne in the course of Le Bras for advanced studies.[45] He regrets that Islam is getting so little attention. With Fr Moubarac's advice, I had proposed him [Khoury] to the Germans and the Africans to try to make sure

---

Coutances—*Commission 5 <Sacraments>*: Mgr Mazerat, bishop of Angers; Mgr de Provenchères, archbishop of Aix; Mgr Guyot, bishop of Coutances —*Commission 6 <Religious>*: Mgr Huyghe, bishop of Arras; Mgr Urtasun, archbishop of Avignon; Mgr Collin, bishop of Digne.

42. AS I/1, 207–210; Siri was very negative about what happened: 'It is difficult to describe the stupefaction and embarrassment caused by this event. The participants are dispersing in an atmosphere of upset and evident discomfort.' '*É difficile rendersi conto dello stupore e del disagio creato da questa vicenda. In un aria di evidente e concitato malessere si disperdono i partecipanti*' (DSri October 12 1962, 360).

43. Fr Moubarac is a participant in and promoter of a group of French theologians who are discussing collegiality (Colson, Pin, Laurentin and Frisque): the journal of H Denis ('La Petite Histoire') speaks about it. For this topic, see Komonchak, 'The Initial Debate' in *Vatican II commence*, 341n.

44. On the participation of the observers from the Taizé community, see É Fouilloux, 'Des observateurs non catholiques' in *Vatican II commence...*, 235–261; Bro Roger and Bro Max had appeared on an Italian TV program, and they were more widely known as a result; see Lercaro's letter of 11 October 1962 in G Lercaro, *Lettere dal concilio 1962–1965*, edited by G Battelli (Bologna, 1980), 63.

45. Joseph Khoury, Maronite Metropolitan; Basil Khoury, the Melkite bishop of Saida, also participated at the Council.

that an Eastern rite bishop should work on the doctrinal Commission that up till now has had a purely Latin perspective.

The pastors [Schutz and Thurian] told me how moved they were by John XXIII's audience with the observers this afternoon. The two observers from Moscow were present.[46]

[Unreadable passage] On the 12th, yesterday, at 7 pm, there was a reception in 'grand style' at the French embassy.[47] I saw a number of French bishops. One or another of them remarked sympathetically about the projected message, which means that they have been informed about it.

[7 r°] *October 15*

I am copying this anecdote reported by Küng (ICI, 15 October).[48] It is said that someone asked John XXIII in a private conversation what he hoped for from the Council. The Pope then opened the window and said: 'That! Fresh air in the Church!'

October 16

After laborious meetings and discussions among 'episcopal conferences' and national groups, there are lists proposing to the bishops the names of people to be elected to the ten commissions. Central and Northern Europe (Austria, Belgium, France, Germany, Switzerland, Holland, Yugoslavia, Scandanavia, Poland) put together a common list (about 350). <The English list only gives one name per commission. Will the English bishops take the other fifteen from the European list?> Moreover {the European list} agrees with the African one (French speaking, and beyond that?) that seems to have used it as a guide.

---

46. *Discorsi messaggi colloqui di SS. Giovanni XXIII*, IV, 604–610. The Russian observers were Vitalij Borovoj and Vladimir Kotiliarov: for them, see *Vatican II in Moscow*, edited by A Melloni (Leuven, 1997); and S Schmidt, *Agostino Bea: Il cardinale dell'unità* (Rome, 1987), 453–4. Articles, interviews, and statements are collected in A Wenger, *Vatican II: Première session* (Paris, 1963), 204–238 and 297–346.
47. The ambassador was Guy de la Tournelle.
48. ICI is *Informations catholiques internationales*.

List for Comm[ission] 1 (doctrine): König (Aus[tria]), Léger (Canad[a]), Charue (Belg[ium]), Garrone (Fran[ce]), Van Dodewaard (Holl[and]), Schröffer (Germany), Seper (Yugos[lavia]), Wright (USA), Guano (Ital[y]).

List for Commission 2 (bishops): Guerry (Fran[ce]), Morcillo (Spain), Schäuffele (Germany), Gargitter (It[aly]), Brown (Ir[e] l[and]), Weyer (England), Veuillot (France).

On the list for Sem[inaries] and Un[iversities]: Weber (France), Döpfner (Germany), Carraro (It[aly]), D'Avack (It[aly]), Cazaux (Fr[ance]), Olachea Loizaga (Spain), Deam (Bel[gium]), etc.

[7 v°] The Italians—with very little discussion—proposed this list for the Commission 1 (doctrine):

Italians: Florit (Florence), Peruzzo (Agrigente), Gaddi (Bergamo), Carraro (Verona), Poma (Mantua).

Non-Italians: Griffiths (aux[iliary] N[ew] York), Franic (Split), Philippe (religious), Fernandez (M[aster] G[eneral] op), Barbado (Salamanca), Van Dodewaard (Haarlem, Holl[and]), Ancel (titular bishop), Ngo-Dinh Thuc (Hue), Muldoon (arch[bishop] of Sydney), Santiago (Silva) (Concepcion, Chile), Lemieux (Ottawa), LoKuang (Taiwan, China).

So in this list of non-Italians there are no Germans, no French (Philippe = Curia), no Austrians. What to make of that?

In all the other commissions, as in this one, they present five names <of Italians>. It is only for this first commission (Doctrine) that they add a list of recommended non-Italians, excluding the Germans and the French. Why?[49]

Portugal (twenty-seven bishops) they only propose one name and only for five of the commissions. No one proposed for the 1st and 2nd commission.[50]

---

49. See DSri 13 October 1963: 'At the Holy Office [...] I found the cardinal [Ottaviani] who introduced me to Mgr Vagnozzi [...]. The assessor, Mgr Parente, came in. We set up a process based on the search for more 'orthodox' names for the conferences. I accept, but want to open up this search.' 'Al Sant'Ufficio [...] Trovo il cardinale [Ottaviani] che mi presenta mons Vagnozzi [...]. Arriva anche l'assessore mons. Parente. Si concorda una procedura bastata sulla richiesta di nominative alle conferenze più 'consone'. Io accetto, ma cerco di far allargare questa richiesta.'

50. Namely, Trinidade for the Clergy Commission, Rendeiro pour the Religious, Da Costa Nunes for the Missions, Alvim Pereira for the Liturgy, Gonçalves Cereijera

[8 r°] It is now official that work will begin with the liturgy. All those who have fundamental criticisms for the doctrinal schemas want work on them to be delayed and they want to begin with pastoral topics.[51]

October 18

Visit with Fr Congar at the Angelicum. Shared information.[52] Fr

---

for the Seminaries and Da Silva for the Apostolate of the Laity. This is why the Portuguese ambassador, referred to as the *minister* on 25 October, had requested an audience with Samoré in the Secretariat of State: 'I want to share a personal reflection on the election of only one Portuguese bishop among the 160 bishops elected for the 10 commissions of the ecumenical council. I have been informed of the Portuguese bishops' thoughts about this by the Cardinal Patriarch and by Cardinal Costa Nunes. I was told that our episcopate had made contact with the Brazilian episcopate who put on their list, in addition to the archbishop of Evora, two Portuguese cardinals–Cardinal Cerejeira for the Commission for Seminaries and Universities, and Cardinal Costa Nunes for the Missions, and also that contact had been made with the Spanish and French episcopates. [...] My personal impression is that our episcopate was not prepared in time for the electoral competition, which on the surface doesn't look very different at the ecumenical council from what goes on in secular assemblies. In any case, seeing only one Portuguese bishop elected alongside 17 French, 13 Spanish, and 6 Brasilians, I decided two days ago to go see Mgr Dell'Acqua.' *'era porém fazer-lhes reflexão pessoal sobra eleição de um unico prelado português entre 160 bispos eleitos paras as 10 commissões do Concilio Ecuménico. Tinha-me informado primeiro junto Snr Cardeal Patriarca e Cardeal Costa Nunes das diligências feitas a este respeito pelo episcopado português, tendo-me sido dito que nosso episcopado havia entrado em contacto com epsicopado brasileiro, que incluira na sua lista além Arcebispo Évora dois Cardeais portugueses—Cardeal Cerejeira para a commissão Seminários e Universidades, Cardeal Costa Nunes para as missões, e bem assim com episcopado espanhol e francês. [...] Minha impressão pessoal é que nosso episcopado não se preparou a tempo para competição eleitoral, que pelos vistos não parece muito diferente no Concílio Ecuménico do que se passa nas assembleias profanas. De qualquer maneira, tendo verificado a eleição de um só bispo português ao lado de 17 franceses, 13 espanhois e 6 brasileiros, propuz-me há dois dias falar com Mons. Dell'Acqua'* (report kept in the archives of the Portuguese Embassy to the Holy See).

51. See A Melloni, 'Giovanni XXIII e l'avvio del Vaticano II', in *1962, Vatican II commence*, 75–104.

52. Fr Congar saw that morning the alternative schema for the *De Ecclesia* prepared by the Louvain theologian G Philips, concerning which it appears he did not speak to Fr Chenu (see CngMJC, 97 for 18 October 1962: 'I had a number of visitors this morning, including Mgr Philips. Cardinal Suenens has asked him to

Trapè,[53] OSAug, will be the editor of the preparatory schema on original sin. Not suprising, since he is not only of the Latin theology type, but also super–Augustinian. Cf *olim* the bull *Unam Sanctam* with Giles of Rome, OSAug.[54]

A manipulation of the election by the Holy Office: they have distributed to all the Italian bishops a list with their seal for the 1st commission where they recommend twelve non–Italians (cf below) among whom there are no Germans, Austrians, and French (with the exception of Fr Philippe).[55]

Fr Congar gave me the report where Canon Laurentin, in summarising recent work by Fr Couvreur (Mission de France), vigorously explained for this time of 'hunger' the classic principle of the primacy of the common destination of goods over the rights of private ownership.[56] I will use this to write a note to send to the bishop of the Canary Islands (Pildain [y Zapain]) for his Spanish colleagues.[57] He came to see me and uttered a magnificent outburst about what ought to be the anguish of Christians in this time of 'hunger' {in the world}. And we remain silent!

---

go over (to complete and correct) with Fr Rahner and one or two others all the texts on the Church [...]. In the afternoon, a good visit from Fr Chenu, who sees a great many people: journalists, African bishops, etc)'

53. Correction by hand of the name misspelled as Tappé, and a marginal note: 'prof[essor] at the Augustinianum and at the Lateran [University]'; the reference is to the preparatory schema *De deposito fidei pure custodiendo* to which Trapè contributed.

54. A point on which Congar insisted in the article 'Église et État' in *Catholicisme*, published in 1952 and reprinted in Y Congar, *Sainte Église* (Paris, 1963), 398–99.

55. A copy in the letters of Bea, Lb 12/2–16; according to Schmidt, *Agostino Bea*, 454. The criterion for the list is explained by one of the members of the Holy Office; see DTcc, 24 October 1962: 'Confidences from *Mgr Lambruschini* during the session: *the Holy Office's list* (Ottaviani–Parente) didn't include any French or Germans: all of them are unsafe!' '*Confidenze di* mons. Lambruchini *durante la seduta: la* lista S Uffizio *(Ottaviani–Parente) non includeva nessuno dei francesi o dei tedeschi: poco sicuri tutti!*'

56. See R Laurentin, 'L'information au Concile' in *Le Deuxième Concile du Vatican (1959-1965)* (Rome, 1989), 359–370.

57. See Duval, 'Le Message...', 113. Fr Chenu had already built a relationship with the Spaniards when on 14 October 1962, C Morillo had assured him that 'some' of the bishops will go for the idea of the message.

[8 v°] *October 19*

Afternoon, private meeting at the place where Mgr Volk (Mainz) resides—a group of theologians and bishops, French and German, seeking a common viewpoint on their extreme reservations about the dogmatic schemas, and a tactic to follow so as to bring about a substantial change and not just simple corrections.

Twenty-four people present, among them: Volk, Bengsch (East Berlin), Garrone, Guerry, Ancel, Weber, Elchinger, (Paul) Schmitt (Metz); the theologians Rahner, Grillmeier, Küng, Schillebeeckx, Philips, Congar, Labourdette, de Lubac, Daniélou and me; Rondet, Semmelroth. <It was Mgr Garrone who specifically asked that Fr Labourdette be invited.>[58]

Presentation by Mgr Volk. Severe criticism of the schemas. In place of their abstract perspective that is out of touch with current problems, substitute the Christian perspective on what is new in the world. To do that, prepare a replacement text ahead of time. After evoking some of the disorders of the contemporary world (*I note*: not so much militant atheism as a world that is organising its ideas without any reference to God as it affirms its values), a presentation of various elements of this schema for the text. Despite the world as it is, reality must be seen as recapitulated in Christ; so: give some meaning to commitment to the presence of Christians in the world.

Rahner spoke up: the schemas can't be corrected. Substitute new texts.

Garrone: in agreement, the schemas are 'incompatible' with the explicit directives given by the Pope on the meaning and objectives of the Council. However, don't go into this in opposition [to the

---

58. See JLbd 19 October 1962: [Labourdette] doesn't say who invited him to the meeting: 'I am rather embarrassed. I can't deny the objections that I had already posed to the schemas and to their style. I wouldn't want the Council to have only that to offer... So I am in profound agreement with most of the views expressed by these theologians *from whom I am habitually quite distant . . . at least I thought so!* But I belong to *quite a different circle* [. . .] that is going to find itself attacked unmercifully with the kind of destructive injustices that such attacks imply. And I can't be part of that. Should I, for all that, hold back?' Fr Congar adds that the presence of the Dominican theologian at the small committee to write the introduction was due to the fact that 'at the last minute, Rahner also invited Labourdette' (CngMJC, 100: 19 October 1962).

procedures], which would only antagonise the fathers—nothing would come out of that. Rather redistribute the viable elements in a new framework.

Philips (*peritus* for Belgium): same position.[59]

[9 rº] Fr Congar. Yes, it's more a question of perspective rather than content. Besides, we don't yet have the schema on the Church, which is a better one.[60]

Fr Daniélou: in complete agreement as to the criticisms. But pick up the work with a kerygmatic and pastoral tone.

Vigorous reaction from Fr Rahner.

Same from Bengsch: we have already tried [modifying the text] at the central Commission. To no effect! Blocked by Ottaviani and Tromp. They took no account of the suggestions of the bishops from the time of the first *vota*. He would consider requesting the Pope through the Commission on Extraordinary Affairs to put a draft schema on the agenda.

Mgr Ancel: Unfortunate approach. Don't get the Pope involved in these discussions. Let qualified and recognised authorities bring the problem to the assembly.

Mgr Guerry: Don't create bad feelings, nor do so ineffectively. Let five bishops representing particular groups get together and, one after the other, present a motion asking for the explicit integration at

---

59. In his journal notes for 8 April 1963, Philips makes no reference to this first meeting; concerning his support, see Cl Soetens, 'La *squadra belga* au Concile Vatican II' in *Foi, gestes et institutions religieuses aux XIXe and XXe siècles*, edited by I. Courtois and J Pirotte (Louvain–la-Neuve, 1991), 159–172. Among Philips' letters, we find only one letter from Fr Chenu dated 30 September 1963 on the *De Ecclesia* (FGL PO28.06).

60. CngMJC 19 October 1962: 'Meeting at 4 pm in Maison Mater Dei, 10 Via della Mura Aurelie, of a number of German bishops and some French ones, some German and French theologians, organised by Mgr Volk. Those present were: Mgr Volk, Mgr Reuss, Mgr Bengsch (Berlin), Mgr Elchinger, Mgr Weber, Mgr Schmitt, Mgr Garrone, Mgr Guerry, Mgr Ancel, Frs Rahner, Lubac, Daniélou, Grillmeier, Semmelroth, Rondet, Labourdette, Congar, Chenu, Schillebeeckx, Feiner, Ratzinger, Mgr Philips, Fransen, Küng. Purpose of the meeting: to discuss and decide on a tactic in relation to the theological schemas. In a long discussion lasting nearly three hours, it became clear that all sorts of nuances were involved. Mgr Volk opened the meeting by reading a kind of draft declaration describing the situation of the Christian in the world today and a view of the history of salvation centered on Christ, in its anthropological, social and cosmological dimensions.'

the beginning of the schemas of the perspective and directives of the Pope.

Discussion of these two tactics, one 'French,' one German. Developing a new draft schema would lead to the rejection of the existing schemas, from which the useful elements will have been kept.

Urgency therefore to compose a preliminary text by a very small group of theologians (Daniélou's plan) that would be enlarged as the work continues with others: Spanish, Italian, etc. For the moment, the group is Rahner, Semmelroth,[61] Daniélou, Congar.

---

61. ST 19 October 1962: 'In the afternoon there was a meeting at 4 pm in which several French bishops took part and, on the German side, in addition to Mgr Volk, Archbishop Bengsch, and Auxiliary Bishop Reuss. I met a number of theologians whom I hadn't known personally before. Fr Daniélou and Fr de Lubac were there. Mgr Philips, who up till now I knew only through his book on the laity. Also Fr Congar, whom I already knew well, and on the German side Professors Ratzinger and Küng. Mgr Volk first made a presentation to which we returned a number of times—and positively. Later this was completed by a proposition from Fr Daniélou that was a lot like his [Mgr Volk's]. People spoke seriously, well, and at a high level, to discuss how best to proceed. I'm happy that we managed to avoid false and unchristian criticisms, but sought to maintain a healthy climate in the Council. However, everybody agreed that the four existing schemas on theology and moral theology simply need to disappear. At the same time it was stressed that we need to come up with a new schema to replace those we have received. We decided to form a commission of theologians, at first very small, to prepare a first draft that would subsequently be discussed by the larger commission. In the meantime, I hope that Fr Schüler will have more or less finished a draft in moral theology. We can't expect much effective help from Fr Hirschmann and Fr Fuchs. They are giving a lot of advice that [Schüler] appreciates. But the formulation and elaboration of the draft is his to do. He has to leave on Monday already. Let's hope that he can produce something usable before then.' *'Nachmittags war dann um vier Uhr eine Zusammenkunft, bei der mehrere französische Bischöfe teilnehmen und auf deutscher Seite an Bischöfen außer Bischof Volk auch Erzbischof Bengsch und Weihbischof Reuß. Ich lernte eine Reihe von Theologen kennen, die ich bisher persönlich noch nicht kannte. P Daniélou und P de Lubac waren dabei. Mgr Philips, den ich bisher nur von seinem Buch über die Laien kannte. Auch P Congar, den ich wohl schon kannte, und von deutscher Seite noch Prof Ratzinger und Küng. Zunächst legte Bischof Volk sein Exposee dar, auf das man nachher mehrfach positiv zurückkam. Später wurde es ergänzt durch einen Vorschlag von P Daniélou, der mit dem seinen eine große Ähnlichkeit hatte. Es wurde ernst und in sehr schönem Ton und mit hohem Niveau besprochen, wie am besten vorgegangen werde. Erfreulich, wie auch Wert darauf gelegt wurde, daß man nicht mit falschen und unchristlichen Attacken vorgehen solle, sondern in einem guten Klima, das Konzil haben und behalten müsse. Aber daß dis bisherigen vier theologischen und moraltheologischen Schemata*

[9 vᵒ] *October 20*

The council fathers begin their session without knowing if the Pope, changing the rules, will decide on a single ballot with a relative majority or a second ballot for the sake of an absolute majority.

Without further discussion, Felici gives the results of the first round with the immediate election of sixteen members by way of relative majorities. The ballots show a spread of 1,800–1,700 to 700 (or even less in several cases). Next, the eight members chosen by the Pope for the Liturgy Commission are announced—they now need to get to work.[62]

Next the message [to the world] is presented for the approval and vote of the assembly.[63] Mgr Rolland kept track as far as he could of the interventions (thirty–two, he said) that were more or less extensive. Only two of them were included by the Praesidium. The fathers had the printed text in their hands.

---

fallen müssen, darüber war man einer Meinung. Aber ebenso wurde betont, daß ein neues Schema ausgearbeitet werden müsse, das an die Stelle der bisherigen zu treten hatte. Man beschloß ein zunächst Gremium von Theologen zu bilden, die einen ersten Entwurf vorbereiten sollen, der dann in dem größeren Gremium besprochen werden solle. Ich hoffe, daß in der Zwischenzeit auch P Schüller einen moraltheologischen Entwurf eingermaßen fertig habe wird. Von P Hirschmann und P Fuchs scheint nicht allzu viel wirksame Hilfe zu bekommen. Sie geben wohl Ratschläge, die er auch schäzt. Aber die Formulierung und Ausarbeitung bleibt bei ihm. Am Montag muß er schon wieder fort. Hoffentlich kann er bis dahin Brauchbares fertigstellen.'

62. AS 1/1, 223–229: The eight named by the Pope are Cardinals P Giobbe, A Jullien, A Albareda and then W Bekkers, B Fey, R Masnou Boixeda, P Schweiger and J Prou; on 3 November 1962 the Pope praised Felici in his notebook for the nomination process: 'I stayed for a long time with Mgr Pericle Felici, Secretary General of the Council: I am still happy with him because he accepts the proposals that I make to him about nominating this one or that one to help him in his energetic work which entails great responsibility. My radio lets me follow all the opinions expressed at the Council. That helps me to decide about everything and to suggest good ideas of a practical nature. The individual interventions of the council fathers help simplify and clarify things. We will certainly have to speed things up a bit.' *'Trattenni pure a lungo mgr. Pericle Felici Segretario Gener. del Concilio: di cui sono sempre contento perchè accetta le proposte che gli facciamo, circa nomine di persone o altro, che facilitano il suo forte lavoro che è di grande responsabilità. La radio in casa mi permette di seguire tutte le voci del Concilio: e ciò aiuta a farmi ragione di tutto, ed a suggerire buone proposte di ordine pratico. Anche questi interventi dei singoli Padri del Concilio inducono a semplificare e a chiarire. Certo converrà che ci affrettiamo un poco.'*

63. AS 1/1, 239–249.

I single out from among the interventions noted by Mgr Rolland:

Several prelates <among them Mgr Guano (Livorno)> observed that if this is addressed to *all* people [*tous* les hommes] and not only to Christians, then there are too many elements that pertain to Christian faith and that it would be better to keep to the themes of peace, justice, fraternity, and love of the poor.[64]

By contrast, Mgr Parente requested that there be an explanation of doctrines.[65]

Two ask that there be an allusion to those who suffer for their faith. <One of these was thinking of Communism. A Hungarian bishop [and] a Lithuanian oppose that, since the message is an appeal to hope and fraternity. Cf 24 October below.> The Praesidium only kept one addition: '*Unanimiter cum Maria* [10 r°] *matre Jesu orantes*' (coming, I hear, from Mgr Ancel) and a correction of some words at the end: '*ab optata pace adhuc* (in place of *semper*) *abest...*' and '*scientiarum progressu mirabilis...*, *sed non semper* (in place of *nundum*) *superiori moralitatis legi* (in place of *subjecto*)'.[66]

The various themes of my text were kept, but in a new version. With the prelates mentioned above, I regret that this version did not respect addressing explicitly *all* people, of whom two billion out of three are ignorant of the faith, and among so-called Christians, three out of four are unaware of the real motivations behind Christian doctrine. I purposely limited myself to great human values: universality, fraternity, peace, love for the poor, duty to maintain justice—all of which are a fruit of the Good News, an 'obediential potency' for understanding it. Cf my project.[67]

So, instead of the sobriety required for newspapers and the radio in a message like this—a bit of sacred rhetoric.

I also regret cutting the paragraph of three lines about agreement with our separated brothers in these issues that matter <for our dialogue>.

However, the *substance* is still there. The message *exists*. It was voted by standing and sitting—passed almost unanimously.

See my dossier.[68] <And also below, 24 October.>

---

64. AS 1/1, 249.
65. AS 1/1, 239–240.
66. G Ferretto and P Fiordelli, AS 1/1, 235–6.
67. See Duval, 'Le Message...', 116–7.
68. Fr Chenu explains his role in his letter to his provincial: see Duval ('Le Message...',

October 21

Fr Congar came to lunch at La Salette and I tell him of my {new} initiative: a letter to Cardinal Suenens expressing my wish for the active presence of an Eastern representative on the doctrine Commission [10 vº] to avoid a serious lacuna for fully grasping the understanding the faith at a time when we are always talking about 'ecumenism'. I wrote to Cardinal Suenens because, in a statement he gave in Brussels before leaving for Rome, he said that in the Commission on which he sat he had always demanded the inclusion of Eastern theology.[69] Further, at any moment, we are awaiting the Pope's designation of eight members for the doctrine Commission. It is urgent that the Pope be contacted directly so that he will choose an Eastern bishop for this group of eight.

We decide to go directly to see Mgr *[sic]* Suenens, who has doubtlessly not yet received my letter. He is away. Mgr De Smedt (Bruges), in charge of ecumenical questions in Belgium, endorsing our view, advises us to go right away to find Cardinal Bea who is the one best placed to make a rapid and effective intervention [with the Pope].[70] Fr Chalencon (La Salette), who is driving us by car, takes Fr Congar immediately to the Brazilian College where Cardinal Bea is staying. (I had to meet Mgr Elchinger.) They arrived at the very moment that the cardinal was going out. Within a few minutes the proposal is made and willingly accepted by the cardinal.[71] Tonight he

---

114–5): 'Through the famous message from the Council to humanity, for which Fr Congar and I took some initiative, I have come to understand the complex steps needed to insert an idea, even one that is accepted, into the apparatus of an assembly and into the collective ethos [*climat*]. The press has informed you about the reactions here and there in the Assembly; however, they voted for it almost unanimously, giving me a joyful surprise. You know me well enough to see that I am not altogether in my element here. But so as to regain my 'natural' element, I think of you and your work; and the news that you send me is an uplifting joy.'

69. Perhaps this refers to the Central Preparatory Commission, or the secretariat *de negotiis extra ordinem* [for extraordinary affairs]; Suenens' secretariat kindly informed me that Fr Chenu's letter unfortunately has not been kept.

70. No data on this meeting with Mgr De Smedt; see Schmidt, *Agostino Bea*, 454–5.

71. CngMJC 21 October 1962: 'At 12.30 pm, Fr Chalencon of the La Salette Fathers, came to collect myself and Fr Chenu to have lunch with them. During the conversation, Fr Chenu spoke of the pain that he felt that there was no one from the East among the members elected to the Theological Commission. I know, for my part, that the Maronites are hurt than none of them has been

has to see the Secretary of State at a reception, and he will convince him to make this request to the Pope. Everything will depend on the intervention of Cardinal Cigognani.

[11 r°] While conversing with Mgr [De] Smedt, he talks to us about the doctrinal schemas. They won't work, he said, in a cold, decisive tone of voice. {We had} a hearty and sympathetic encounter with him, despite the unplanned nature of our meeting at this incongruous time of day (2.30 pm).

From 3.45 to 5 pm, a visit and a long conversation with Mgr Elchinger, who came to see me. We talk again of the French–German gathering on the 19th about the doctrinal schemas.

Fr Congar tells me that in the small group that took on writing a draft for a new schema, he is expected to write the text.

---

elected to the Commissions, and that the Melkites occupy all the places. At the Preparatory Commission I myself had said several times that it was necessary to hear the Eastern point of view. Nothing had been done, and the presence of Mgr Hermaniuk had not been enough to fill this void. It seems to me that we must use the last chance we have: that the Pope should appoint someone from the East (a Maronite?) among the eight theologians that he is to appoint to complete the Commission *de fide et moribus* [the Doctrinal Commission]. We reached a decision: to arrange for a cardinal to speak to the Pope. We thought of Cardinal Suenens who had said, in an interview, that he had been concerned, at the Central Commission, about the Eastern point of view. We went, at once, by car to the Belgian College. The cardinal had withdrawn for three or four days to *somewhere* in Rome. So, I saw Mgr De Smedt, Bishop of Bruges, who is a member of the Secretariat. I had my name announced. He was having his siesta, he had left the table. But he came. Excellent welcome. He felt we should approach Cardinal Bea, and he authorised us to present ourselves to the cardinal in his name. Off we went! We dropped Fr Chenu on the way as he had an appointment. We were lucky. When we reached the Brazilian College where the cardinal was staying, we were told that he would be coming down, as he was going out. In fact, the car was waiting for him. He appeared after about twenty minutes. In two minutes, I had explained to him the purpose of my visit. I made the point (it seemed to find its mark) that the Easterners would very much appreciate the fact that the POPE had appointed one of them. Luckily, the cardinal is going this evening to a reception given by Cardinal Agagianian at which Cardinal Cicognani would also be present. He promised to raise the matter with both of them.' On 24 October 1962, Cardinal Suenens wrote to Fr Chenu: 'The idea of an Eastern theologian [on the commission] strikes me as a good suggestion. If it hasn't happened, then this idea needs to come from one of the members. I will speak to them about it.'

October 22

Lunch at Santa Sabina to pay my respects to the Master General. Saw Fr Hamer, Fr Dondaine (who spoke of his work), Fr Dumont (who confirmed for me that the 'secretariat' for church reunion has been transformed into a Commission; so right away there are schemas being prepared that will be passed around, but not yet presented to the Council).[72]

When I return, Mgr Rolland tells me about the morning's session on the liturgy. Cf the newpapers. He was shocked by Spellman's contribution: '*Lingua latina est lingua catholica*' [The Latin language is the Catholic language].[73] On the whole, the remarks were very favorable to the schema, to the adaptation to a statutory (*statuere* and not only *proponere*) role for episcopal conferences, and the use of modern languages.

---

72. A similar judgment is found in DTcc: 'Two significant facts today: 1) the practical transformation of Cardinal Bea's secretariat into a genuine conciliar commission, with the advantage that its members are not being chosen by the C[ouncil], but are those [he wanted, who had been] proposed by the Cardinal President for the preparatory period; 2) the breakdown of the opposition between North Central Europe and the countries of Latin culture (presupposing that such existed) in the discussion on the general principles of renewal for the S Liturgy.' *Due i fatti salienti della giornata: 1) la pratica equiparazione del Segr del Cardinale Bea ad una vera e propria Commissione Conciliare, col vantaggio che i membri di esso non sono stati lasciati alla scelta del C, ma sono quelli [voluti] proposti dal Cardinale Presid per il periodo preparatorio; 2) La rottura dei fronti opposti Europa Centro Nord e Paesi di cultura latina, se mai vi sono stati, nella discussione sui principi generali del rinnovamento della S Liturgia.'* For the operation of the secretariat and its creation of schemas, see M Velati, 'La proposta ecumenica del segretariato per l'unità dei cristiani', in *Verso I Vaticano II*, 273–343.

73. AS 1/1, 316–319; John XXIII had noted on 24 October 1962: 'The question of [using] Latin certainly separates [bishops] who have never left home or Italy from those from other nations, especially in missionary lands, or even Italians who are living and sacrificing themselves in distant places. On this matter of Latin in the liturgy we will have to proceed slowly and by degrees.' *'La questione del latino divide senz'altro quanti non sono mai usciti di casa, o d'Italia, da quanti appartengono ad altre nazione, specialmente se in terra missionaria, o che pur essendo Italiani si trovano a vivere e a sacrificarsi nella regioni lontane. Su questo punto del latino nella liturgia occorrerà procedere lento pede e per gradi.'*

[11 v°] *October 24*

La Croix confirms and gives details concerning what I said about the reception of the message by the Assembly. Mgr Fiordelli, the bishop of Prato, had proposed including some allusion to the 'church of silence'. A Hungarian bishop and then a Lithuanian bishop in exile remarked that the message, as an appeal for hope and fraternity, shouldn't lend itself to polemical possibilities. So the text was left as it was on the recommendation of the Praesidium. At the vote by sitting or standing, some prelates remained seated, notably some bishops expelled from China.[74]

---

74. The polemic surrounding this minor resistance stretched out over several days in the press: a note from DTcc of 21 October 1962 describes it as follows: 'Friday night, a long conversation of Mgr Morcillo with a limited group of people from the press, mostly priests, at the Spanish Documentation Center for the Council (Via Gregorio VII, 58): he told us about this document [the message], being clearly in favor of it. From Mgr Mayer of ICI I learned that the writer was Fr Chenu. Rev Montero, director of *Ecclesia* (Madrid) said that it had to be either Fr Chenu or Fr Daniélou, who would have received the commission principally from Mgr Morcillo himself. However, it seems that the initiative came from the Central Europe group, perhaps with Spanish support. [. . .] Next Mr. Mayor pointed out, as Fr Brêchet told me, that the text approved by the C wasn't altogether the same as the one prepared by Fr Chenu: the Council of Presidents had changed it on certain points, weakening it a bit. Undeniably the rather summary procedure left the impression of a *fait accompli*. But it seems to me that *Il Tempo* exaggerated the bad feeling of the Fathers, and it is certainly false that many remained "nailed to their seats". I only succeeded in seeing very few—perhaps five out of the entire left side of the aula.' '*Venerdi sera, lungo colloquio di Mons Morcillo, con un limitato gruppo di rappresentanti della stampa, per lo più sacerdoti, al Centro spagnuolo di documentaz. sul C (Via Gregorio VII, 58): praticamente ci aveva annunciato questo documento [scil il messaggio], mostrandosi chiaramente favorevole. Dal Sig Major, di ICI vengo sapere che l'estensore è stato il P Chenu. Il rev Montero, dir di Ecclesia (Madrid) sa che deve essere stato o P Chenu o P Daniélou, per incarico principalmente di mons. Morcillo stesso. Pare invece che l'iniziativa sia partita dal gruppo Centro-Europa, sia pure col consenso spagnuolo. [...] Il sig. Major sosterrà poi, a quanto mi riferisce P Brêchet, che il testo approvato dal C. non corrisponde del tutto a quello preparato dal P Chenu: il Cons di pres lo avrebbe modificato in alcuni punti, estenuandolo un po'. È innegabile che la procedura alquanto sommaria ha lasciato l'impressione di un giuoco già fatto. Ma mi pare che anche su questo punto Il Tempo abbia esagerato i malumori dei Padri, e certamente è falso che molti siano rimasti "inchiodati al lor seggio": io non sono riuscito a vedere che*

Someone tells me also about the remark of Mgr Lefebvre (ex–Dakar): 'The Church shouldn't be concerned about such material problems.'

October 27

Fr Congar tells me that he received a phone call from Cardinal Bea's secretary about the Pope's designating an Eastern theologian to the doctrine Commission (cf 21 October): the cardinal made the request [at an] opportune [moment].[75]

Others had already done so: Cardinal Agagianian. And also the Maronites, who don't have a place anywhere [on the commissions].

Mgr Rolland, in telling me about the morning's meeting of the Assembly, observed that Mgr Kobayashi, bi[shop] of Sendai in Japan, said that he spoke in his own name and in the name of all the Japanese bishops. Mgr Thiandoum, arch[bishop] of Dakar, said he spoke in his own name and in the name of all the bishops of Black Africa (250).

By contrast, Mgr De Vito, an Italian Capuchin, bishop of Lucknow in India, spoke for himself. He requested keeping the western rites and [12 rº] in Latin.

Observation: what a different weight between the opinion of the first two who represented the body of entire churches and the private opinion of the bishop of Lucknow, a diocese of only 4,600 faithful, despite its huge territory.

I composed a note that I sent to Mgr Jenny,[76] member of the Liturgical Commission, to the effect that in reflecting on the

---

qualcuno rarissimo: forse cinque in tutta la parte sinistra dell'Aula.'

75. CngMJC 123 on 27 October 1962: 'At 4.30 pm, lecture to the Melkites on Tradition. Their outlook on the question is quite different from that of the French bishops, and several of them asked me very penetrating questions, which were enriching for myself too, but fairly remote from academic and scholastic analytical questions; not very "usable", in fact. So, authentically Eastern. That makes me glad. At 6 pm, lecture to the La Salette missionaries (on adult faith), followed by Benediction (including the Rosary) lasting thirty–five minutes, then supper with them and with Fr Chenu.'

76. This note has apparently not been kept in the archives of the CNPL; the inventory of the Diocese of Cambrai, where Jenny was the auxiliary, has not yet been published; see AM Abel-Ribaut, 'État present du répertoire des archives du concile Vatican II en France', in *Mélanges des sciences religieuses,* 47 (1990): 157–161.

opinions and the amendments 'sententiae non solum numerandae sed ponderandae sint' [statements need to be not only *counted*, but also *pondered*].

October 29

I visited Fr Rondet, SJ, at the {Jesuit} Generalate. He told me that he had been rehabilitated thanks to his provincial, who was pleased to announce that he could teach historical topics, but not dogma. [Rondet] said that he was sorry but he refused to admit such a separation. The affair was finally settled. He will teach, outside Fourvière {the Jesuit seminary in Lyons}, at the Catho[lic Faculty of Theology] of Lyons, in the 5th year of theology.

At this moment the list of nine (no longer eight) members named by the pope, beyond the sixteen who were elected, arrived in the hands of Fr Lucas (Vatican Radio).[77] We met in Fr Rondet's cell: de Lubac, Semmelroth,[78] Grillmeier, Hisrchmann, and me. Hirchmann briefed us—he is a *scriptor* in touch with what's going on, and he informs the 'political bureau' (*ipse dixit*) of the German prelates many of whom are alumni of the Germanicum.

The Pope's intentions in making these nominations are: 1) to appoint members of the Curia, beginning with the Secretaries of the Congregations, and starting with Parente at the doctrine Commission [12 v°]; 2) reintroduce members of the preparatory

---

77. AS 1/1, 559–562.
78. ST 20 October 1962: 'In the afternoon, visiting Fr Grillmeier, I met a group of theologians, and it was important and pleasant for me to get to know them: Frs Hirschmann, Chenu, OP, de Lubac, Rondet and Grillmeier, all engaged in discussing the list of members of the commissions who had been named by the Pope. The outcome was disappointing in one way. But it is difficult to predict clearly what it means. Anyway this widens the circle of those whom I've met and it is very valuable to know them. The Council helps me personally a lot in this way.' 'Nachmittags traf ich beim besuch bei P. Grillmeier eine Reihe von Theologen, mit denen zu konferiern mir sehr wichtig und angenehm war; P Hirschmann, P Chenu OP, P de Lubac, P Rondet und P Grillmeier waren dabei, die Liste der vom Papst ernannten Mitglieder der Kommissionen durchzusprechen. Das Ergebnis war zum Teil einigermaßen enttäuschend. Aber es ist schwer Eindeutiges vorauszusagen. So weitet sich der Kreis derer, die ich kennelerne und sie kennezuleren sehr fruchtbar ist, immer mehr aus. Für mich selbst bringt das Konzil aus diese Weise jedenfalls sehr viel Gewinn.'

commissions that the fathers (as electors) dropped; 3) give greater presence to religious superiors; 4) give a place to underrepresented nations (Burma, <Ethiopia, Thailand, Malaysia>, Japan, etc.) and to the East (thus, following the initiatives taken cf 27 October, an Oriental on the doctrine Comm[ission], and one on the Commission for bishops, without mentioning the Comm[ission] for the Oriental Church itself).

Whatever the Pope intended, the result is the return of a great number of Italians, few of whom were elected: twenty-four people are nominated but among them not one German, Austrian, or Dutch, and only three French (not counting members of the Curia). So, for certain Commissions—Doctrine, Universities—an influx of conservative elements.

Next Fr Hirschmann[79] went over the persons he knew with 'notes' about each one and significant anecdotes. He recalled that at the morning session, Peruzzo, the bishop of Agrigente, said: the liturgical movement has been corrupt from the beginning since it began with Erasmus and Luther; further, any desertion of the use of Latin will lead to schism and to heresy.[80]

Mgr Guano, bishop of Livorno, who was set aside by the Italian conservatives, was named by the Pope to the Commission on the Laity.[81] I note that he was someone who (among others) during the

---

79. No trace can be found in F Hirschmann of direct contacts with Fr Chenu.

80. AS 1/3, 594–597: '*Motus antiliturgicus mihi non placet, ratione originis. [...] Si fons inquinata, difficiliter fiet pura. Istis principiis innixus, ante oculos habeo origines motus anteliturgici: qui patres, qui auctores. Hic motus ortus habuit sub fine saeculi XV e initio saeculi XVI. Primi antiliturgici fuerunt humanistae, pagani in Italia, meliores in Gallia et in terris nordicis, duce Erasmo, sed omnes non sicuri in fide. Ipsos secuti sunt cursu magno multi Fratres nostri, qui postea se ab Ecclesia catholica separaverunt.*'

81. In reality his being a candidate for two commissions put him in a difficult position; DTcc explains on 24 October 1962: 'Mgr Guano would have been "burned" in the elections because he had been proposed by the Central Europe group for the theological commission and by the [Italian] Felici list for the Ap[ostolate] of the Laity: this is my fault (!) and that of the Italians who excluded him from the laity commission. But Mgr Glorieux assures me that the Holy Father "fished him out". '*Mons. Guano sarebbe stato "bruciato" nelle elezioni perchè proposto dal Centro Europa per la "teologica" e dalla lista [italiana] Felici per l'ap. dei laici : colpa mia (!) e anche degli italiani che lo hanno excluso dall'ap. dei laici. Ma mons Glorieux m'assicura che lo "ripesca" il S Padre.*' For Guano's contribution in the preparatory phase, see Turbanti, *I laici nella chiesa e nel mondo*, 222–239 and *Emilio Guano*

brief discussion about the message had regretted that confessional elements were introduced [13 r°] into a text being sent for the most part to non–Christian and non–believers. I find his fidelity to the point of the message as I had imagined it significant.

[Hirschmann] tells about the meeting of CELAM in Bogotà last year: at its opening, during a violent address by Cardinal Camara (Rio), Mgr Samoré and the cardinal (Agagianian), prefect of the Congregation in Rome, got up and left. The whole group of South American bishops are deeply critical of running CELAM as an organism of the Curia.

Before I left, P Rondet gave me the text of the reply to the hateful calumnies of Spadafora, a disciple of Romeo, against the biblical movement today; especially against the Biblical Institute. Spadafora's pamphlet, simply reproducing two articles already published, has been sent confidentially to many bishops at the Council. The reply to it is signed by the Biblical Institute itself.[82]

L'Espresso published (28 October) an article, '*Verso la nuova teologia: Prevalgono i Padri conciliari favorevoli al rinnovamento*' [Towards the New Theology: Council Fathers favorable to renewal predominate] with a photo of Cardinal Liénart (a French cardinal). There is half a column about me, both complimentary and compromising. It is inexact in its details. Useless to talk about it here. It is signed Carlo Falconi (a priest who left the Church).[83]

[13 v°] *October 30*

Concerning the message to the world—*La Croix* today.

A dispatch of the press agency had said that the bishops expelled from China were among those who didn't approve the message and

---

uomo della Parola (Rome, 1977).

82. H Rondet, SJ, had been named by his provincial as peritus to Bishop Dalmais of Tchad; see Prudhomme, 'Les Évêques d'Afrique . . .', 181. The attacks in *Settimana del clero* and *Divinitas* were responded to in a duplicated manuscript intitled *Pro memoria sugli attacchi contro il Pontificio instituto biblico* (Rome, 1961), and reprinted in Tafi, *Mezzo secolo a servizio della chiesa.*

83. C Falconi will go on to publish a translation and notes in his *Documents secrets du Concile* [Secret Documents of the Council]: *première et deuxième session* (Munich, 1965). See CgrMJC 31 October 1962: 'In the afternoon, a good visit from Fr de Lubac. He told me that last week's *L'Espresso* spoke of one school (Lubac, Congar, Chenu) against the Ottaviani–Parente school . . .'

who remained seated during the vote.[84] In fact, several of them sent a correction to say that they joined the majority of the fathers.

By contrast, Mgr Malanczuk, Exarch for the Ukrainians in exile, wanted people to understand that the fifteen Ukrainian bishops, 'enduring the suffering of their persecuted church, wished to make clear to the world that the dramatic situation imposed on their church, was very much on their minds. They did not stand up, judging that the message was not sufficiently clear about this situation.'[85]

Fr Congar, returning from a visit with Mgr Elchinger who lives with several bishops, among them some Ukrainians, told me that these Ukrainians refused to talk to their colleagues who had conversed with the two Russian observers–delegates at a reception.[86]

Concerning this morning's session, Fr Congar told me how obscure he finds Anglo–Saxon liturgical pragmatism: Cardinal Godfrey (Westminster) argued that saying successive Masses was reason enough to propose that a homily should be given only to the degree possible (a pragmatism that sacrifices the Word to sacramentalism). By contrast, there was a fortunate intervention by the aux[ilary] bi[shop] of Trier about the *duplex mensa* [two tables] of which the *mensa Verbi Dei* [table of the Word of God] is one.[87]

Fr Congar tells me about a schema, not yet officially registered, prepared at the Pope's request [14 rº] about world order.[88] The Rector

---

84. There is a summary of the religious situation in A Dupuy, *La Diplomatie du Saint-Siège après le IIe concile du Vatican* (Paris, 1980), 223–7.
85. On the Ukrainian situation, see BR Bocirkiw, 'The Uniate Church in the Soviet Ukraine: A Case Study in Soviet Church Policy', in *Canadian Slavonic Papers* 7 (1965): 89–113.
86. CgrMJC 30 October 1962: 'After this long morning, Mgrs Elchinger and Schmitt took me off to lunch with them. We chatted. I also saw there a dozen Italian bishops, about ten English and above all SCOTTISH bishops, and four or five Ruthenian bishops (from America): these stopped speaking to the four French bishops after the latter invited the two Russian Observers to join them at table. These bishops told me that one of the benefits of the Council is that one sees the Curia up close and can see how small–minded it is: that is all! Immediately on my return, a visit from Fr Chenu. We chatted.'
87. AS 2/1, 10–11.
88. This is the schema *De ordine internationali* that was not submitted to the Central Preparatory Commission and so remained unofficial. Its argument became centrally important again after the Pope's intervention on 16 October 1962 in the Cuban Missile Crisis between the US and the USSR. The day after the Pope's message that seemed to have a positive effect upon the relations of the

of the Angelicum has worked actively in preparing it.[89] [There are] two paragraphs against the atomic bomb—not only its use, but also its manufacture as part of the arms race. A very strong condemnation. *Le Monde* revealed that there is a petition going around requesting the Council to take up this problem. Fr Congar has signed it.

From the same conversation: concerning the problem of overpopulation, during discussions in the preparatory Commission, the old bishop of Agrigento, Peruzzo (cf above 29 October) stood up and spoke out very emotionally, saying that he was scandalised to see that there was no confidence in Providence: If, because of the problems of overpopulation, people die, it's because that is the disposition of Providence.

There is a trace of this same thing in a note of the preparatory schema (on the morality of the family, page 147), where an allusion is made to this controvery and this 'dogmatic' solution proposed by some: God said in Genesis, 'Increase and multiply'—so let the law of Providence be! Fr Tromp takes this position. On the contrary, Mgr Griffiths defends a 'sociological' position for this problem, including its earthly considerations.[90]

---

superpowers, Fr Pavan was charged to take up questions concerning world order again in a document that would later become the encyclical *Pacem in terris* on 11 April 1963; see Burigana, *Progetto dogmatico*, 27.

89. Fr Chenu left space in his manuscript next to the name R. Sigmond that he didn't fill in. Tromp, in his journal, notes for 28 February 1961: 'First meeting of the Comm. *De ord. mor. Sociali* at the Angelicum. Tromp presiding, plus Pavan, Ferrari, Toniolo, Hurth [sic], Sigmond, Gundlach, Jarlot. I explained the general situation of the Commission and the twofold Subcommissions on the moral order. [...] I divided up the subject matter for the group to work on: fundamenta 1–4: Gundlach, Pavan; family and matri[mony]: Sigmond; the proper ordering of social reality: Jarlot and Ferrari; politics: Pavan, Gundlach for principles, Sigmond for errors.' *'Prima session de* Comm. De ord. mor. Sociali *in Angelicum. Praes. Tromp, Pavan, Ferrari, Toniolo, Hurth [sic], Sigmond, Gundlach, Jarlot. Explicavi situationem generalem de Commissione et Subcommissionibus et in specie de Subcommissionibus duabus de ordine morali. [...] Statuta materia facta fuit divisio laboris: fundamenta 1–4: Gundlach, Pavan; familia et matri.: Sigmond; recta ordinatio rerum socialium: Jarlot et Ferrari; res politicae: Pavan, Gundlach pro fundam,; errores Sigmond.'*

90. *Schemata constitutionum et decretorum de quibus disceptabitur in concilii sessionibus*, series 1, 147. DTrm describes on 31 May 1961 that *'Actum est cum fructu de jure proprietatis. Mgr Pavan offert novam redactionem de fundamento ordinis socialis "Multiplicatur" et statim dabitur P Gundlach (qui fecit primam redactionem) ut faciat observationes.'*

A very significant incident at this morning's session. Cardinal Ottaviani was saying: With all that the liturgical movement is doing and its adaptations, there won't be anything left of the tradition or of its substance. [14 v°] Scripture doesn't suffice to assure this substance. (Cardinal Alfrink had just talked about the scriptural content of the Mass). Ottaviani went over his time limit and Alfrink, the president, interrupted him at the end of fifteen minutes. Part of the assembly applauded.[91]

November 3

Conversation with V Peri, *scriptor* at the Vatican Library. In Milan he participates in the Catholic youth movement that is attentive to the new problems for the Church, including the political role of Christians in the world. Faced with the country's opening to the left, the courageous pastoral bishops in Italy are embarrassed by the developments in the Curia. Long refusal of dialogue, categorically

---

91. Here is the account in AS 1/2: '(Alfrink:) "Excuse me, Your Eminence, but your fifteen minutes are up; (Ottaviani:) I'm finished, I'm finished, I'm finished! [Applause in the aula.]" Semmelroth only learns the details on 11 November: '*Il Tempo* and *Messaggero* reported the Ottaviani affair. Cardinal Alfrink, who was presiding at the General Congregation, stopped Cardinal Ottaviani shortly after he went over his time limit. There was then a strong wave of applause in the Plenum [assembly]. That annoyed Ottaviani so badly that he said that he wouldn't set foot in the aula until he had gotten an apology [*literally, satisfaction*]. Ottaviani is not at all liked because of his ideas. That made the affair easier to handle. But Ruffini, who is quicker on his feet, is even more dangerous than he.' '(Alfrink:) "*Eminentiam vestram habeat me excusatum; quidecim momenta praeterierunt; (Ottaviani:) Ego iam finivi, iam finivi, iam finivi!* [In Aula fit plausus.]" *Semmelroth ne apprende i dettagli solo l'11/11: 'In Tempo und Messaggero steht ein Bericht über die Affaire Ottaviani. Vor kurzem hatte Kardinal Alfrink, der gerade den Vorsitz der Generalkongregation hatte, dem Kardinal Ottaviani das Wort entzogen, als dieser die Redezeit überschritt. Dabei gab es im Plenum allgemeinen großen Beifall. Das muß Ottaviani so erzürnt haben, daß er erklärt hat, er werde keinen Schritt mehr in die Konzilsaula tun, bevor ihm Genugtuung geschehe. Ottaviani ist wegen seiner Auffassungen sehr unbeliebt. Das hat sich in dieser Affaire Luft gemacht. Gefährlicher als er scheint aber Ruffini zu sein, der zudem sehr viel geschickter ist.'*

upheld by Cardinal Siri.[92] Then one day John XXIII brought about change. So now they have to accept what they had explicitly condemned before.

Mgr De Luca, a personal friend of John XXIII, met with Togliatti who gave him an explanation for this evolution. John XXIII's political interests are 'pastoral', not doctrinal (that doesn't interest him).[93]

November 4

A Mass at St Peter's for the fourth anniversary of the Pope's coronation. Mgr Rolland comes back disappointed, distressed, and shocked [15 r°] by the solemn celebration with its pompous formalities and archaic and lifeless rituals, and its lack of any community involvement. At the very moment that we are recovering the active and informed participation of the faithful in the liturgy, we 'assisted' at Mass in the most passive sense of the term. The Christian people are only 'spectators'.

I'm told about the remark of Mgr Khoury, arch[bishop] of Tyre (picked up by Dom Rousseau): 'A solemn Mass before the Holy Father exposed'.[94]

Fr Chalencon, general secretary of the Congreg[ation] of La Salette, tells me this. About two years ago as superior of the house, he received one day an order from the cardinal–vicar of Rome addressed to all the superiors and all the parish priests to come to a meeting. It was just before the elections. After a few words from the cardinal, a journalist[95] from the Oss[ervatore] Rom[ano] gave a conference about the parties in the election. Shocked by this {political} campaign, Fr [Chalecon] got up and left. The cardinal lashed out against those who were absent. The day before a similar conference had been given to the houses of religious women.

---

92. See the minutes of the Italian Episcopal Conference in F Sportelli, La Conferenza Episcopale Italiana (1952–1972) (Galatina, 1994), 129–168.
93. On De Luca's role in relations with Togliatti, see A Riccardi, Il Vaticano e Mosca (1940–1990) (Rome–Bari, 1992), 241.
94. O Rousseau is a monk of Chevetogne.
95. Unidentified at present.

November 5

I gave a conference to the fathers and students of Holy Cross (my account of the missionary experience of the church in France).[96]

I had supper with Mgr McGrath, the bishop of Panama, former prof[essor] of the Univ[ersity] of Santiago, Chile <and member of the doctrine Commission>. I have already made note of his intervention in the discussion on the liturgy.[97] [15 v°] A passionately interesting conversation. He has been made liaison between the Latin American episcopate and the North American bishops. Cardinal McIntyre (whose comments on the liturgy were painful),[98] like Cardinal Spellman, doesn't represent at all the mentality of the whole group.[99]

Reflections on what is being done for a new schema on the Church, in particular the chap[ter] on the Church and the new world (Congar, Rahner, Ratzinger, de Lubac, Colombo . . .).[100]

---

96. It seems not to have been published, but several presentations on this theme between 1954 and 1961 are listed in A Duval, 'Bibliographie du P M-D Chenu', in *Mélanges offerts à M.-D. Chenu, maître en théologie* (Paris, 1967), 10–29.

97. AS 1/1, 515–519: On 27 October 1962 Mgr McGrath spoke against the phrase '*nihil velle dogmatice definire*' [wishing not to define anything dogmatically] in the constitution *De liturgia*.

98. The intervention of the Archbishop of Los Angeles on 5 November 1962 (AS 1/2, 108–9) supported the claim that giving up Latin would cause scandal among the faithful, and he contradicted the Pope's proposition in the Apostolic Constitution *Veterum sapientia* in February.

99. Cardinal Ritter's intervention at the 5th General Congregation had already shown a sign of a plurality of views; see DTcc 23 October 1962: 'Today, with Cardinal Ritter's intervention, we saw clearly that Spellman and McIntyre are not the whole USA; another view is breaking in. All we need now is to hear some voice favorable to liturgical reform from among the people in the Curia, and then there won't be any more blocks or closed factions.' '*Oggi, col l'intervento del Cardinale Ritter, si è visto chiaro che Spellman e McIntyre non sono tutti l'USA; altro fronte che si spezza. Non resta che sentire qualche voce favorevole alla riforma liturgica anche tra i "curiali", e allora non vi saranno più blocchi e fronti chiusi.*'

100. At this point the strategies of different groups are being clarified: the difference is not yet evident between the Rahner–Ratzinger group (who want a kerygmatic preamble and to set the preparatory schemas aside) and the others (whom Philips will join) who think that it is possible to reuse and re-arrange the chapters from the preparatory commission with a new outline that will diminish the impact of substantial modifications and corrections; on this topic see J Komonchak, 'The Initial Debate about the Church', in *Vatican II commence*, 329–352.

November 7

Fr Congar gave a conference to the bishops of black Africa on tradition. It was lucid and full of evangelical passion. His conclusion severely criticised the schema. At the end, conversation [between] Mgr Zoa (secretary for the whole group of bishops), Fr Congar, Fr de Lubac, Fr Martelet, and a Dutch bishop: opposition to the prepared schemas is very extensive; but how can we proceed when discussions have to be raised in terms of the texts of these very schemas? Is it possible or timely to request the substitution of another text prepared in private? Won't it be necessary to multiply and focus criticisms on the text[s] presented until this leads to a rewrite? Will sending the text back to the Commission achieve anything, since Ottaviani is controlling the structure there?

They speak of the text prepared by Rahner and some others. Fr Congar says that it is very good. After a period of extreme discretion, it must become known. Mgr Zoa and Fr Martelet leave for the Germanicum to ask for it.[101]

---

101. Rahner's view can be seen in DTcc 11 November 1962: 'I invited Fr Rahner to lunch. After recreation we talked, among other things, about [an alternative schema] a paper critical of the schema *De fontibus revelat.* given to the Fathers, edited at the request of Cardinal Döpfner and others. Fr Rahner thinks that a new schema, being prepared by Ratzinger and himself in Latin, has little chance of being considered. That's why he has [also] prepared [various things]: [a fundamental critique of the schema] plus various amendments to help the text given to the council Fathers to become at least passable. He is pessimistic because the prohibition of his publishing anything without previous oversight by the Holy Office has not yet been resolved. In leaving us, he said while smiling: "If the Council finishes by going in the direction that the Holy Office wants, then the only thing left for me to do is to become a Carthusian!"' '*Ho invitato P. Rahner a pranzo. Dopo la ricreazione, ci ha parlato, tra l'altro, di [uno schema sostitutivo di quello] un memoriale critico sullo schema* De fontibus revelat., *consegnato ai Padri, redatto per desiderio del Cardinale Döpfner e di altri P Rahner considera che [tale] un nuovo schema, [da] prepara [to] rsi da Ratzinger e da lui in latino, ha poche chances di essere preso in considerazione. Perciò ha anche preparato [vari] [questa critica di fondo] vari emendamenti intesi a rendere almeno passabile il testo proposto ai Padri Conc É pessimista, anche perché come ci ha detto non gli è stato ancora risolto il problema dell'obbligo fattogli di non pubblicare nulla senza previa revisione del S Uffizio. Nell'accomiatarsi ci diceva ridendo: "si il Concilio finisce per andare nel senso auspicato dal S O non me resterà che farmi certosino!"*'.

[16 r°] They say that Fr Tromp, who is watching his schemas being threatened, says about the bishops who are discussing all this: '*Questi esteri!*' [These foreigners!][102]

November 9

Conference by Fr Martelet to the French–speaking bishops of black Africa {about} the organic vision of the economy of salvation in an intellectual grasp of faith's meaning [*intelligence de la foi*] according to the three resources indicated by Vatican I. The Christological center and the eschatological meaning. Severe criticism of the preparatory schemas that were thought through and composed in a way completely outside this perspective.[103]

Opposition to the schemas is more and more widespread. However at {this} time when the {schemas} are about to be discussed publicly, we have no idea what to do about bringing this problem to the assembly. Is it possible to raise the preliminary question, especially for the 2nd schema, *De deposito fidei?*[104]

102.CgrMJC 7 November 1962: 'At 4.30 pm, lecture to the French–speaking bishops of Africa. Very remarkable secretary of this group, Mgr Zoa. After my lecture (on Tradition), followed by quite a lot of questions, I chatted for a while with Frs Chenu, de Lubac, and Martelet. We must speed up the preparation of the battle over the dogmatic schemas on the part of the African and the French bishops. We agree that Martelet will see Karl Rahner and Cardinal Liénart.'

103.See G Martelet, *Les Idées maîtresses de Vatican II: Introduction à l'esprit du Concile* (Lyons, 1966).

104.In SChn there are two notes from September 1962: 'Schema de deposito fidei— Cap I De cognitione veritatis (27)—*Sub titulo "De fide et de deposito fidei", cap I 'De cognitione veritatis' jam ab initio propositum, magis redolet quamdam metaphysicam quam scientiam salutis et objectum proprium fidei de quo agitur. Istae metaphysicae assertiones praesupponuntur quidem ad assensum fidei; sed haec prae–suppositio se habet non tanquam introitus ad fidem, sed ad modum implicitae cognitionis, cujus explicatio formalis inconvenienter in terminis philosophicis quaestionem vertit, quando agitur expresse de processu reali et religioso actus fidei. / De facto, assertiones hujus paragraphi statim ad vocabula et conceptus rationis philosophicae vertuntur, cujus tamen praecisam et subtilem discretionem non servant. V gr quando dicitur (lin. 12) "Ecclesia firmiter agnoscit hominem facultate pollere intelligendi res prouti in se sunt", haec assertio philosophica non tantum longe distat a dignitate et religioso valore textum Sacrae Scripturae excellenter citatae in initio paragraphi; sed affirmationem satis summariam et vulgarem continent de objectivismo absoluto cognitionis humanae. Quod verae methodo philosophiae repugnat; imo et incoherentiam parit, in detrimentum et irrisionem fidei. / Revera,*

There is a rumor going around about a tactic to be used by those who solidly support these schemas. Under the pretext of revising the amendments proposed by the liturgy Commission, let them be revised by[105] the doctrine Commission—which would not be ready to do that; so the votes would be put off to the second session (January? April?), which would lead to suffocating the desire for reform manifest in the Assembly and simultaneously to pressure them to accept the doctrinal schemas.[106]

---

in par. 4 de primis principiis, tanquam de propositionibus "quae mutationi non sunt obnoxiae" (lin. 26), magis ac magis apparet inconveniens transitus fidei ad rationem philosophicam, cujus tamen exegentiae non serventur. Enuntiationes enim principiorum difficillimam rectitudinem apud philosophos jugiter praestant, extra "spontaneam" "perspicuitatem" (lin. 29). V. gr. Principium rationis sufficientis nemo ignorat metaphysicam leibnizianam implicare, nullo modo thomisticam, et amplius christianam philosophiam. / Quando dicitur (lin. 31) 'Ipse ordo doctrinae fidei quodammodo' non tollit, praesertim quando concluditur in nomine Ecclesiae "principia illa a nemine in dubium ullatenus vocari posse" (lin. 32). / Et ideo convenientus videtur hoc caput tollere, et opportunius praesupposit fidei de cognitione veritatis in terminis generalibus et scripturisticis asserere, et in alio capitulo integrare' 'Cap 4. De revelation publica – 20. Revelatio et manifestatio Christi. *Haec paragraphus intendit repellere "tendentias... quae indebite efferent adspectum mysticum fidei indebiteque deprimunt adspectum ejus doctrinalem"* (nota 10, 43). / Recte quidem; sed, a contrario, iste textus deprimit adspectum *mysticum fidei et indebite effert adspectum* doctrinalem. *Ad redarguendos enim quosdam theologos protestantes, indebite "experientiam" extollentes, ipstmet in alterum excessum cedit, ita ut videatur reduceri* testimonium *Christi (vita, mors, ressurectio) ad* doctrinam *(lin. 11–12). Revera, haec defectuosa disjunctio pervertit, cum verbis ipsis, positionem quaestionis, in detrimentum notionis integrae fidei, in qua "doctrina" non habet vim extra 'testimonium'. Revelatio est ipsamet manifestatio Christi (lin. 6), in qua doctrina est enuntiatio testimonii. / Fides est* simul *"auditus" (magisterii) et "lumen". Quod lumen certo certius non est effectus cujusdam experientiae subjectivae; est tamen qualitas supernaturalis infusa, extra quam propositiones, conceptus, verba, imo et doctrina objectiva, valorem non habent. Fides est testimonium Spiritus in nobis. Infeliciter igitur illuminatio fidei deprimitur, sub praetextu auctoritatis magisterii proclamandi. Positio polemica inducit hanc declarationem in quemdam abusum intellectualismi, qui non cohaeret cum ultimis verbis descriptionis (lin. 24) de "fruitione obscura mysterii". Imo, jam in catechesi ipsa, secundum traditionem patristicam et liturgicam, instructio doctrinalis* intra *initiationem mysteriorum transmitti debet. / Cum objectivitas revelationis firmiter et sufficienter in aliis articulis schematis asseritur, videtur haec paragraphus obscurus non retinendus.'*

105. Ms.: put them in contact with...

106. John XXIII's concern is no different; on 5 November he writes in his notebook: 'The prolongation of individual speeches by the council fathers, without their

The doctrine Commission as well as the Holy Office is taking to itself the right to review and correct the decisions and texts of the other commissions and dicasteries.[107]

[16 vᵒ] *November 10*

A visit from Don G Dossetti, who brings Dom Olivier Rousseau with him.[108] Intense conversation about the state of the Italian episcopate.

---

seeing the results of serious work from the Commissions that have to prepare the texts that will be brought to a definitive vote, leaves things uncertain and perplexing as to the rapidity of the work's progress. If all the work continues at this rate, the year 1963 will not be enough to satisfy everyone. The temptation to impatience grows and spreads! We need to clearly see where we have to modify the system [*modus*] so as to facilitate good work and prepare the resolutions. *Sic Deus nos adjuvet*'; then again on 7 November he writes: 'The Council's voice gets clearly to me here in my room. A current is developing that wants not so much repetition, but summation. At the end of this work on the "Liturgy" I am thinking of proposing and seeking with my cardinals a more expeditious way of doing things. Please God that will happen.' *'Il prolungarsi delle letture dei singoli Padri del Concilio, senza scorgere il lavoro intimo che deve svolgersi delle Commissioni, che devono preparare il testo difinitivo delle proposte da presentarsi alla votazione definitiva, lascia un po' incerti circa la speditezza del lavoro, incerti e perplessi. Se si va di questo passo neppure tutto intero il [[lavoro]] il 1963 potrà bastare al desiderio del mondo intero. La tentazione di impazienza, guai, se si diffonde! Converrà dunque vederci ben chiaro e ove occorre modificare il [[modus]] il sistema così da facilitare il buon lavoro, e preparare le risoluzioni.* Sic Deus nos adjuvet'; *'La voce del Concilio arriva chiarissima al mio orecchio qui in camera. Una corrente di invito a non ripetere, a sunteggiare, pare che si avvii. Al termine però di questa trattazione sulla "Liturgia" sto pensando a proporre e a cercare coi miei Cardinali un modo di procedere più sbrigativo. Faxit Deus che riesca.'*

107. In fact, this is a fear without factual foundation, but it reveals the state of mind of [these private] debates.

108. Chenu kept a note that came from Dossetti, very close in spirit to the 'message': '*Pro memoria per una dichiarazione orientativa* [position in favor of an orientation declaration] / Beyond the particular questions being discussed at the Council, no matter how important, there is from now on a supreme problem more important than all the others: How shall the Council define in a realistic and concrete way its objective and its future work? / This problem is particularly serious because it is clear that the preparatory phase was a failure. In a sense, it's as though the preparation for the Council only began a few days ago. It's not just the inadequacy of this or that doctrinal schema nor the unacceptable quality of a whole group of schemas. The entire preparation of the Council was lacking in *spirit*—in its *formal cause*—because the fundamental decisions that should have established with clarity and proportion the essential objectives of relating the Church's

Except for four or five (Lercaro, Montini, then Guano, Bartoletti), the

---

contemporary situation to the world were not taken into consideration. (These are described in the Apostolic Constitution that convoked [the Council], *Humanae salutis*: according to the great tradition of councils, we could have expected that it would have given the Council its specific and concrete themes. It is enough to look at the Bulls of convocation of Trent, for example. Another, no less significant symptom, is the fact that more than a month after the Council elected Commissions, they cannot function for the most part because the dozens of schemas prepared by the corresponding preparatory commissions are not yet under scrutiny.) There was a certain amount of material and quantitative preparation (that was very inadequate) that consisted in the endless accumulation of every possible problem—the classic pile of stones—but (with the exception of the Secretariat for Christian Unity and the schema on the Liturgy) the overall preparation—the definition of its historic mission and the potential objectives of the Council—were lacking. The real preparatory phase only began with certain remarks in the opening address of the Pope. The preparation was deficient in another sense as well: three years were not enough to bring to maturity a fundamental prior agreement within the central bureaus of the Church: up to now this Council has not been a dialogue between the Pope and the Episcopate, between the Holy See and the Local Churches, but rather a hesitant and confused dialogue between the Pope and a large party within the Roman Curia, between the President of the Council and his most immediate collaborators who have not wanted to or have not known how to understand the intentions of the Pope. / All things considered, then, rather than say that the preparatory work failed, it is more correct to say that in a certain sense *it could not succeed* because logically *a council can't be prepared* ahead of time. Certain choices can be made to circumscribe the agenda (especially if this is not imposed by the necessity of dealing with specific 'heresies'), and some materials can be prepared ahead, but the Council can't be prepared. Perhaps the text to cite is Luke 21:15–15 *"So make up your minds not to prepare your defense in advance; for I will give you words and a wisdom..."* The Council starts preparing when it begins, that is, when the Pope and the Bishops in the act of coming together *make themselves present* to the Spirit, the Lord and Giver of life. / That seems to be what has happened between 11 October and now. / So there is a meaning to this failure of the preparatory phase in that you can see how Providence is using it to bring about a more authentic success for the Council. / But that will happen only under precise conditions. / First, the Holy Father himself needs to clarify and concretise the mission and the agenda of this Council, or at least be open to what can come from the Council. The absence of any heresy that needs to be condemned does not legitimate the Council addressing everything—every topic in dogma, all the questions in morality, all the institutions and all the historical problems of our times. / Basically it would be enough to take on only two or three themes, for example, "The Church and the poor", "the Church and the new Christendoms outside the West", and grasping some essential and vital aspects of these two themes, to define some rare and incisive doctrinal orientations related to them and some imperative and concrete points of institutional reform. In this way the

[Italian] bishops are completely kept in hand by Cardinal Siri, the

---

Council would best do its job, at least the urgent and possible aspects of this job. At the most it should again be concerned to create a *provisional* structure *ad experimentum* for permanent consultation between the Pope and the episcopate to keep the flame burning and to insist on the effective and faithful execution of fixed rules. / On deep reflection, it doesn't seem that [the Council] needs to do anything else: it's not necessary, for example, to take up theological problems like the nature of the Church, or the question of the relation between the Pope and the episcopate, or that of the orientations and the inspiration of new biblical and theological research. / All these questions are not yet ripe [*mûrs*]. If they are taken up, they could be treated in way that would be *more likely to close down options rather than open them up*. So not bringing them up not only doesn't compromise anything, but on the contrary confirms implicitly and clearly that we are looking for openness, not closure. Everything else will ripen according to its own rhythm. Because it's a question of a maturation that can't happen in the area of doctrine, but can in the area of events and of life. For example, the problem of the realtionships between the Pope and the episcopacy will never develop as much as a result of a dogmatic Constitution as by the very fact of the Council as an event, and also by that other event that could occur from the creation of episcopal conferences and from some kind of representation of the episcopacy of the universal Church before the Pope. Such facts, then, whether desired or not, will develop by themselves by the nature of things in the world and within the center of the Church. / The second condition for the Council not to fail in its historic mission is that it becomes conscious right away of this state of affairs and that it formulate an orientating declaration, even if very preliminary, before the end of the present session. This very preliminary declaration should in substance only recall the most significant phrases of the Pope's opening address and, so to speak, *canonize* these phrases as the absolute rule for future work, affirming that today it is not the Council's mission to legislate in all the areas of doctrine, morality, and ecclesiastical institutions, but only to work on two or three synthetic aspects of the Christian and human situation of our time and to indicate these few topics as the object for reflection and study for the Commissions and especially for the *Deputatio Concilii* that will be meeting during the intersession period. When the Council reconvenes, perhaps in a single session it can approve two or three documents on the teaching about and on concrete commitment to the evangelisation of the poor, on the de facto universality of the Church, and on its transcendence with respect to all cultures and civilisations and, similarly, its maternity in relation to all peoples. The documents [*actes*]— which will have to contain doctrinal texts and essential and incisive directives for reform—should be synthetic and sober, but be such as to exclude formulas that are vague or compromised, and they should touch on central and critical points. If Vatican II does that, it will have done a lot. Perhaps it will discover how to be discreet and leave with confidence an even greater task for the following Council, which would not be able to be postponed for many years.' Dossetti, a canonist, then an organiser and leader of Christian Democrary, retired from political life to promote theological and historical studies. See D Menozzi, 'Alle origini del

president of the episcopal conference named by Pius XII.

---

centro di Documentazione' in *Con tutte le tue forze: Saggi sui nodi della fede Cristiana oggi*, edited by A and G Alberigo (Genoa, 1993), 333–69. Regarding his activities for Lercaro, G Alberigo, *L'esperienze conciliare di un vescovo*; see *Per la forza dello spirito: Discorsi conciliari* (Bologna, 1984), 9–62.

'Pro memoria per una dichiarazione orientativa. / *Al di là dei singoli problemi – per quanto di grande importanza – in discussione al Concilio, vi è ormai un problema supremo, che comanda tutti gli altri: come il Concilio può delimitare— secondo realismo e concretezza—l'oggetto del suo impegno e del suo lavoro futuro? / Il problema si pone con particolare gravità perché si deve ormai prendere atto che la fase preparatoria è fallita. In un certo senso è come se la preparazione del Concilio fosse cominciata solo da pochi giorni. Non si tratta della inadeguatezza di questo o di quello schema dottrinale e nemmeno soltanto della inaccettabilità di tutto un gruppo di schemi. E' tutta la preparazione del Concilio che è mancata nella sua* anima, *nella sua* causa formale, *perché sono mancate le scelte elementari che dovevano fiassarne con chiarezza e misura gli scopi essenziali in rapporto alla situazione odierna della Chiesa e del Mondo. (Questo è bien rilevabile della Constituzione Apostolica* Humanae salutis *di convocazione: secondo la grande tradizione conciliare sarebbe spettato ad essa dare al Concilio i suoi temi definiti e concreti. Basterà per convincersene confrontarla con le Bolle di convocazione, per esempio, del Tridentino. Altro sintomo non poco significativo è il fatto che da oltre un mese il Concilio abbia eletto delle Commissioni che nella maggior parte non possono funzionare perché ancora non sono state rese note le varie decine di schemi che sono state preparate dalle corrispondenti commissioni preparatorie.) C'è stata (e anche questa molto difettosa) una certa preparazione materiale e quantitativa, che è consistita nell'accumulare senza discrezione tutti i problem possibili, il classico mucchio di pietre, ma (se si eccettua l'opera del Segretariato per l'unità dei cristiani e lo schema sulla liturgia) è mancata la preparazione sostanziale, l'individuazione del compito storico e degli obiettivi immediati possibili di questo Concilio. La vera fase preparatoria è cominciata solo con alcune espressioni della allocuzione papale d'apertura. La preparazione è mancata anche in un altro senso: nel senso che tre anni non sono bastati per fare maturare un accordo preventivo di base all'interno degli organi centrali della Chiesa: questo Concilio sinora non è stato tanto un dialogo tra Papa ed Episcopato, tra S Sede e Chiese locali, quanto piuttosto un dialogo reticente e confuse tra il Papa e una larga parte della Curia Romana, tra il Presidente del Concilio e i suoi più immediati collaboratori che non hanno voluto o saputo intendere la mente del Papa. / Perciò,* tutto considerato, *forse più che dire che i lavori preparatori non sono riusciti,* é corretto dire che in un certo senso non potevano riuscire, *perché a rigore un concilio non si prepara. Si possono preparare alcune scelte per circoscrivere l'agenda del Concilio (specialmente se questa non è imposta di necessità dall'insorgenza di 'eresie' determinate) e si possono preparare dei matieriali, ma non si prepara il Concilio. Forse è il caso di dire anche per esse:* "Ponite ergo in cordibus vestris non praemeditari quemadmodum respondeatis: ego enim dabo vobis os et sapientiam" *(Lk 21: 14–15). / Il Concilio si prepara quando incomincia la sua celebrazione, cioè quando il Papa e i Vescovi nell'atto della loro riunione* adsunt *allo Spirito Signore e vivificante. / Sembra ben essere*

D[ossetti] tells me about a statement of Siri *after* the famous

---

ciò che è accaduto dall' 11 ottobre ad oggi. / Quindi vi è un senso di questo fallimento della così detta fase preparatoria, per cui esso può essere una premessa provvidenziale a une più autentica riuscita del Concilio. / Tutto questo però a condizione ben precise. / Prima di tutto che lo stesso S Padre chiarisca e concreti di più—o almeno accolga quanto dal Concilio può venire, perché si chiarisca e si concreti di più—il compito, l'agenda di questo Concilio. Non è possibile che la mancanza di una eresia definita da condannare, possa ancora lasciar credere che allora questo Concilio deve occuparsi di tutto, di tutti i capitoli del dogma, di tutti i capitoli della morale, di tutte le instituzioni e di tutta la problematica storica del nostro tempo. / In fondo basterebbe prendere duo o tre temi soltanto, per esempio "la Chiesa e i Poveri" et "la Chiesa e le nuove cristianità extraoccidentali" e, cogliendo alcuni supremi e vitali aspetti di sintesi di questi due temi, statuire alcune poche e incisive orientazioni dottrinali in ordine ad essi, e alcuni tassativi e concreti punti di riforma instituzionale. / Con questo il Concilio avrebbe più che esaurito il suo compito, e almeno la parte urgente e possibile del suo compito. Al più si dovrebbe proccupare ancora di esprimere un organo provvisorio *e ad* experimentum *di consultazione permanente tra Papa ed Episcopato, allo scopo di mantenere accesa la fiamma e di insistere per l'effettiva e fedele esecuzione delle norme fissate. / A ben riflettere non sembra necessario che faccia altro: non sembra necessario, per esempio, che affronti problemi teologici come quello della natura della Chiesa, e quello dei rapporti tra Papa ed Episcopato e quello delle direttive e della inspiratione della nuova ricerca biblica e teologica. / Tutti questi problemi non sono maturi. Se affrontati non potrebbero esserlo altro che in modo* più *capace di* chiudere che di aprire. Mentre non affrontarli non solo non compromette nulla, ma anzi confermerebbe in modo implicito ma inequivoco che si vuole la aperture e non la chiusura. Il resto maturerà a suo tempo. Perché si tratta di una maturazione che non può avvenire tanto in sede di dottrina, quanto di fatti e di vita. Per esempio il problema del rapporto tra Papa ed Episcopato non farà mai tanta strada per effetto di una Constituzione dogmatica quanta ne potrà fare per l'evento già accaduto del Concilio e per l'altro evento che protrà accadere di una certa presenza di fatto delle Conferenze Episcopali e di una qualsiasi rappresentanza dell'Episcopato universale presso il Papa: questi fatti ormai, si voglia o non si voglia, cammineranno da sè per la forza delle cose nel mondo e nel seno stesso della Chiesa. / La seconda condizione perché il Concilio non fallisca il suo compito storico è che esso prenda subito piena coscienza di questo stato di cose e arriva a formulare una dichiarazione orientativa in senso sia pure molto preliminare, prima della fine della presente sessione. Une diachiarazione molto preliminare che in sostanza, soltanto, richiami le frasi più significative del discorso di apertura del Papa, e per così dire* canonizzi *quelle frasi come la regola assoluta del lavoro futuro, affermando non essere oggi compito del Concilio legiferare in tutti i campi della dottrina, della morale e delle instituzioni ecclesiastiche, ma solo di cogliere due o tre aspetti sintetici della problematica cristiana e umana del nostro tempo e indicare quei pochi aspetti come l'oggetto di meditazione e di studio per le Commissioni e soprattutto per la Deputatio Concilii che dovrà sedere durante l'intervallo. Alla ripresa il Concilio potrà, anche in una sola sessione, pervenire all'approvazione di due o tre documenti sulla dottrina e*

opening address of the Pope (*Orizzonti*, 18 October).[109] Siri presents himself as someone in the Pope's confidence and expressing the thinking of the Italian episcopate. The content {of the Pope's address}: the complete disappearance of a pontifical perspective. 'De–westernisation?!' Not the right word. It is crucial to banish this, even when one opens it to accommodation. A pastoral Council? Of course. But all Councils have been pastoral. It is an error to give to the term pastoral an *impegno nuovo* {new meaning—literally 'commitment'} and to believe that by doing so you can put doctrine and truth aside. <See the text in my dossier.>

Siri alone has the administrative structure and the material means to inform and teach the bishops. Dossetti showed me one of his circular letters about the current discussion of the liturgy. It was put together by him without consultation with the national liturgical commission headed by Lercaro. It proposes that the Holy See create a 'Code for the Liturgy' that would be uniform, even though local bishops would be able to make applications and changes of detail.

At the election for the liturgy Commission, the Italian bishops scratched out [17 r°] Lercaro from their list. One of the bishops came to the cardinal and told him: 'I'm sorry; I was obliged to do that by obedience.'

Continuing the conversation about a procedure for opposing the schema. Dossetti, who is qualified to talk about how to influence an assembly, said that *procedure* is the effective area for doing battle.

---

l'impegno concreto della evangelizzazione dei povere, della universalità di fatto della Chiesa e della sua trascendenza rispetto a tutte le culture e civiltà e della sua pari maternità nei confronti di tutte le genti. Gli atti—che dovrebbero contenere una parte di dottrina e una essenziale incisive parte di riforma—dovrebbero essere sintetici e sobri, ma tali da escludere ogni formula vaga e compromissoria e da toccare i punti nodali e dirimenti. / Se avrà fatto questo il Concilio Vaticano II avrà fatto moltissimo. Forse tanto più quanto più saprà essere discreto e riservare con fiducia un compito—ancora più grande—per il Concilio successivo, che non potrà così tardare molti anni.'

109.Siri elaborated on the distinctions already sketched in his journal for 11 October between good and bad use of the [Pope's] address, about which he stressed the Pope's concessions and his citation of Vincent of Lérins. This is one of the statements that made the Pope react in his Christmas address to the College of Cardinals by taking up again passages that he considered important as a sort of response to a greeting of welcome that he himself had edited and corrected.

'That's where I have always won.'[110] Here, at least for the second schema

110. On Dossetti's experience as a facilitator of groups in the Italian post-war era, see
G Dossetti, *La ricerca costituente (1945-1953)*, edited by A Melloni (Bologna,
1994), and G Alberigo, 'Concilio acefalo?' in *Il Vaticano II fra attese e celebrazione*,
edited by G Alberigo (Bologna, 1995), 193–238. Dossetti gave Fr Chenu the
following note, now in his archives: '*Observations and Propositions concerning
the Government of the Council*. As the Council unfolded, the importance of
regulations has been underestimated, as well as the importance of stable and
clear procedures. This has often led to obstacles in defining the exact functions of
different conciliar operations, in elaborating a stable practice (despite needed
adaptations based on experience); and all this has led to confusion and slowness,
and above all it has become an obstacle to clear work habits and to orderly and
constructive dialogue between the Council and the Pope. For this reason I
suggest that before the end of the session the following changes should be made:
1) *Normalizing Rules and Procedures.* It is understandable that in the opening
weeks it was necessary to adjust regulations, and we can draw lessons from that
for the future. But it is of the greatest importance that changes are not made daily,
but only on the rarest of occasions and especially that they are not made *viva
voce*, but only according to form, following written norms that are thoughtful
and organic, properly coordinated with the text of the *motu proprio
Appropinquante Concilio*, which set up the regulations. This is not just a demand
of form and legislative technique, but a substantive necessity: it sets the conditions
for serious work and for the agenda of the Council, the maturing of the awareness
of the Council and of the conciliar fathers, and the adjustment and the rectitude
of the rapport between the Pope and the Council. 2) *Improving the Force of Article
65 § 3* by which the president of each commission should designate the recording
secretary [*rapporteur*] who will edit and interpret the schema 'according to the
ideas of the Commission'. Up till now, this norm has not been faithfully observed:
the fact that the presidents of the commissions are the heads of the congregations
plays a large role here. Without doubt, on the whole, this procedure—which is
being done here for the first time: it was not like this at Vatican I—has not
contributed to and cannot contribute to the correct functioning of the Council.
In the final analysis it will not contribute either to the prestige and the authority
of the congregations themselves. If it were possible, it should be proposed to
everyone's advantage (at least for the end of the session) to distinguish the
competencies of the Council, the Pope, and the Congregations. But even if this
situation is from here on definitively compromised, it is necessary to insist at
least that in each commission the recording secretary be chosen not by the
president, but (as is more just) by the commission itself; and even better, at least
when the commission sees the possibility, there should be two recording
secretaries: one from the majority and the other from the minority. The possibility
for the minority to make its voice heard and its reasons understood constitutes
not only a greater guarantee for the freedom and extensiveness of the debate, but
also a means to speed up the work because the minority, both in the commission
as well as in the general assembly, can in this way find its ideas expressed in an
orderly and reasoned way that will forestall many disorderly interventions that

(*De deposito fidei*), the preliminary question is about procedure; the

---

are often not well thought out. Most experienced and mature assemblies have adopted a measure like that in their government. 3) *An Absolute Insistence upon the Norm of Article 39 § 1* that requires a two–thirds majority for every decision. From time to time you hear someone suggest the possibility of a reduced majority. But it is necessary for a Council, insofar it is an assembly of divine right representing the Church, to be clearly different from a democratic assembly. That is why the simple majority of an ordinary democratic process won't work here. If the Council represents the Church, which lives in Christ, then the principle of a simple majority can't suffice, but rather only unanimity—even if it is not a material but only a moral unanimity. Moral unanimity is only slightly different from absolute unanimity. That is why one could reasonably imagine needing an even stronger majority than two thirds, at least for doctrinal decisions. In any case, it is unacceptable for doctrinal decrees to pass with a majority less than two thirds (which is what is actually established in the rules). 4) The need for a *Deputatio generalis Concilii* for the interval between the two sessions. It has already been announced that there will be about six months between the first and second session and that during this in–between time the commissions will continue to work. In this way Vatican II is faced with something new in the history of councils: there never was such a long interval (if you accept the case of the interruption of councils). If the commissions of the Council were the only ones to work during the interval, then probably the situation described for the preparatory commissions would repeat itself, that is, that each commission closed in upon its own specialty would tend to lose perspective on the needs of the whole and on the concrete function of the Council with respect to the Church and the world of today (such as the sovereign pontiff described in his opening address and according to the commitments made by the conciliar fathers in their message to the world). For the rest, from the beginning of the work of the preparatory groups there was clearly a need for a central commission. Even more now since the Council has opened and begun to express its general orientations— going beyond particular sectors—it will be necessary during the long period of suspension to maintain a global representation of the Council: a general deputation of at least 40 fathers who are not themselves already members of commissions, all of them elected by the Council. It is clear that this deputation ought to be completely elected by the Council; and to represent the Pope there remains the Council of Presidents, and eventually also the Secretariat for Extraordinary Affairs, all designated by the Pope. The deputation will have to hold periodic meetings and, without deliberating, it will be able to follow the work of the Commissions, hear from the recording secretaries and forward to the Commissions the votes, the ideas, and the suggestions of the deputation (see the following point). 5) *A Vote on a Declaration of Orientation* before the end of the session. It is impossible for the Council to suspend its activity while leaving the situation in the same conditions of uncertainty that prevailed at the beginning with respect to the essential purpose of the Council, the overall criteria, and the agenda for the work to be done. After the experience of this first session, the absence of concrete preparatory work is evident, going all the way back to the

first [schema] (*De fontibus Revelationis*) may be revised by way of

an*tepreparatory phase. The Council has to speak so as to affirm once for all for
the future session[s] and for the Commissions and the general deputation—how
the objective of the Council needs to be understood in the current situation of
the church in the world: for this, a brief declaration which specifies exactly the
goal of the Council in terms set by the opening address of the Pope and the
Message to the World will suffice. Beyond that, the Council can effectively recall
that the preparatory schemas need to be reduced in number, concentrated and
regrouped, and then can fix certain criteria and principles concerning the mode
and the spirit of their formulation. 6) *Revive the Traditional Principle according to
which the Pope,* as long as the Council is in session, abstains from making any
innovations in the legislative area, at least at a certain level. He should delicately
be reminded that during councils pontiffs used to abstain even from creating
new cardinals. But above all it seems to be the case that according to traditional
practice, during a council, popes abstain from legislative acts at least in the areas
and about questions that, at the pope's initiative or that of the Curia, had been put
on the agenda of the Council. // Annex n. 1 *The need for a Secretariat for Rules.*
Normalising rules and procedures calls for an *ad hoc* organism that is fully
adequate: otherwise there is the risk of going back to what happened during the
first session, where incessant regulatory modifications showed the insufficiency
and the inadequacy of the study and preparation of issues of conciliar government.
Experience in the assemblies of modern systems has led to setting up in each
assembly and *ad hoc* organism—distinct from all the others functioning—for the
study and control of the aspects and the needs for good operating procedures
that are the most profound or the least contingent. It is not easy to make it evident
that this requirement is fully justified: in the case of the Council there are not a
great many precedents nor much wisdom or experience concerning the running
of assemblies. In the extreme case, if it proves impossible to convey the
importance of this proposition, it will be necessary to propose an alternative:
namely, that the function that would best be served by a special Secretariat be
formally handed over to the Secretariat for Extraordinary Affairs. In truth this
could not be other organs of the Council, even those named by the Pope;
however, the Pope himself is in charge of regulations: this is exactly why it makes
sense that there should be an appropriate organ of the Council—one entirely
elected by the Council—because a uniquely consultative organ would be able to
express in a responsible and reflective way what the Council has drawn from its
experience concerning its ways of working together. The secretariat, composed
of 14 members all elected by the Council, could have as its president the Cardinal
Secretary of State, the better to assure an explicit (not implicit and improper as at
present) contact with the sovereign pontiff. The observations and propositions of
the Secretariat should be presented to the pope in writing, but deliberated in a
formal way following the rules of the majority established for procedure in the
commissions (article 37 and 39 of the rules). Evidently the Pope also is free to
consult other groups within the Council (particularly the [the council of]
presidents). However, as a rule, he should always pay attention to the Secretariat
before making any modification of the norms of governing the Council.'

discussion.

'Osservazioni e proposte sul regolamento del Concilio. *Nella svolgimento del Concilio, sinora l'importanza del regolamento e della stabilità e chiarezza della procedura. Questo ha impedito spesso il precisarsi delle funzioni dei vari organi conciliari, il costituirsi di una prassi stabile (pur negli opportuni adattamenti alla esperienza), ha ingenerato confusione e lentezza, ha soprattutto ostacolato il formarsi di un limpido costume di lavoro e di un ordinato e costruttivo dialogo tra Concilio e Papa. Pertanto si suggerisce di fare, prima della fine della sessione, le seguenti richieste. 1)* Normalizzazione del Regolamento e della procedura. *Si può capire come nella prime settimane si sia reso necessario qualche ritocco al regolamento ed altri possa consigliarne l'esperienza futura. Ma è di importanza capitale che le modificazioni non avvengano quasi quotidianamente, ma solo in occasioni sempre più rare, e soprattutto non avvengano in modo informe per decisioni date* vivae vocis oraculo, *ma solo in modo formale con ponderate e organiche norme scritte, debitamente coordinate al testo del* motu proprio Appropinquante Concilio, *che ha sancito il regolamento. È questa una esigenza non solo di forma e di tecnica legislativa, ma è una esigenza di sostanza: che condiziona la serietà e l'ordine del lavoro conciliare, la maturità della coscienza del Concilio e dei Padri Conciliari, la correttezza e la moralità del rapporto tra Papa e Concilio. 2)* Perfezionamento della norma dell'art. 65 §3 *per quale il Presidente di ogni Commissione deve designare il relatore che proponga ed illustri lo schema* juxta mentem Commissionis. *Sinora questa norma non è stata osservata fedelmente: è uno degli aspetti sui quali ha influito più pesantemente il fatto che Presidenti delle Commissioni siano i capi delle Congregazioni. No vi è dubbio che nell'insieme questa identificazione—che avviene per la prima volta: neppure al Vaticano I fu così—non ha giovato e gioverà al corretto funzionamento del Concilio: anzi si può dire che alla fine non gioverà neppure al prestigio e all'autorità delle stesse Congregazioni. Se fosse possibile bisognerebbe (almeno per la fine della sessione) proporre una distinzione delle competenze, con vantaggio di tutti, del Concilio, del Papa e delle Congregazioni. Ma se questa situazione risulta ormai definitivamente pregiudicata, allora bisogno almeno insistere perchè in ogni Commissione il relatore venga designato non dal Presidente, ma, come è più giusto, dalla Commissione stessa; e più precisamente, almeno quando la Commissione ne riconosca la opportunità, vengano designati due relatori: uno della maggioranza e uno della minoranza. La possibilità anche per la minoranza della Commissione di fare sentire la sua voce e le sue ragioni, costituisce non solo una maggiore garanzia per la libertà e completezza del dibattito, ma anche un mezzo di acceleramento dei lavori, perchè la minoranza, sia in commissione sia nell'assemblea generale, può così trovare una espressione più ordinata e qualificata, sostitutiva di molti interventi disordinati e non sempre ben qualificati. Tutte le assemblee più esperimentate e mature hanno adottato un simile mezzo nei loro regolamenti. 3)* Inflessibile difesa della norma dell'art. 39 §1 *che stabilisce la necessità della maggioranza qualificata dei due terzi per ogni decisione. Ogni tanto si sente qualcuno accennare alla possibilità che questa maggioranza venga ridotta. Orbene bisogna assolutamente tenere fermo che un Concilio, come assemblea di diritto divino rappresentante tutta la Chiesa, si differenzia in questo da un'assemblea democratica: per esso non può*

D[ossetti] asked me to send him information, notes, critiques, and

---

valere il semplice sistema maggioritario del formalismo democratico. Se il Concilio rappresenta la Chiesa, che è in Cristo, non può valere per esso il principio della maggioranza, ma quello della unanimità sia pure una unanimità non materiale, ma morale. Unanimità morale è quella che si differenzia soltanto per una esigua frazione dell'unanimità assoluta. Perciò si sarebbe potuto ragionevolmente auspicare la garanzia di una maggioranza anche maggiore dei due terzi, almeno per le decisioni dottrinali. Ma in ogni modo non sarebbe ammissibile per i decreti dottrinali accontentarsi di un maggioranza inferiore ai due terzi, attualmente previsti dal regolamento. 4) Richiesta di una Deputatio generalis Concilii per l'intervallo tra una sessione e l'altra. L'annunzio già dato che intercorreranno quasi 6 mesi tra la prima e la secunda session e che nel frattempo continueranno a lavorare le commissioni, pone il Concilio Vaticano II di fronte a un fatto nuovo nella storia dei Concili: mai si è verificato un intervallo così lungo (se si eccettua il caso di una vera e propria interruzione). Si le commissioni conciliari fossero le sole a lavorare nell'intervallo, probabilmente si riprodurrebbe la situazione già verificatasi per i lavori preparatori e cioè che ogni commissione, rinchiudendosi nella propria specialità tenderebbe a perdere di vista le esigenze di assieme e la fundazione concreta di questo Concilio in rapporto alla Chiesa e al mondo di oggi, come è stata definita dal discorso del Sommo Pontefice e dall'impegno assunto dai padre conciliari con il loro messaggio al mondo. Del resto persino durante i lavori preparatori si è sentito il bisogno di una commissione centrale. A fortiori dopo che il Concilio si è aperto ed ha incominciato ad esprimere degli orientamenti generali— trascendenti i singoli settori—occurre che durante la lunga vacanza permanga una rappresentanza complessiva del Concilio: una deputazione generale di almeno 40 padri, che non siano già membri delle Commissioni, eletti tutti dal Concilio; come ovvio questo Deputazione deve essere eletta tutta dal Concilio, mentre a rappresentare il Papa resterà il Consiglio di Presidenza e eventualmente anche il Segretariato de negotiis extra ordinem, entrambi designati dal Papa. La deputazione dovrà tenere riunioni periodiche e, senza nulla deliberare, potrà seguire il lavoro delle Commissioni, ascoltarne i relatori e fare pervenire alle Commissioni voti, indicazioni, suggerimenti (cfr punto seguente). 5) Votazione prima della fine della sessione di une dichiarazione orientativa. Non è possibile che il Concilio sospenda la sua attività lasciando la situazione nelle stesse condizioni di incertezza in cui si è aperto rispetto al fine essenziale, ai criteri supreme e all'ordine dei suoi lavori. Questo, dopo l'esperienza fatta in questa prima sessione e alla prova palese della mancanza di concretezza dei lavori preparatori, vorrebbe dire tornare indietro, tornare addirittura alla fase antepreparatoria. Occurre che il Concilio si pronunzi affermando una volta per tutte per le sessione future e, intanto, per le Commissioni e par la Deputatio generalis—come debba essere inteso il fine del Concilio, nella presente situazione della Chiesa e del mondo: basterà al riguardo una breve dichiarazione che limiti esattamente lo scopo del Concilio nei termini fissati dal discorso di apertura del Papa e dal Messaggio al mondo. Oltre a questo il Concilio potrà efficacemente ribadire che gli schemi preparati debbono essere ridotti di numero, concentrati e raggruppati e fissare alcuni criteri di massima per il modo e lo spirito della loro formulazione. 6) Richiamare il principio tradizionale

documents whether from me or from other theologians. He wants me to do this without my putting my name on it, since he doesn't hide the fact that my name alone would lead the Italian bishops to refuse even to consider what I say.

As he was leaving he gave me a copy of a large volume, *Conciliorum Oecumenicorum Decreta,* prepared by the documentation center founded by D[ossetti] in Bologna. Published in recent days by Herder, the first edition (2000 copies) was sold out in two weeks.[111]

---

per il quale il Papa, Concilio sedente, si astiene dal fare atti innovatori specie legislativi, almeno di un certo rilievo. Conviene delicatamente ricordare che durante i Concili i Pontefici si astenevano persino dal creare nuovi cardinali. Ma soprattutto sembra sia il caso di fare presente che non corrisponderebbe alla prassi tradizionale il porsi, durante il Concilio, di atti legislativi del Papa almeno in campi e questioni che a iniziativa del Papa o della Curia sono stati posti all'ordine del giorno del Concilio. // Allegato n 1. Necessità di un Segretariato del Regolamente. La normalizzazione del Regolamento e della procedura richiede un apposito organo, veramente adeguato: altrimenti si rischia di verificarsi quello che è già avvenuto in questa prima sesssione nella quale le continue modificazioni regolamentari mostrano l'insufficienza e l'inadeguatezza dello studio e della preparazione dei problemi regolamentari. L'esperienza assembleare degli ordinamenti moderni ha portato alla costituzione in ogni assemblea di un organo ad hoc—distinto da ogni altro che eserciti già altre funzioni—per lo studio e il controllo continuo degli aspetti e dalle esigenze più profonde o meno contingenti del suo funzionamento. Non è facile che questa esigenza venga pienamente difesa: non soccorrendo nel caso del Concilio una grande somma di precedenti e una vera maturità di dottrina e di esperienza assembleari. In ipotesi estrema, se proprio non si riuscisse a fare comprendere la portata di questa proposta si dovrebbe proporre in via subordinata che venga affidata formalmente al Segretariato de negotiis extra ordines la funzione che meglio competerebbe a un Segretariato speciale. In verità non possono essere il Papa stesso che dispone in materia di regolamento: ma proprio per questo conviene che vi sia un organo apposito del Concilio—in questo caso tutto eletto dal Concilio perchè organo solo consultivo, che possa esprimere responsabilmente e meditatamente le indicazioni che il Concilio trae dalla sua esperienza in ordine al proprio modo di lavorare. Il Segretariato, di 14 membri tutti eletti dal Concilio, potrebbe avere come Presidente il Cardinale Segretario di Stato, proprio per assicurare meglio un contatto esplicito (non implicito e improprio come è stato sinora) col Sommo Pontefice in questo campo; le osservazioni e le proposte del Segretariato, da presentare al Papa per iscritto, dovrebbero essere da esso deliberate in modo formale con le norme di maggioranza stabilite per il procedimento nelle Commissioni (art. 37 e 39 del Regolamento). Libero—come è ovvio—Papa di consultare anche altri organi del Concilio (specialmente la Presidenza), Egli dovrebbe però di regola sentire sempre il Segretariato prima di ogni modifica regolamentare.'

111.This volume had been given to the Pope on 1 October, and he wrote in his

<M Saraceno (an expert in Italian public planning)[112] told me about the sermon of the priest in a small village where he goes on vacation. Here was the priest's view of the Council: 'What can the Council do? The Council by itself? Nothing. The Council with the Pope? Something—even in important matters. The Pope alone: Everything.'>

[17 v°] *12 November*

Visit from Vogel (editor at ICI) with Dom Lemercier, OSB, theologian of the bishop of Cuernavaca in Mexico. He told me about his Benedictine foundation in Mexico—a very original arrangement. He circulated a long paper on psychoanalysis (cf my dossiers) not only for treating the sick, but as a general resource for people to get to know themselves.[113]

He told me that Spadafora (Lateran) gave some lectures to the Mexican bishops. [Lemercier] went to the first lecture and raised some objections. The cardinal asked him not to come back to the others.[114]

---

journal: 'Most noteworthy and important on this October 1 is my meeting with the Lord Cardinals. Today I received four of them [...] Cardinal Lercaro from Bologna told me about his Documentation Center—Don Dossetti was there—that promises to do excellent work. They gave me their most precious flower, *Conciliorum Oecumenicorum Decreta*. I encouraged them and blessed them heartily.' *'Più nobile e importante in questo I ottobre è l'incontro coi Signori Cardinali. Oggi ne ricevetti quattro. [...] Cardinale Lercaro di Bologna che mi informa del suo Centro di documentazione—presente don Dossetti—e compagni bella promessa di eccellente lavoro. Mi offrono il loro fiore più prezioso* Conciliorum Oecumenicorum Decreta. *Incoraggio e benedico di cuore.'*

112.The economist Pasquale Saraceno, one of the editors of the *Codici di Camalduli*. For his work as a 'meridionalist', see P Saraceno, *Studi sulla questione meridionale (1965–1975)* (Bologna, 1992).

113.G Lemercier was Prior of Santa Maria de la Resurección, a priory erected in Cuernavaca on 15 January 1950; the bishop there was S Méndez Arceo.

114.This is perhaps Cardinal J Garibi y Rivera. See also the report that Schmidt gave to Tucci in DTcc on 8 November 1962: ' Mgr Spadafora ranted and raved about the Biblical Institute and about Fr K Rahner (a formal heretic!) with the Mexican bishops. For their part, they were not impressed by his dogmatism and fanaticism; that led them to ask Cardinal Bea to come speak to them about the biblical problems. [...] The Mexican bishops then let Mgr Spadafora know, when he wished to continue his presentation, that they had no desire to listen

November 14

'Big' session. The first doctrinal schema. Cf the newspapers.[115]

The growing opposition [to the schemas] is becoming a sensation. This is happening not only because of some stars (bishops and theologians), but because of entire clusters of bishops in working groups, and because of the courses given to the bishops by theologians.

Replacement schemas are in circulation. The one by Rahner and Ratzinger is very attractive in my view.[116] The French bishops are somewhat reserved, at least in their way of going about this.

---

to any more. If that's true, then he learned the lesson that he deserved.' *'Mons Spadafora ha pestiferato sul Biblico e su P K Rahner (eretico formale!) di fronte ai vescovi messicani. Questi sono rimasti male impressionati dal suo dogmatismo e fanatismo, per cui hanno pensato di chiedere al Cardinale Bea di venire a parlare loro sui problemi biblici [...] I vescovi messicani poi hanno fatto sapere al mons. Spadafora, che voleva continuare la sua esposizione, che non avevono più intenzione di ascoltarlo. Se è vero, è la lezione che si merita.'*

115.The daily newspapers were very important for Fr Chenu: his letters leave traces of press articles like the one he alludes to here, and that often have been lost. It is clear that *La Croix* and ICI are the two vectors of information to which he most often turns.

116.This is the *Disquisitio brevis de Schemate 'De fontibus revelationis'*, a mimeographed copy is present in many archives and in DTcc, document 14; a version containing Fr Congar's comments is published by D Favi. Even the Pope records in his notebook: 'An interesting introduction for the debates on the *sources of revelation*. It is likely to open up some controversy: on the one hand the draft of the proposition does not fully take into account the exact intentions of the Pope in his official addresses. On the other hand, at least 8 cardinals are focusing on it in order to discredit the principal point of the proposition. May the Lord help us and bring us together.' *'Interessante la introduzione delle discussioni circa* le fonte della rivelazione. *É prevedibile l'aprirsi di qualche contrasto: da una parte la stessura della proposta non tenne conto delle precise intenzioni del Papa nei suoi discorsi ufficiali. Dall'altra ben 8 Cardinali appoggiata su quello misero in discredito il punto principale della proposta. Che il Signore ci assista e ci riunisca.'* The German proposal also struck the bishop of Rafaela, DZzp, 13 November 1962: 'This afternoon discussion about Rahner at the Pio Latino and with Pironio tonight. People are tense about the schema *De fontibus*; its complete withdrawal is being asked for. Rahner is a mature person, strong and also very learned. He is German in his way of explaining things. He has insisted that the schema be totally abandoned and has sent us some of his crazy ideas.' *'Por la tarde charla de Rahner en el Pio Latino y Pironio por la noche. Tirantez por el esquema De Fontibus. Se solicita el rechazo total del esquema. Rahner es un hombre maduro; vehemente y muy doctor; aleman en su manera de exponer. Insistió en rechazar el esquema de plano y nos entregó unas folias suyas.'*

The French bishops had a meeting about the first schema. Ninety of them voted to reject it, thirty to amend it, and one approved it (Dubois from Besançon? Lefebvre ex–Dakar?, Rupp?).[117]

Bea, who spoke firmly against the schema, reportedly said: 'I have to wager [*jouer*] [18 r°] my authority, my purple, my life.'[118] In fact, if the schema were to pass, Cardinal B[ea] would have to 'close down his house' (biblical studies, ecumenism).[119]

On the morning of the 15th, loaded headlines in *Il Tempo*: 'Favorable Speeches by Ruffini, Siri . . . French Opposition'. They conjured up the opposition of some cardinals, including that of Ritter, as favorable.[120]

15 November

Fr Docks (OP, Belgian)[121] brought the Melkite Patriarch Maximos to visit me. Mgr Hakim and Keramé were present. Fabulous conversation. Maximos is vehement, fairly unconcerned about the tactics of the assembly. In particular, {he delivered a} diatribe against the phoniness of the consistory [of cardinals] this morning for three canonisations;[122] he didn't go to it. (Mgr Rolland didn't go either, explicitly refusing to attend ceremonies lacking real content.)

Mgr Hakim asked me to write a paper for him in the name of the Melkite Church in preparation for his intervention against the schema; not repeating the various motives for rejecting it, but dismissing it as foreign to the Eastern tradition that it totally ignores.

Lunch at the Holy Office at the invitation of Fr Verardo, an assessor who defended me last year in an Italian Dominican publication. I saw

---

117. At this session Himmer proposed creating a secretariat for external relations (*ad extra*), in the same way as there is one for unity, and Daniélou 'proposed the draft of the schema' (CngMJC 14 November 1962).

118. JCgr/CngMJC speaks about this and Schmidt confirms it (*Agostino Bea*, 455).

119. See Schmidt, *Agostino Bea*, 455, which repeats JCgr.

120. The writer for *Tempo*, an organ of the cerical right, was G Svidercoschi. On the newspapers, see M Marazzitti, *I papi di carta. Nascita et svolta dell'informazione religiosa da Pio XII a Giovanni XXIII* (Genoa, 1990). Semelroth was nabbed for the cover story of November 11 treating the Alfrink–Ottaviani incident.

121. Belgian Dominican, founder of the International Academy for the Science of Religion to which Chenu will also belong after 1964.

122. See SEdb 15 November 1962: 'Some of our bishops went to the ceremony. Most, along with S B, preferred to take advantage of a free morning.'

Fr Giraudo.[123] [18 v°] Very friendly conversation. We didn't touch on burning questions except a little at the end, without getting aggressive or too precise. A bit of teasing about their work at the Holy Office.

Visited Mgr Louis (Périgueux). {His view:} Not just change but reject the schema. From his first reading, he thought it was bad. But he finds the Rahner project too difficult; it's good personal work, but not irenic.[124]

Ottaviani maintains his right as {Prefect of the} Holy Office to review the work of the other Commissions, as he does in ordinary times with the other Congregations. He delegated Gagnebet to represent him at the Liturgy Commission as it writes its amendments. <G[agnebet] will tell me, day after tomorrow, that he was not warmly welcomed by the Commission.>[125]

November 16

I had lunch with the Patriarch Maximos and the Melkites. I brought my text for Mgr Hakim's intervention. Well received. I eliminated a paragraph that was too technical about 'the aristotelianism of the scholastics' confronted with the platonic themes ('participation') of the Eastern Fathers.[126] [Maximos] tells me, among other stories, this

---

123.Verardo, an assessor at the Holy Office, was a confidant of John XXIII; see his contributions to *Memorie domenicane* (1961), 119; (also [1960], 71; [1960], 284; [1962], 154; [1962], 215). Marco Giraudo was Verardo's assistant and a consultor at the Holy Office; he had been a student at Le Saulchoir in Belgium between 1937 and 1939.

124.This is the opinion of Fr Congar which spread rapidly even among those who opposed the dogmatic schemas.

125.See F Gagnebet; according to Bea's secretary his job was to be a spy. See DTcc 28 October1962, the request comes from the liturgy commission: 'All the *periti* of the preparatory Commiss. work in the liturgical Commisssion, but Larraona handed over the theological revisions to Gagnebet, [Cecchetti] Van den Eynde, Masi and Vaggagini (in the first meetings, the first three of these were silent spies for the H[oly] O[ffice], says S[chmidt]!' *'Nella Commissione liturgica lavorano tutti i periti che già furono nella Comiss. preparatoria, ma Larraona ha confidato la revisione teologica a Gagnebet, [Cecchetti] Van den Eynde, Masi, e Vaggagini (i primi tre nelle prime riunioni silenziosi spioni del SO, dice S[chmidt]!).'*

126.'If I speak now, it is not to repeat what many eminent bishops have perfectly well said about the doctrinal schemas; I only humbly add my explicit support to the criticisms that they formulated and which led them to think that these schemas should not be amended, but redone if we wish to be faithful to the apostolic goals

one. Gregorios, his predecessor at Vatican I, considered the definition

of this Council. I just want to bring a voice from the East and from its patristic tradition into this, and to say that the doctrinal schemas actually being studied are foreign to this venerable and authentic tradition in their composition, their structure, their perspective and their conceptualisation. The schemas surely contain riches and values of Latin theology, and we are pleased to pay warm homage to the magnificent *intellectus fidei* that this theology gained for the church; but we regret that by completely ignoring the catechesis and the theology of the East—that of Cyril of Jerusalem, Gregory of Nazianzen and Gregory of Nyssa, Maximus, John Damascene and so many other eastern Fathers—the authors have apparently monopolised the universal faith in their project for the benefit of their own particular theology and thus can seem to want to erect as the exclusive perspective of the Council concerning God's Revelation what is a valuable perspective, but local and partial... In eastern theology—where liturgy is the effective vehicle for the transmission of the faith, where initiation takes place within the sacramental mystery and not in abstract instructions lacking links to the symbols—the mystery of Christ is proposed directly as an *oeconomia*, flowing from history, prepared for by the Old Testament, accomplished in Christ, and realised in the time of the Church. Theoretical explanations, as legitimate and necessary as they may be, are never detached from the framework of Scripture and the witness of the Fathers. This concrete character of the Word of God is made manifest in its presence in the world. The Church, the Body of Christ, is precisely the authentic place and the living magisterium of its transmission. Any rupture, even apparent, between Scripture and Tradition, such as that created by the project *De fontibus* submitted to the Council's consideration, will be seen by many as doing violence to the effective unity of the ways of transmission which are never split apart in oriental theology and that we are unable to conceive of as separate. The schemas presented are exclusively the fruit of scholasticism— beautiful and truthful fruit certainly—but produced from only some elements of the church's Tradition. The ecumenical character of the Council invites us not to enclose the Word of God within particular categories and not to eliminate by force of omission another *intellectus fidei*. Here are some examples to illustrate what I am saying: eastern theology gives full play to the definition of the human being as *imago Dei*; that leads to a different way of thinking than the abstract distinction of the Latin church between nature and grace, and so a different way of seeing the relation between God and human beings, including in terms of Revelation. Another example: oriental theology considers the 'paschal mystery' in its totality—death and resurrection, whereas the Latin theology weighs more heavily the aspect and the theory of satisfaction... I am listing these examples quickly to show the catholic approach of eastern theology whose truth and orthodoxy are clearly incontestable. That is why, brought up on this authentic tradition, I feel estranged from the writing and the structure of the proposed schemas; and so I understand even more clearly—and I formally support—the criticisms that have been made from a pastoral and evangelical perspective. *Dixi.* [I have spoken.]'

of infallibility inopportune. At the audience closing the Council, he kissed the foot of Pius IX according to protocol. Then Pius IX put his foot on Gregorios's head [19 r°], saying: '*Questa testa dura*' [What a hardhead]. Gregorios never put foot inside the Vatican again. A harmful and disgusting gesture—doubly inacceptable in the East— even kissing the Pope's foot.

When the patriarch [Maximos] was supposed to kiss the [Pope's] foot in receiving the pallium, he omitted doing so. The Master of Ceremonies insisted, but John XXIII intervened, saying: 'Leave him alone. He's an Oriental.'[127]

November 17

Today Mgr Hakim's speech to the Assembly opposing the schema, following my prepared text. In French.[128]

---

127. John XXIII had received the Armenian Patriarch Batanian from Licie on 12 November and on the 18th gave him the pallium; in his notebook the Pope writes of no incident of this kind: 12 November: 'Tonight Cardinal Agagianian [came] with the new Patriarch Batanian and 8 bishops, then Cardinal José Garibi y Rivera [from Guadalajara] with 40 Mexican bishops. Great joy of fraternity.' '*Stasera il Cardinale Agagianian col nuovo Patriarca Batanian e 8 Vescovi[.] Poi il Cardinale José Garibi y Rivera [di Guadalajara] con 40 Vescovi del Messico. Grande gioia di fraternità.*' On 18 November: 'A little before noon I gave the pallium to the new Armenian Patriarch from Cilicia who was accompanied by several bishops among whom was Mgr Kiregian from Istanbul, a good and dear friend.' '*Poco prima di mezzodi diedi il pallio al nuovo Patriarca Armeno di Cilicia, accompagnato da parecchi Vescovi, fra i quali mgr. Kiregian di Istanbul mia buona e cara conoscenza.*'

128. The Pope notes in his agenda for 16 November: 'This morning [I] listened to the Fathers of the Council. Boring debate concerning the sources of Revelation. Despite the efforts of the Ottaviani block, they are not succeeding in containing the opposition which is very strong. Even good old Mgr Battaglia from Faenza rose to his support, but in an unfortunate way. *Melius erat si locutus non fuisset.* {It would have been better for him not to speak.}' '*Al mattino ascolto dei Padri del Concilio. Dibattito increscioso, circa le fonti della Rivelazione. Nonostante gli sforzi per la corrente Ottaviani, esse non riesce a contenere l'opposizione che si rileva molto forte. Anche il buon mgr Battaglia di Faenza si levò in suo soccorso: ma infelicemente. Melius erat si locutus non fuisset.*' 17 November: 'In the morning, continued to listen to the discussions at the Council. Still heated. The liveliest segment, the young and those who come from far away, are constantly appealing to the instructions of the Holy Father in his introductory speeches at the Council, *about which part of the Fathers prefer to remain silent.* But the one who has to be the most silent is *me.*' '*In mattinata ripresi l'ascolto delle discussioni del Concilio. Sempre vive. La parte più vivace, giovani e lontani, si tiene in continuo richiamo*

In the afternoon, a visit to Mgr Koury and Mgr Doumith, Maronites. A long conversation in which their rivalry with the Melkites {was apparent}. Mgr D[oumith] told me about the meeting of the Theological Commission (the only one up to now) in preparation for the debate. Fr Tromp, the secretary, gave a very long report in defense of the schema that made Mgr D[oumith] very impatient. Then a remark from Mgr Peruzzo[129] in pious advocacy for the schema. Cardinal Léger intervened, calling for freedom from any pressure before the debate that seems to present the schema as authoritative because the Pope approved its presentation [to the Council], as if making it impossible to reject. That argument has been widely spread by those in favor of it. But in reply: the Council is the one with full authority, and it is not bound to the preparatory texts.

[19 v°] Mgr D[oumith] also told me that at the request of Cardinal Cicognani, Ottaviani suggested that the Doctrinal Commission make a briefer version of the second schema, *De deposito fidei* (since the fathers and the theologians are even more negative about it than about the first one). Who wants to do this work? Nobody wanted to take it on. So Cardinal Ottaviani asked Cardinal Browne to do it, and he accepted.[130] Mgr D[oumith] (and others!) were not at all happy about this. Evidently Cardinal Browne will do this work with 'his own' theologians.

Supper tonight with Mgr Carlo Colombo, Cardinal Montini's theologian, at the house of V Peri (a *scriptor* {document writer} at the Vatican whom I knew in Paris). C[arlo] C[olombo] was extremely discreet—not a word about the Council. He was more forthcoming about the Italian clergy, bishops included. Very serious cultural inadequacy [–] the causes [*sic*]; we talked about the meetings for study of the other episcopates. The Italian bishops had only one 'official' meeting on Tuesday under the authoritarian leadership of Siri. The bishops of Lombardy have had some meetings, but it was unthinkable to open them up to the others. If the other Italian bishops were invited to {such} meetings, only twenty out of four hundred would come.[131]

---

delle istruzioni del S.P. nei suoi discorsi di introduzione al Concilio, su cui una parte dei Padri ama tacere. *Ma chi tace di più devo essere io stesso.'*

129. *Perozzi* in the manuscript.

130. See Congar, *My Journal of the Council* (14 November 1962), 166. Minutes taken by Tromp in the *Relatio 8*, page 7. Based on Fenton's journal: Komonchak, 'The Initial Debate...', 341.

131. See AM Negri, *Mons Carlo Colombo fra Chiesa e società* (Milan, 1993); DCcl

Received a note from Don Dossetti (cf 10 November) giving me a rundown on the meeting of the Italian bishops last Tuesday [13 November] about [20 rº] the debate over the first schema. Remarks by Ruffini, Fares, etc, to urge its acceptance against the 'new modernists' and the Franco–German project—a kind of 'romantic' fantasy, he said. Mgr Guano, who spoke up to object to that sort of attitude, was asked to get in line with the immense majority of the episcopate.[132] Cf in my notes Don Dossetti's text.[133]

---

makes note of the progress of the debates, but not private meetings, such as the one with Fr Chenu, that remain unverifiable.

132. In G Dossetti's note, he had said: 'All those who spoke (Cardinal Ruffini, Mgr Fares, Mgr Carraro, etc) spoke as if they were preaching a crusade against the "new modernists". The Franco–German project was not read out, but presented in a ridiculous way: they only read the titles of some paragraphs and made fun of them, as though of a sort of romantic fantasy lacking any doctrinal content. [...] In this atmosphere Cardinal Urbani, the Patriarch of Venice, proposed that Cardinal Siri be charged to declare complete opposition to the project in the name of the entire Italian episcopate. Only Mgr Guano tried to express a reservation. Mgr Carraro, the bishop of Verona, opposed [Guano] and defended Cardinal Urbani's proposal saying that Mgr Guano's reservations were worthless in the light of the attitude of all the others, because "one swallow doesn't make a springtime". [...] This atmosphere of crusading and ridicule impeded any serious evaluation of the worth and the reasonableness of the proposal: also pay attention again to the fact that with regard to the theological schemas, it is not reasonableness that will prevail, but the sheer force of numbers.' *'Tutti gli oratori hanno parlato (Cardinale Ruffini, mons Fares, mons Carrero ecc.) hanno parlato come predicando la crociata contro i "novi modernisti". Il progetto franco–tedesco non è stato letto, ma presentato in modo ridicolo: ne sono stati letti soltanto i titoli di alcuni paragrafi ridicolizzandoli, come una specie di fanstasia romantica, senza nessun contenudo dottrinale. [...] In questa atmosfera il Cardinale Urbani, patriarca di Venezia, ha proposto che venisse dato incarico al Cardinale Siri di dichiarare a nome di tutto l'episcopato italiano la netta opposizione al progretto. Il solo mons Guano ha tentato di presentare una riserva. Ma si è opposto a lui e ha difeso la proposta del Cardinale Urbani, mons Carraro, vescovo di Verona dicendo che le reserve di mons. Guano non avevano valore di fronte al parere di tutti gli altri perché "una rondine non fa primavera". [...] Questa atmosfera di crociata e di ridicolo impedisce qualunque serra valutazione del valore e del fondamento delle ragioni: perciò ancora una volta si richiama l'attenzione sul fatto che a proposito degli schemi teologici non saranno le buone ragioni a prevalere, ma la forza del numero.'* Siri noted in his journal, 'The Guano rigmarole' (DSri 380).

133. Kept with the council letters of Fr Chenu with the annotation 'Two notes (mid-November 1962) from G Dossetti, whose role in Italy as expert and counselor for Cardinal Lercaro is well known. Strong reaction against the preparatory schemas. A 3rd note at the end takes the Italian episcopate to task for categorically refusing

November 18

A reception for all the theologians at the Gregorian [University].[134] Very nice gathering. I 'saw' people whose works I have read for a long time (Lyonnet, to whom I expressed my deep sympathy for the conflict at the Bib[lical] Inst[itute]; Haering *[sic]*, CSR, who told me that the 3rd schema on morality is even worse than the others, despite some improvements made:[135] Vignon, SJ, and others).

---

the initiative of the German and French episcopates for another orientation for the Council.' These notes are respectively: *Pro memoria per una dichiarazione orientativa*, 4 f° ds; *Osservazioni e proposte sul regolamento del concilio*, 5 f° ds + 1 joint, 2 f° ds; *La riunione dell'episcopato italiano*, 1 f° ds. There are other convergent opinions about the meeting of the Italian bishops, for example, DTcc, 18 November 1962: 'I heard next that at the [plenary] assembly of the Italian bishops, the same Carli had strongly exhorted them to vote for the schema presently under discission so as not to leave the Council and the Church in the hands of the Germans.' *'Ho sentito poi dire che all'ultima riunione [plenaria] dei vescovi italiani, il medes. Carli li avrebbe fortemente esortati a votare per lo schema attualmente in discussione, per non lasciare il Concilio e la Chiesa nelle mani dei tedeschi.'*

134. See ST 18 November 1962: 'At 5 pm there was a gathering at the Gregorian for all the theologians in Rome for the Council. There were a lot of people, and I was able to once again meet certain persons whom I didn't yet know personally. However I didn't mix in enough so that that would be easily possible. But it wasn't either necessary or prudent, because it would only have been a brief and superficial hello.' *'Um fünf Uhr war ein Empfang der Gregoriana für alle Theologen, die zum Konzil in Rom sind. Es war eine große Menge Leute dort, und ich habe wieder etliche kennengelernt, die ich noch nicht persönlich kannte. Allerdings habe ich mich dann doch nicht genug unter die Leute gemischt, um so viele zu begrüßen, wie es an sich möglich gewesen wäre. Aber das ist wohl auch nicht nötig und sinnvoll, da es sich ja doch nur um eine oberflächliche und kurze Begrüßung hatte handeln können.'* At 4 pm, there was a meeting of theologians for editing new schemas (Fr Daniélou, Fr de Lubac, Fr Grillmeier, Fr Häring, Prof Ratzinger, Prof Feiner) in which neither Fr Chenu nor Fr Congar nor the Beligians took part.

135. After sending the first two schemas *De ordine morali individuali* and *De familia et matrimonio* to the bishops during the summer, there remained a third schema— *De ordine sociali*. In its turn this text was finally joined to the third draft: after its approval by the theological commission and then by the central preparatory commission, it was passed on to the judgment of the sub-commission for amendments. Häring's criticisms (notes in FHä, 1911-1912, 1922-1923, 1928, 2570 and 2571, these last requested by the French bishops) are summarised in the article 'Sur l'ordre moral', in *Études et documents du Secrétariat general de l'épiscopat* (28 March 1963), n 7, 1–8.

Conversation with Fr Tucci, the new director of *Civ[iltà] catt[olica]*;[136] I had heard that his orientation is completely different from that of the old directors. Right away, a matter of fact conversation. He brought up Pius XII's orders for the magazine; however, today with John XXIII it has elbowroom, at least on this side {the left?}. He told me that he learned a lot in going through records from past years. *Civ[iltà] catt[olica]* had published a review that highly praised my '*Intro[duction] à l'étude de S. Thomas*' in 1951. The editor received this criticism: 'Doubtless the work is good, but the author is bad.'[137] When the review of Fr de Lubac's '*Méditation sur l'Église*' was ready, the editor held up its publication; it was only printed (if I understood correctly) when it received rave reviews everywhere else, including from Fenton.[138]

One of the professors at the Gregorian, Fr Vignon, who has taught *De fide* for a long time and went on to teach the Eucharist, told me about his contacts with Fr Garrigou on the topic of the supernatural motive of theological faith. Fr G[arrigou] was happy with Fr Vignon's position that adopted the Thomist thesis of faith's substantial supernatural character ('formal object'). Garrigou told him, 'When I see you, I think of the formal object! For me you are the formal object in person!'

It was Fr Vignon, I think, who also told me: 'You know, things have changed a lot at the Gregorian. We have a different approach to problems now.' Fr Tromp is completely isolated. So are Frs Huerth and Lennerz, who were the theologians of Pius XII.

November 19

In the Assembly, among the interventions on the schema *De fontibus Revelationis*, Mgr De Smedt (Bruges) denounced its serious

---

136.See DTcc, 18 November 1962: 'At 5 pm, meeting of theologians at a reception given for them at the Gregorian. I met Fr Chenu. Brief conversation with Fr Arnon and Fr Vogt about the articles that Cardinal Bea prepared on the historicity of the gospels to be distributed to the bishops and then, perhaps, to be published in *C[iviltà] c[attolica]*.' '*Alle 17, incontro di teologi ad un ricevimento per loro alla Gregoriana. Ho conosciuto P Chenu. Breve colloquio con P Arnon e con P Vogt sugli articoli che il cardinale Bea ha preparato sulla storicità dei Vangeli per distribuirli ai vescovi e poi, forse, pubblicarli su* C[iviltà] C[attolica].'
137.See *Civiltà cattolica* (1955)/2, 310–11.
138.In fact *Civiltà cattolica* remained silent; see De Lubac, *Entretien...*, 78–83 and 308.

insufficiency concerning the reality [21 r°] and the promotion of ecumenism. He was roundly applauded despite the recent reminder not to give in to applauding. This was bad news for the schema.[139]

Somebody gave me an article from *The New Yorker*, October 20 1962, 'Letter from Vatican City,' which is being talked about in American circles. It it strongly critical of the Curia and its governance.[140]

139.AS 1/3, 184–187. H Fesquet wrote (*Le Monde*, 21 November 1962) that this is one the 'great moments of the Council.' See G Ruggieri, 'La discussione sullo schema Constitutionis dogmaticae de fontibus revelationis durante la 1 sessione del Concilio Vaticano II', in *Vatican II commence*, 315–328: 'The Pope heard the interventions and noted on the same day in his agenda: 'Again today I listened with interest to all the opinions at the Council. For the most part they are criticisms of the schemas proposed (by Card Ottaviani), although prepared collectively; but they reveal nonetheless the too preponderant fixation of one person and his permanent mind–set incapable of letting go of the tone of a scholastic lecture. His blindness in one eye shadows his entire vision. Naturally the reaction is strong, perhaps too strong. But I think good judgment will prevail in the end.' *'Anche oggi ascolto interessante di tutte le voci del Concilio. In gran parte sono di critica agli schemi proposti (Cardinale Ottaviani), che preparati da molti insieme, rivelano però la fissazione un po' prepotente di uno solo e il permanere di una mentalità che non sa divincolarsi dal tono della lezione scolastica. La semicecità di un ochhio è ombra sulla visione dell'insieme. Naturalmente la reazione è forte, taloro troppo forte. Ma penso che la buona intesa finirà per prevalere.'* Semmelroth likewise notes (ST 19 November): 'This morning in the general congregation some very powerful things must have occurred. Mgr De Smedt, the bishop of Bruges, very effectively represented the interests and the views of the Secretariat for Christian Unity. With good reason he struck some harsh blows on the Theological Commission and underlined that it had made it impossible for the Secretariat for Christian Unity to be in contact with it. He must have gotten some strong applause. For the moment in any case it seems pretty sure that there will be a negative vote on the schema *De fontibus revelationis*.' *Heute morgen muß es in der generalkongregation recht massiv zugegangen sein. Bischof de Smedt von Brügge hat die Interessen und Anliegen des Sekretariats für die Einheit der Christen sehr Wirksam vertreten. Er hat mit recht starken Geschossen gegen die Theologische Kommission geschossen und betont, daß diese es dem Einheitssekretariat unmöglich gemacht habe, Kontakt mit ihr zu nehmen. Er muß dann starken Beifall bekommen haben. Im Augenblick sieht es jedenfalls so aus, als wenn das negative Votum zum Schema De fontibus revelationis ziemlich sicher wäre.'*

140.The author was Fr Murphy, writing under the pseudonym Xavier Rynne. This article, revised and enlarged, is reprinted in *Letters from Vatican City: Vatican Council (First Session)—Background and Debates* (London, 1963), 60–94. The article also treats some bishops who in September wrote to the Secretary of State to ask for a message to the world. 'They later learned with considerable

November 20

Mgr Rolland came back from the session of the Assembly gloomy, disappointed, and practically angry. It quickly became evident that a great many bishops are saddened and disturbed as well. At the session, the president proposed a *dubium* with this formula: 'Should the discussion of the schema be interrupted?' The response *placet* would mean to choose the interruption; and the *non placet* would mean to choose to continue with the schema as it is. The language betrayed the ambiguity in the way it formulated the question, ie, those who *refuse* the schema vote *Yes*, those who *support* the schema vote *No*.[141]

2,209 were present for the vote: 1,368 *placet*, 822 *non placet*, 19 null.

However, two–thirds (1,473) was needed to suppress the schema. So it remains, and they continue. So a minority imposed continuing its consideration even as a strong majority rejected it.

[21 v°] Further, it's clear that none of the chapters of the schema could be accepted with such a small minority of support, since two–thirds is required. The discussion is just going to get bogged down. Already it is going nowhere.

For three or four days, since the remarks of Mgr De Smedt, opposition to the schema has grown strong.

Tonight at a reception at the American Embassy, the representative from Bonn to the Vatican—an echo of the German bishops—strongly expressed everyone's disappointment.[142]

Some wonder if an intervention from the Pope will relax the tension.

---

satisfaction that this idea had come from two Dominican theologians, Fathers Chenu and Congar, who had drawn up a document with this end in mind, and that they sent it to six cardinals in different countries' (91, citing also the interview in *La Croix* with Guerry on 10 January 1963).

141.AS 1/3, 220–221 and 254–255: the question posed by Felici for this vote about a dubium was confusing. It was translated into French by the sub–secretary J Villot: 'The following *dubium* [doubt] is being put to a vote by the conciliar fathers: 'Should the discussion of the dogmatic schema *De fontibus revelationis* be interrupted?' Those favorable to interrupting the discussion need to vote *Placet*; those opposed to the interruption—that is, those who want the discussion to continue—need to vote *Non placet*.'

142.The Ambassador of the Federal Republic of Germany was Hilger Scherpenberg.

November 21

I was at the exit [of the bishops] from the session at St Peter's. Most of the bishops were lively and joyful. Mgr Rolland with great joy and enthusiasm told me the news: the Pope intervened. Seeing the large majority and wanting to alleviate the fathers' upset, John XXIII in a message to the Council decided to interrupt the discussion on the schema, and he announced the formation of a new Commission of bishops charged to prepare another schema together with the Commission on Unity (Bea) and the Theological Commission (Ottaviani). General relief. We are out of the impasse.[143]

Yesterday afternoon the South American bishops (600) [22 r°] appealed to the Pope to make him understand the ambiguity of the vote, the huge difficulty of making progress with such an ambiguity, and the need to clarify the situation.[144]

143.See A Melloni, 'Giovanni XXIII e l'avvio del Vaticano II' in *Vatican II commence*, 86–97. The Pope noted in his agenda for 23 November: 'This morning I listened again to the presentations of the council fathers in St Peter's. As far as I can see, a good flow has been reestablished. Everyone is blessing the Pope for having decided to form a special Commission presided by Ottaviani and Bea on the question of the *Fontes Revelationis*.' *'Al mattino sempre audizione delle parole dei Padri del Concilio da S. Pietro. A quanto pare la buona corrente ha ripreso il sua alveo natural. E tutti benedicono il Papa perchè vi ha provveduto formando una Commissione speciale presieduta da Ottaviani e Bea sulla questione delle* Fontes Revelationis.'

144.Not found in the AS, nor do I find any trace of this in the letters of Wenger, Descalzo, Rynne and Caprile. That evening Fr Chenu gave a conference attended by Zazpe; see DZzp, 21 November 1962: 'Tonight I went with Mejia to the Sala Augustiniana in the priory where Luther studied for a conference by Fr Chenu, OP. Ambiance of young people, intellectuals, and journalists. I introduced myself to a very friendly Pastor from Geneva and to the journalist for *Informations Catholiques*. All of them concerned about questions internal to the Council. Fr Chenu spoke about the situation of the church in the contemporary world. A loss not only of Christianisation, but also of sacramentalisation. Secularity in the [?]. This is why the church itself has to become missionary again. Priest-worker experience. Return to the pure Gospel, and the church's place in society to be decided by the laity. In the dialogue after the discussion, I spoke about the dialectic of history applied to the church, and the dynamism of the church because it is the people of God. Interesting. Daring. It's a shame that I missed a lot because of the French. Mejia introduced me and told me to see Num [?] Marty of the Mission de France. [Chenu] is extremely smart, cultivated, confident and daring. Very nervous. He pleased the pastor.' *'Por la noche fui con Mejia a la Sala Agustiniana, del convent donde estuvo Lutero, a una conferencia del P*

A day for celebration: Today the war in India ended—the Chinese moved their troops fifty kilometers back from the border. In Cuba, Castro accepted the American demands, and the Americans gave up control.[145] The French also: the Gaullists carried the first round of the elections.[146]

November 22

In *Le Monde* for 13 November:

> Theologians have something to say in this matter that touches upon doctrine. Up to the time of the Council, John XXIII was rather evasive. 'Are you a theologian?' he asked an important non-Catholic guest. 'No?— Well, *Deo gratias!* I'm not either, even though I have to pretend to be. You see for yourself how many problems professional theologians inflict on the Church by their subtlety, their pride, and by their narrowness and their obstinacy.' Doubtless these words shouldn't be taken too seriously. Better than anyone, John XXIII knows

---

Chenu O.P. Ambiente de gente joven, intellectual, periodistas. Me presentó a un pastor de Ginebra, muy simpatico y al periodista de Informationes Catholiques. Todos preocupados por las cuestiones internas del Concilio. El P Chenu habló sobre la situación dela Iglesia en el mundo contemporaneo. Perdida no solo de cristianización, sino de sacralización. Laicismo en la [?]. De ahí que la Iglesia se haya hecho misionera ella misma. Experiencia de los sacerdotes obreros. Volver al Evanglio Puro, y ubicación decidida de los laicos en el mundo. En el dialogo posterior a la charla, habló de la dialectica de la historia, aplicada a la Iglesia; del dinamismo de la Iglesia, por ser el pueblo de Dios. Interesante. Audaz. Lastima que perdí bastante por el frances. Mejia me lo presentó y me dijo de ver a Num [?] Marty de la Misión de Francia. Es inteligentisimo, preparado, seguro y audaz. Muy nervioso. Al pastor le gusto.'

145. On 20 November the Pope received 'Mr Jerzy Zawieyski, a Polish confidant of Cardinal Wyszynski, who had seen Mr Gomulka who asked him to bring his greetings to the Pope and to tell him that the liquidation of the terrible Cuban affair is considered due to the Pontiff himself.' *'Il sigr. Ierzy Zawieyski polacco confidente del Cardianle Wyszynski, e bene accetto al Sigr. Gomulka il quale lo incaricò di portare il suo salute al Papa, e di dirgli che la liquidazione del terribile affare di Cuba egli la ritiene dovuta allo stesso Pontefice'* (Agenda).

146. See E Di Nolfo, *Storia delle relazioni internazionali 1918-1992* (Rome-Bari, 1994), 1069-1087 and 1152.

that a religion that values reason can't do without theology and that only good theology can get you out of the mistakes of bad theology. But {these words} point out the style of a pontificate that values spirituality and ministerial needs above everything else.

[The Pope's guest was] the Anglican Canon Pawley, the Anglican observer at Rome even before the Council.[147] He told this to a bishop. I may add that his wife is very pretty, and the Roman Monsignori have noticed her.

[22 vº] *November 23*

Press conference by O. Cullmann. The hall is full.[148]

At the beginning, Mgr Willebrands announced, discreetly but firmly, that the Secretariat for Unity in no way endorses statements made outside of its authority.[149] He evidently meant the declaration

---

147. The Anglican theologian told the story of the preparatory work in a small book (B Pawley, *Looking at the Vatican Council*, London, 1962) that came out in April.

148. See *La Documentation catholique*, 16 November 1962, 1619–1626. JCng includes the English text.

149. See Riccardi, *Il Vaticano e Mosca*, 238–249, and Wenger, *Vatican II: Première session*, 234–238. *Osservatore Romano*, 25 November 1962, published an article in which the 'Secretariat for Christian Unity insists on clarifying that all the observer-delegates were invited by this same secretariat that was happy to welcome them all. All of them without exception manifested a sincere religious and ecumenical spirit. So the secretariat regrets anything that might be published in opposition to the spirit of open and loyal relations with the observer-delegates. The secretariat has no choice but to dissociate itself from anything like that.' *'Il Segretariato per l'Unione dei cristiani tiene a precisare che tutti gli Osservatori–Delegati sono stati invitati dal medesimo Segretariato, che è stato lieto di accoglierli. Tutti, senza eccezione, hanno manifestato une spirito sinceramente religioso e ecumenico. Il Segretariato è dolente, pertanto, di quanto è stato pubblicato in contrasto allo spirito che ha animato i leali contatti avviati e in atto con gli Osservatori–Delegati. Il Segretariato non può fare altro che dissociarsene.'* DTcc 25 November 1962 notes that 'This declaration was read yesterday by Mgr Willebrands before giving the floor to Professor Cullmann for the press conference at the Council's Press Bureau (23 November 1962). Clearly it aims to diminish the consequences of the declaration that the Ukrainian bishops made to the press some days ago.' *'Questa dichiarazione fu letta ieri da mons. Willebrands prima di cedere la parola al prof. Culmann per la conferenza stampa svoltasi all'Ufficio Stampa del Concilio (23 nov. 1962). È chiaro che mira a ridurre le conseguenze della dichiarazione dei vescovi ucraina data all stampa*

by the Ukrainian bishops protesting against the persecution and deportation of Mgr Slipyj, but also explicitly accusing the Patriarch of Moscow of being hostage to the Communist government; hence {the Ukrainians} regret the presence at the Council of the observer-delegates from the patriarchate.[150]

November 25

At lunch with the Fathers of La Salette, Pastor ...*[sic]*, observer-delegate at the Ecumenical Council intelligent and youthful. Very cordial. Without illusions, having a healthy religious fervor.[151]

That evening, I met by chance two Dutch theologians: one, an OP who had been the student of Frs Barendse and Schellekens, the other

---

pochi giorni fa.'

150.*La Croix* (22 November 1962): 'A Declaration from Fifteen Catholic Ukrainian Bishops: Fifteen Catholic bishops of the Byzantine–Ukrainian rite published a declaration on Wednesday regretting that observers from the Russian Orthodox Church had been invited to the Council while a Catholic bishop, the Metropolitan Josy Slipyj, Archbishop of Lviv (Poland), is languishing in a Siberian prison. Introducing a discordant note concerning the presence of the Orthodox observers—up to this point graciously received—the 15 bishops stated that their presence stirred up 'a feeling of uneasiness, unhappiness, and discouragement' among their clergy and their flock. For certain areas of world public opinion, said the 15 bishops, it seems that the arrival of the Orthodox observers has been greeted with great attention, while the absence of Metropolitan Slipyj and his imprisonment were passed over in silence. According to this declaration, Mgr Slipyj was 'illegally deported and has been imprisoned in Siberia for seventeen years'; he is the only survivor among 11 Ukrainian Catholic bishops sent to Siberia. The Ukrainian bishops also severely criticised the Russian Orthodox Church, claiming that the patriarchate of Moscow (to which the observers belong) is 'a docile and useful instrument in the hands of the Soviet government.' Moreover, says the declaration, the patriarchate 'has assumed jurisdiction over four and a half million Catholic Ukrainians against all divine, ecclesiastical or human law, in overt collaboration with the atheistic civil power because it is the only way to suppress and liquidate the Ukrainian Catholic Church.'

151.Perhaps H Roux, for whom the description of a clear-sighted enthusiasm applies perfectly. The high quality of the [Protestant] pastors had been pointed out explicitly in the official lists by WD Schaw of the Presbyterian alliance.

a diocesan priest working with Cardinal Alfrink.[152] They kindly told me in confidence that the cardinal was deeply interested in the initial message and had carefully examined the provisional draft. Then, after the vote in the Assembly, he took a long time in considering the Dutch version to be given to the press. This confirms my insistence on the great importance that must be given to <the editing of> a text meant to be made public.

[23 rᵒ] *November 26*

A mischievous idea of Mgr Newman[n], the bishop of Burma, a La Salette residing at the generalte. With quiet humor, he suggests that, given the lively discussion about the two sources of relevation, Scripture and Tradition (to which the majority of the Fathers are opposed), perhaps this: Since the Scriptures are solemnly brought in at the beginning of each session,[153] so Tradition can be solemnly brought in as well—that is, Cardinal Ottaviani wheeled in on a little wagon.

November 27

Conversation with Fr Congar.

1) He told me about his adventure at the Capranica Seminary, where he gave (in Latin) a conference on Tradition. At the end, in response to the invitation to ask questions, the bishop of Benevento,[154] who came in only for the second part of the conference, got up. In the tone of voice of a Nazi officer, he launched into a diatribe against ecumenism, insisting that absolute truth contradicts the errors of Protestants and schismatics. {He insisted on} neat formulas 'such as those in the manuals you are criticising.' Fr Congar answered in making necessary distinctions [*discernements*]. Then, following a new attack from the archbishop [*sic*], Congar asked him to point out where he failed to represent the truth. The archbishop kept silence. The seminarians in the audience broke out into applause. Afterwards, they came [23 vᵒ] to apologise for the bishop's behavior.

---

152. See JYHA Jacobs, *Met het oog op cen andere Kerk* (Baam, 1986).
153. The tradition ritual of enthroning the Gospels was observed at Vatican II.
154. Bishop Raffaele Calabria.

This affair became known in the corridors of the Congregations. Abbé Poupard from the Secretary of State's office, meeting Fr Congar, spoke to him and said that, whatever else, it was an excellent contribution to enlighten the young generation of Italian priests.[155]

2) A Czech bishop told Fr Congar: 'We came with the authorisation of our government. But the government expects us to get from the Council a declaration in favor of peace.'[156] I think that the initial message, with its paragraph on peace (stressed by the press), already satisfies this request in a very timely way.

Further, it is urgent not only 'politically' but also in terms of the Gospel, that the various projects favoring the Council's taking a stand on war and peace should succeed. A schema on this has been prepared, but it hasn't been put on the agenda by the Central Commission. [There are] initiatives by Jean Goss,[157] the plea by Fr Pyronnet and the [conscientious] 'objectors', and the project of Abbé Boulier favorably welcomed by Cardinal Feltin.[158]

3) Some information about the new mixed Commission in the controversy over the doctrinal schema. Ottaviani has chosen only narrow and sectarian [24 r°] new members for the Commission *De fide* who are all in his style {literally, in the pay of O. – tr}, such as Felton.[159]

---

155. See CgrMJC 22 September 1962: the college's chronicle laconically reports: 'Conference by Fr Congar on ecumenism.'

156. On the Czechoslovak declaration, see H–J Sthele, *Eastern Politics of the Vatican 1917–1979* (Athens–London, 1981), 332–341.

157. Jean and Hildegard Goss–Mayr had circulated a mimeographed paper about *Propositions concernant la paix et la guerre préparées en vue du 2ᵉ Concile du Vatican* in two drafts (kept in the papers of K Rahner among others). J Pyronnet was the secretary of the Movement for Non–Violent Action.

158. See H Fesquet, *Journal du Concile* (Paris, 1966); see also DTcc, 4 December 1962: 'Mr Piser gave me a copy of a proposal for a schema *De jure belli et pacis* by an [American] ex–Jesuit, distributed especially for the use of the French bishops (doc 41)' '*Mr. Piser mi ha dato copia di una proposta di schema* De jure belli et paci, *redatto da un ex–gesuita (Americano), distribuito soprattutto ad uso de vescovi francesi [doc. 41].*'

159. This is probably Fenton, whose name, even though well known, Chenu forgot. Semmelroth had only noted on 23 November that: 'The new commission has been formed. Mgr Volk is part of it. The presidents are Cardinals Bea and Ottaviani, the vice-presidents the Cardinals Liénart and Ruffini. At the Secretariat for Christian Unity it was said that a bishop cried out: *duo fontes* (two sources).' *'Die neue Kommission ist gebildet. Bischof Volk gehört auch zu ihr. Präsidenten sind*

Fr Congar reminded me of the intervention of Mgr De Smedt

Kard. Bea und Ottaviani, Vizepräsidenten Kard. Liénart und Ruffini. Als es im Sekretariat f.d. Einheit der Christen verkündet wurde, soll ein Bischof dazwischen gerufen haben: duo fontes'; and two days later (ST 25 November): 'This morning we had a discussion at the Germanicum with Mgr Volk, Fr Alonso–Schökel of the Biblical Institute, Fr Rahner, Dr Thyssen, another theologian from the Secretariat and Bea and me, about what (from a biblical point of view) ought to be absolutely thrown out of the schema *De fontibus revelationis* and what ought to be changed. We worked for three hours without interruption.' *'Vormittags hielten wir hier im Germanikum eine Besprechung mit Bischof Volk, P Alonso–Schökel vom Bibelinstitut, P Rahner, Dr Thyssen, noch einem Theologen des Sekretariats Bea und mir über das, was von biblischen Gesichtspunkt am Schema De fontibus revelationis unbedingt wegfallen bzw. geändert warden muß. Wir arbeiteten drei Stunden hintereinander.'* Tucci, as always through Schmidt, knows about another reason for the origin and the composition of the commission, 22 November 1962, n: 'Fr V Galli learned from a good source that Cardinal Frings and Cardinal Bea had been to see the Pope to convince him to make this decision. Fr Galeota told me that at the Congr. for Seminaries as well as at the Cong. for Religious they say that it happened because of Cardinal Bea's intervention (21 November 1962). Fr Schmidt told me last night (22 November 1962) that things didn't happen quite that way. Cardinal Cicognani, present at a reception given by Prime Minister Ikeda of Japan, learned the exact results of the voting. As he left, he asked Cardinal Bea to come with him and asked his advice on how to get out of such a delicate situation. That's where the idea came from, and it was accepted and owned by the pope. Cardinal Bea had the support of Cardinal Frings and Liénart. So the commission will be composed of the following: Ottaviani, Bea (co–presidents)—Lefebvre, Liénart, Frings, Browne, Meyer. Beyond these there will be all the bishops from the doctrinal Commission and all those from the Secretariat for Unity; 6 periti per group.' *'P V Galli ha appreso da buona fonte che il Cardinale Frings e il Cardianle Bea sono stati dal Papa per convincerlo a prendere questa decisione. P Galeota mi dice che sia alla Cong dei Seminari sia alla Cong. dei Religiosi attribuiscono la cosa ad un intervento del Cardinale Bea (21 nov 1962). P Schmidt mi diceva stasera (22 nov 1962) che le cose non sono andate proprio così. Il Cardinale Cicognani, trovandosi al ricevimento offerto dal Primo Ministro del Giappone, Ikeda, seppe i risultati esatti della votazione. Uscendo, chiese al Cardinale Bea di accompagnarlo e gli demandò un parere sul come uscire da una situazione così delicata. Di qui la proposta, poi accettata e fatta sua dal Papa. Il Cardinale Bea ebbe il consenso del Cardinale Frings e Liénart. La Commissione sarà così composta: Ottaviani, Bea (copresidenti)—Lefebvre, Liénart, Frings, Browne, Meyer. Inoltre tutti i vescovi della Commiss. de doctrina e tutti quelli del Segret. dell'Unità; 6 periti per parte.'* According to the official list announced on 25 November 1962: 'The Commission for the revision of the schema *De divina Rivelazione* has been constituted as follows: Presidents Cardinals Alfredo Ottaviani and Augustin Bea, elected members Cardinals Achille Liénart, Joseph Frings, Ernesto Ruffini, Albert Meyer, Joseph Lefebvre, Michael Browne. Further taking part in the commission will be the members of

(Bruges) who made public Ottaviani's constant refusal during the preparatory work to collaborate at all with the other Commissions. Ottaviani's closed mind very much shocked the Americans who are used to fair play in formal meetings, and it influenced their vote against Ottaviani's texts.[160]

Ottaviani is extremely skilled in running the Commission. He gets major texts passed quickly like foundational truths that can be taken for granted—then he allows long discussion, for 'freedom' of speech, about the details.

4) In the schema *De Ecclesia*, the writing in the chapter 'De Magisterio' is substantially from C Colombo, Montini's theologian. The ch[apter] on ecumenism was done by Witte (Dutch). Fr Congar sent in a written contribution.[161]

---

the theological Commission and of the Secretariat for Christian Unity.' *'È stata costituita la Commissione per la revisione dello Schema* De Divina Rivelazione. *Ne sono presidenti i Cardinali Alfredo Ottaviani e Agostino Bea. A Membri della Commissione sono stati eletti i Cardinali Achille Liénart, Giuseppe Frings, Ernesto Ruffini, Alberto Meyer, Giuseppe Lefebvre, Michele Browne. Della Commissione faranno parte inoltre Membri della Commissione Teologica e de Segretariato per l'Unione dei Christiani.'* DTcc adds: 'As you can see, the name of Cardinal Ruffini has been added to the list, something told me by Fr St Schmidt and confirmed by Fr Dhanis.' *'Come appare, è stato aggiunto il nome del Cardinale Ruffini alla lista communicatami viva voce da P St Schmidt e confermatami da P Dhanis.'* On the composition of the commission, see G Caprile, *Cronache del Concilio Vaticano II*, II (Rome, 1966), 358.

160. This had been the constant position taken in the preparatory work. See, for example DTrm 23 February 1961: *'Mane venit mgr Willebrands. Vult Commis. mixtas pro natura hierarchia Eccl., pro membris Ecclesiae, pro laicatu in Eccl Ego dixi mihi valde displicere modum agenda Cardinale Bea, qui propaganda fecit pro theoria valde disputabili de membris, dum scit nec praesidem Comm Theol nec secretarium publicum contra eum disputare posse. Deinde dixi commissiones mixtas esse impossibiles quia non fit cum secretariatu; deinde ne fieri commissionem mixta de re pure dogmatica: eos spectare unice ad Comm theologicam. Sed si vult Secr. de Unione dare votum id libenter acceptari, vel etsi haberi posse amicalia colloquia'*; DTrm 3 March 1961: *'Mane colloq cum E mo Cardinale [Ottaviani] de epistola accepta a Secr Comm Liturg ad faciendam Comm mixtam de fundamento ontologico partic act in Liturgiam. Non fiat Commissio mixta. Habebitur Sessio Subc. de dep et de font feria V proxima ad vivendum quid respondeatur in casu'*; DTrm 7 March 1961: *'Teleph Mgr Gawlina. Volunt facere documentum de emigratione in quo etiam de principio religionis. Rogat Comm. Mixta vel sufficit documentum mittere pro reunione. Responsum dedi: faciatis et mittatis documentum.'*

161. See R Burigana, 'Progetto dogmatico', 167–177.

This morning, a big and beautiful session on the schema *Ut unum sint* (Commission on the Eastern Churches).[162] {This schema} was unfortunately developed before a mixed Commission with the Secretariat for Unity (expressly asked for) was established. The Secretariat for Unity for its part {also} prepared a text.

Interventions by Maximos [IV Saigh] of Nabaa (Melkites) and [25 v°][163] several other Eastern prelates. Mgr [George] Hakim read Maximos's French text in Latin. These interventions made a fine impression and were listened to attentively. {They} all stress episcopal 'collegiality', the structural foundation of the Church in the East. Patriarchs ought to have preeminence over cardinals.

A phrase of Mgr Nabaa's to describe ecumenical work: '*in caritate ad veritatem*' {(moving) toward the truth in love}.[164]

November 28

Lunch with Abbé Laurentin and Fr Hamer.[165] 'Chronicles' from behind the scenes of the Council. Fr Hamer is rather overwhelmed by the 'skulduggery' that he has seen.

{We} reflected together on the way a conciliar assembly should be governed. Talked about M Martimort's way of evaluating presentations [*voix*] by the impact of leaders of groups:[166] I put my products forward like a wine merchant from Algeria.

Fr Hamer {was at} the first meeting of the new mixed Commission Ottaviani–Bea, chosen as an expert by Bea. He said that Cardinal

---

162. Either Fr Chenu is reporting here on Fr Congar's opinion, or this entry indicates his direct assistance with the work in the aula.

163. Pages 24 v° and 25 r° of the notebook had been lightly pasted together at the beginning and so Fr Chenu left them blank.

164. AS 1/3, 616–621, with an intervention by Maximos, according to whom: 'If we want to speak effectively with the Orthodox East, we need to speak first of all about the Catholic doctrine concerning the collegiality of the Church's pastors— the collegiality of the pastoral life of the Church!' AS 1/3, 624–627 for the intervention of the Melkite archbishop who had also written several articles in the course of the year; above all F Nabaa, 'Il Concilio Ecumenico Vaticano et gli Orientali', in *Oikum*, 2 (1962): 3, 95–122; 'The Council and Christian Unity', in *Unitas* [English], 14 (1962): 92–104, 186–200.

165. Laurentin published his chronicles in *Le Figaro* very quickly, see R Laurentin, *L'Enjeu du Concile: Bilan de la première session, 11 oct.–8 déc. 1962* (Paris, 1963).

166. Martimort classified the interventions of the speakers in terms of the number of faithful whom they represented.

Frings expressed two provisos about his collaboration: the weakness [*maladie*] of his eyes and his determination to work on a new schema other than the one rejected by the assembly. Ruffini spoke up. He warmly expressed his good wishes concerning the cardinal's eyes, ending by insisting on keeping the old schema under the pretext that the Pope used the word *refeciatur* [should be re–done], and so that means revising the old one, not looking at a new one. People are talking about the bitter remark Ruffini made after the famous session that turned down Ottaviani's schema: 'Protestantism is at our doors.'[167]

The reflections of Fr Fernandez, the Dominican Master General, shared with Fr Hamer after Fernandez had read the new schema prepared by Rahner and some others (cf my documents): 'This is a text for a spiritual retreat (*retiro*), not for deliberation by a Council.' Very significant remark, revealing his lamentable separation of theology (abstract intellectualism) from spirituality (living faith, Gospel).

New texts for the schema *De Ecclesia* recently distributed:[168] There is a noticeable contradiction between two theologies of the episcopate: one a theology based on jurisdiction, the other a theology based on orders. On the one hand, titular bishops become marginal; on the other hand, the sacramentality of the episcopacy becomes clear (the position and the writing of Fr Lépicier whose fine discretion was responsible for the text being adopted by the Preparatory Commission).[169]

This morning at the assembly, the interventions of the Maronites, in particular that of Mgr Khoury.[170] Mgr Rolland told me that a good bit of his intervention was unintelligible if you didn't understand that he was speaking in opposition to the Melkites on several points that they had presented yesterday. In particular [26 vº] he deemphasized the difference and the apostolic autonomy of the Churches of the East with respect to the Church of Rome, and he insisted on the unity in the Roman Church. This is the 'Latinism' of the Maronites.

---

167. On the attitude of the cardinal of Palermo, see FM Stabile, 'Il Cardinale Ruffini e il Vaticano II: Le lettere di un "intransigente"', *Cristianesimo nella storia*, 11 (1982): 83–113.
168. The schema *De Ecclesia* had been distributed for discussion on November 22; see Komonchak, 'The Initial Debate...', 329–352.
169. See Burigana, 'Progetto dogmatico', 176.
170. Joseph Khoury, already cited above {see page 73}.

November 29

Lunch with a little group of Italian lay people interested in problems of development at the initiative of Don Rosario Scarpati.[171] Passionate, remarkable conversation. They are all smart, committed Christians, concerned to the point of anxiety about the church's presence in the new world that they see coming about.

Then, at the invitation of Abbé Houtart[172] who was present, I took part in a meeting of thirty bishops of several nationalities interested in creating a climate favorable for the a new 'secretariate' for problems facing the present–day world: population growth, underdevelopment, hunger and poverty, peace. Presided by Cardinal Suenens who will present this project tomorrow to the cardinals' Commission for Extraordinary Affairs.[173] This creative activity is being guided by the

---

171.*Scarfati* in the manuscript. See his position at the Congress of Religious Sociology in Trent 21-23 October 1962: R Scarpati, 'Il Concilio nel "Social Change" contemporaneo', in *Atti del primo symposion di sociologia religiosa a cura del centro USE (Quaderni di 'Humanitas')*, (Brescia, 1973), 71-78.

172.We can't find notes from Houtart about this meeting; see Cl Soetens, *Concile Vatican II et Église contemporaine (Archives de Louvain-la-Neuve)*, I, *Inventaires des Fonds Ch Moeller, G Thils, Fr Houtart* (Louvain-la-Neuve, 1989).

173.That didn't happen if we are to believe the notes that Siri made about this meeting of the secretariat *de negotiis extra ordinem* for 30 November in Lai, *Il papa non eletto*, 354-355. The problem is taken up again by Fr Chenu in a letter to Suenens on 15 December 1962, SChn: 'Your Eminence, Mgr Rolland, bishop of Antsirabé (Madagascar), after having invited me to assist as his counselor for his conciliar work, has now asked me insistently to continue to help him during the intersession. He fears for himself and for the other bishops of Madagascar that geographical and psychological distance will make them lose contact with the benefits of the first session while they must, according to the wish of the Sovereign Pontiff, actively prepare for the second session. Mgr Rolland has asked me therefore to keep him apprised of the progress of the work and to obtain for him and his colleagues materials for a timely reflection in common during these nine months. For this reason I think that it would be good to send him some major texts from the first session. Among these I think particularly of your intervention at the time of the 33rd congregation on 4 December; I believe that it presents powerfully the exact purpose of the Council, and so gives the axis for its work and the principal themes that need to be treated. I would like to send this text in its complete form to the bishops for their reflection (not only the bishops of Madagascar, but those of Africa as well). So I allow myself to request from your Eminence the text of this intervention. I dare to think that my request is not indiscreet, since it aims to make the positions that you presented to the conciliar assembly fully efficacious for this group of bishops. In case other texts

famous auxiliary bishop of Rio, Mgr Helder Camara.[174]

---

or notes, today or later, might enrich the work of the episcopal conference of Madagascar, I would be deeply grateful to you to allow me to have them. Please accept, Eminence, my thanks in my name and in the name of the bishop of Antsirabé, and my best wishes and fond respect. M.M. Chenu. / On this separate page, because it treats another matter, I am adding this reflection and this proposal. Explicitly or implicitly some problems enter into the Council's agenda that confront us collectively with harsh realities and that demand a Christian attentiveness and judgment insofar as the church has to proclaim the Gospel *ad extra*. Problems concerning population growth, underdeveloped countries, hunger and suffering, war and peace. For a thoroughly responsible consideration of these problems, it seems opportune, given the object under discussion, to turn to lay experts—people who from experience, have treated these problems *ex professo* and who, as well, are known to have dealt with these questions in the perspective of the faith and a Christian understanding of the world. Like experts from the FAO that is centered in Rome. Also someone like M Veronese who, formerly president of UNESCO, had been brought in to counsel Pius XII. Despite the wish of many, the lay faithful have not been invited to participate officially in the preparatory work of the Council that would be of concern to them (Commission on the Laity). It seems that, while still respecting the established norm, some of them might be designated as 'experts'—outside the Commissions, but officially available to be called into the Commissions—in cases where the object being considered is formally within the competence of faithful committed to the construction of the world.'

174. Helder Camara had given a press conference on 25 November 1962: see *La Documentation catholique*, 16 December 1962, n. 1390, 1611–1613; there is a similar passage from the Bishop of Sées, Pioger, in *Semaine religieuse*, 23 November 1962. On the day after this meeting, Fr Chenu took part in the 5th gathering of the group 'Jesus, the Church and the Poor' at the invitation of Himmer and Hakim. He himself wrote on the mimeograph that announced the 5th gathering of the group: to the list of participants Fr Chenu added his own name and made this note: 'Except for Dossetti, whose 'adventures' are well known, no Italian bishop.' There is also attached an appendix 1 f° ds, with signature and date to fill in for 'The Church of the Poor' in October 1963. Zazpe was there also and notes in DZzp, 14 November: 'Studied until 5.15 pm and then left to go hear Congar. [...] There is a group that meets at the Belgian College and that is preparing a revolutionary schema about an authentic poverty in the entire church. M. Bogarin told me about it. I will try to go to it. Congar: thin, mature, spiritual and balanced. He was magnificent on Tradition. I learned a lot. Came back with M. Marengo.' *'Estudié hasta las 17.15. en que fui a oír a Congar. [...] Hay un grupo que se reune en el Colegio Belga, y que prepara un esquema revolucionario sobre una verdadera pobreza en toda la Iglesia. Me lo dijo m. Bogarin. Trataré de ir. Congar. Delgado, maduro, espiritual y equilibrado. Estuvo magnífico sobre Tradición. Aprendí mucho. Volví con m Marengo.'* November 20: 'This afternoon I went to a meeting at the Belgian College about proposing to the Council the problem of the Church's relation to the poor and to poverty. C

In my view it would be desirable that the different initiatives popping up on all sides, especially concerning peace, could be effective and find their place at the table.

[27 r°] This morning I had written to Mgr Ancel who is linked to this group [of bishops] to stress the importance of *evangelisation* and not only philanthropy for a simple 'apologetics'.[175] In the evening I met

---

Gilier [?] presided. Participants were Mgr Ancel whom I met on the street, Mgr Veuillot, and other bishops well known in the church. Interesting.' *'Por la tarde assisto a una reunión en el Colegio Belga para proponer al Concilio, el problema de la Iglesia frente a los pobres y la pobreza. Preside el c. Gilier [?]; assisten mgr. Ancel quo lo encontré en la calle; mgr. Veuillot; y otros Obispos de mucha fama en la Iglesia. Interesante.'* November 30: 'I went next to the Belgian College for the meeting on poverty. Fr Congar spoke to about 40 bishops. Fr Gauthier told us about his work. Afterwards with Iriarte we walked and stopped for a coffee while arranging our trip to Germany, Belgium, France and Spain. At the house we had a meeting on the schema "Church" guided by Fr Mejia.' *'Después fuí al Colegio Belga a la reunión sobre la Pobreza. Habló el P Congar y estaban presentes unos 40 Obispos. El P Gauthier nos dió un trabajo suyo. Después con Iriarte, estuvimos caminando y tomando café, arreglando el viaje, para Alemania, Belgica y Francia y España. En casa tuvímos una reunión sobre el esquema "La Iglesia", a cargo del P Mejia.'*

175. See the letter to Ancel of 29 November 1962, SChn: 'Yesterday's *La Croix* made public the hope formulated for some time now by various bishops and groups of bishops for the creation of a Secretariat (or of a Commission, which would be even better) for the critical problems facing people today. Problems whose common denominator is an *evangelisation* matched to real needs, especially evangelisation of the poor, the privileged clients of the Good News. / For reasons of discretion, I won't dare to flesh out the proposals being made here and there, including among the African bishops with whom I mix. It gives me great joy to find out that these proposals have a chance to move on to an institutional status. / I remained however disappointed to see that the preparatory implementation of the Council's organs (commissions) had been made almost exclusively with personnel from the Curia, people in roles created during centuries past and unfamiliar with burning problems that we have today. The numerous *Vota* [wishes] of the bishops, collected in the volumes of the *Acta et Documenta*, have lost their sap and their apostolic initiative in a debriefing process that shoved them into prefabricated slots. Chapter X of the constitution *De Ecclesia* remains a long way from the mark... It shows, I think, a serious lack in the preparation and orientation of the Council. The refusal by (Cardinal Ottaviani) Commission *De fide* to be open to 'mixed' working groups managed to break apart and isolate within narrow abstractions the problems raised by 'pastors'. It would be good when the bishops go back to their respective dioceses at the end of the first session for them to clearly to take the perspective of these great problems that trouble Christians (and non-Christians as well), rather than the perspective of

(M Pastore), the minister for economic development for southern Italy. I was brought to him by M Rossi—a smart Christian who has been in unionising work for twenty-five years. {We talked} about the politics of the opening to the Left. {They were} deeply satisfied with the nationalisation of electricity finally voted yesterday in the Senate.[176] Full of hope that the Council can pull the Italian Church out of its clerical paternalism.

November 30

Regarding a declaration of the Ukrainian bishops (cf *La Croix* 23 November):

> A declaration that some have considered a protest against the presence at the Council of observer-delegates from the Moscow was attributed to the Ukrainian bishops in exile, in which the Ukrainian

---

the technical details of the the current debates, however important they may be./ This is, I think, not only a question of tactical opportunity or of simple apostolic utility—but really a *basic problem* in the Church's very *structure*. The Church is a *community of faith*, in order to be and before being a *community of [worship]*, even if the worshipping community [Eucharistic] is the only complete community. The transmission of the faith, authentic witness to the Word of God, is the *first* function of the Church, whether in the Body or in its sacred hierarchy. Many of the schemas are dealing with sacramental ministry; none of them is addressing directly the evangelising function of the Word of God (the text of the Commission *De fide* mentioned above is very insufficient on this!). This question was posed, however, in a consistent if diffuse way in the preparatory reports of the bishops. The problems envisaged for the work of a new Commission find their theological (as well as their practical and human) expression in this theological primacy of the Word of God, that is, in evangelisation as such. Theology of the faith *at work* is evangelisation. This is theology that finds itself integrating human needs into its light of faith, not surely because of some lax naturalism, nor for purely practical reasons, but rather because of the structure proper to and according to the nature of faith. Your Excellency, please see in these summary remarks an expression of the apostolic joy with which I share your hopes and a proposal that is dear to your own heart. Please accept the expression of my respectful and profound good wishes.'

176. Giulio Pastore, minister in Fanfani's fourth government; for his activities, see V Saba, *Giulio Pastore, sindicalista: dalle leghe bianche alla formazione della Cisl (1918–1958)* (Rome, 1983).

bishops supposedly said that they would only believe in the sincerity of these observers when their own bishops being held captive in Communist countries were set free. Although it has been more or less denied, this declaration—whether true or exaggerated—has been addressed directly by the Secretariat for Christian Unity. Concerning the {Russian} observers, the text says: 'All of them, without exception, have shown a sincerely religious and ecumenical spirit. So the secretariat regrets what has been published in contradiction to that spirit, given the genuine contacts that it has had with these observer–delegates and that it cannot ignore. and it dissocciates itself from {the Ukrainian} declaration.'[177]

[27 v°] *December 1*

A visit from Mgr Glorieux and an excellent conversation about the idea, the plan, and the perspectives for his history of theology in the Middle Ages (a project for Desclée).[178] He led me to expect, with his usual discretion, a strong intervention by Cardinal Liénart against the schema which is coming under discussion.[179]

Tonight a conference by Fr de Lubac on Teilhard de Chardin at the cultural center of the Augustinian College. Right in the middle of the Council! Fr de Lubac is not very optimistic about 'Ottaviani's Defeat', such as *L'Espresso* headlined it yesterday.[180] He confirmed the rumor

---

177.Excerpted from *La Croix*. Fr Caprile made a note that is similar on 14 December in the margin of DTcc 8 December 1962.

178.A Glorieux, *Histoire de la théologie du Moyen Âge* (Paris).

179.That intervention took place on 1 December 1962 (AS 1/4, 126–127).

180.See De Lubac, *Entretien {ST}* [De Lubac] returned in a less guarded context to what he had said at the Germanicum on November 11: 'Tonight Fr de Lubac gave a beautiful and delightful conference about some French Jesuits whom he had known well and who were important in theology after Modernism: Frs Grandmaison, Lebreton, Huby and—someone most important for him and for his listeners—Teilhard de Chardin. Although he spoke in French—or perhaps precisely for that reason—it was a genuine pleasure to listen to him.' *'Abends hielt P de Lubac im Germanikum einer sehr schönen und genußreichen Vortrag über einige französische Jesuiten, die er gut gekannt hat und die seit dem Modernismus in der Theologie bedeutend gewesen sind: P Grandmaison, P Lebrton, P Huby*

that Ottaviani wanted to chase Fr Rahner out of Rome. Perhaps also Fr de Lubac and Fr Congar. There was an allusion to this in an article in *La Libre Belgique* written by an Assumptionist.[181] Fr Garrastarin meeting Fr de L[ubac] in a corridor of the {Jesuit]} generalate told him that a bishop had asked him if Fr de Lubac hadn't left Rome. To which Fr G[arrastarin] answered: 'Oh no, I saw him this morning in the refectory.'

Monday, December 3

A good session, said Mgr Rolland, with strong and peaceful criticism of the fundamental ideas of the schema *De Ecclesia*. An Italian bishop, having made an unkind allusion to those who insinuate that there is error in the church, using a citation from St Paul, provoked unhappy murmuring. 'The first insult at the Council,' the American bishop of Hartford [28 r°] told me tonight.[182]

At two-thirty, following a phone call, I went to see Mgr Hakim and the Melkites (Fr Kéramé) to edit his intervention for tomorrow. The schema completely leaves out the Eastern theology of the Church as mystery and it tumbles into the juridicism of an idea of the Mystical Body that is identical with a visible social body with rights and powers. The same thing is true in its treatment of the episcopacy.[183]

---

und—worauf es ihm und Zuhören vor allem ankam—P Teilhard de Chardin. Obwohl er französisch sprach—oder vielleicht gerade deswegen—war es ein Genuß ihm zuzuhören.' (ST--Semmeroth, *Tagebuch*.)

181.Stiernon had referred in the issue of 21 November 1962 to the polemics tied to the 'new exegesis' represented by four theologians—Congar, Rahner, Schillebeeckx and de Lubac—that was appreciated by the bishops of central Europe, but which prompted 'integrist elements' to desire their being sent out of Rome; in the issue of 26 November 1962 Stiernon said that if these anonymous elements had tried to pressure the Pope, their efforts remained 'unsuccessful'.

182.B Musto cites the *'Tu vero vigila'* (AS 1/4, 206–208); AS doesn't report on the murmuring, but from the words of the president at the end of Musto's intervention (*'Est libertas loquendi hinc et illinc; propterea omnes libenter audimus'*) you can deduce the lively reaction in the hall. The American bishop who spoke with Chenu was Henry J O'Brien.

183.AS 1/4, 3580360: [Kéramé using Chenu's text-tr] 'Venerable Brothers, dear Observers. I would like, after a general introduction, to have you listen one more time to the voice of the East concerning the schema that we are studying, and then I will conclude. *Introduction*. We all came to this Council as though carried by the hope of great things that would be done and that we would do despite our

At five-thirty, I took part in *Nuova Italia's* presentation to

---

weakness and our insignificance. This hope comes to us certainly from our Pope, the beloved John XXIII, for whom we wish a prompt and complete recovery. In his appeal *Ad Petri Cathedram* in convoking the Council and above all in his opening address at the Council, he laid out a particular line of conduct. The Pope has certainly opened up a new pathway that corresponds to the hopes of the world, this world that St Paul describes as suffering the pangs of childbirth, this world that looks to the church to be a universal mother—'the church for all people, but especially for the poor,' as the Holy Father said on 11 September and as His Eminence Cardinal Lercaro has also reminded us in moving terms. Certainly the full effects of our Council will not be felt for ten or fifteen years. What will the world be like, what will the church be like at that time? Whether we want it that way or not, a Council at the end of the twentieth century must be a Council for the twenty-first century—for a time when humanity will have doubled in size reaching six billion persons, when hunger will also have doubled... Where then will evangelisation take place for that world? That is why we would like to find in the schema on the Church not texts from manuals of years gone by, however precise they might be, but rather something that today's world is waiting for. We ask to speak the language of our own century, we ask that Vatican II do for the episcopate what Vatican I did for the papacy; that we speak like John XXIII, or to put it simply, like the Gospel. It would be so comforting to speak of the Church as the *Mater amabilis* of papal primacy and of episcopal power seen as *service*, as a response to the Lord's loving question: "Peter, do you love me more than these?" That kind of language would be understood by everyone, by Christians and non-Christians. *Eastern Thinking.* Now I come to my point about an eastern point of view—and I am grateful to His Em. Cardinal Frings to have already said this with a clarity that is all his own and an unequaled force. As with *De fontibus*, so the *De Ecclesia* does not take eastern thought into account: it is conceived solely in juridical categories, and the Mystical Body itself is reduced to only visible realities. A simple but telling detail: in the 300 or more notes and references in the schema that take up more than half its pages, only 5 references mention the Greek Fathers. Yet doesn't the Catholic Church want to be enriched by this thought that is part of its patrimony, to be genuinely catholic and therefore more open to ecumenical dialogue? What do we see here? The realism of Greek theology is atrophied by the juridicism of the schema. Here are two examples: 1) First, the Church according to the Eastern Fathers is the continuation of the *mysterion* of Christ. This mystical reality, into which someone enters by an initiation and which is nourished by the liturgical mysteries, does find its structure and its authenticity in a visible society with its powers and its magisterium. But this essential visibility does not absorb the mysterious substance of the ecclesial body. Never did Chrysostom, Basil, the two Gregorys in their catechesis, or John Damascene whose feast we celebrated on the 2nd and who is the author of the first theological summa (that we would do well to consult more often), never did these Fathers reduce St Paul's teaching on the Mystical Body to a system where authority, on the one hand, and obedience, on the other, might suffice to define the attitude of the faithful. So we read with painful surprise the chapter

the public of the Italian translation of the special issue of *Esprit*. Pro[fessor] Jemolo chaired the meeting. Forcella identified himself as a non–believer deeply interested in the phenomenon of the 'Council'; M. Rossi spoke about the problem of the laity in the church; and I, from the perspective of a religious sociologist, commented on the meaning of the slogan 'a *pastoral* Council.'[184]

---

on evangelisation that is presented only as an incontestable right, and not first of all as the proclamation of the Good News to people of good will and as the identification of Christ with the poor when he said, "*I* was hungry and you gave me to eat". 2) Secondly, following the perfect logic of the ecclesial mystery, bishops are not defined first of all by their juridical authority, but by the mystery itself of which they are, by their consecration as as successors to the Apostles, architects and strategists (as a third century hymn puts it). So the episcopal body emanates from Christ, and jurisdiction only localises by pontifical power a function that belongs in the whole Body of Christ as such and collectively. This collective responsibility is exercised in an extraordinary way in the Council, but it pertains to each bishop as such, beyond his own proper diocese; he is in solidarity with the entire work of salvation that Christ confided to the apostolic college with Peter at its head. It is a serious matter to diminish this truth! We affirm it with the vigor of eastern theology that has always expressed this [collegiality] in its doctrine and in its synodal institutions. The Church is a community within the mystery, and it transcends the juridical apparatus. We find these ideas in the texts of John XXIII, so why not in the schema? *Conclusion*: I suggest that this schema, just like the one for *De fontibus*, should be sent back to a commission that includes experts in eastern theology—and very happily there are many of them among our Latin brothers here from whose love and estime for our Tradition and our Fathers we orientals have drawn. Finally, allow me to say, so as to calm one or another council father, that if I appeal to the Eastern Fathers I do so not out of a chauvinist fanaticism, but rather to return to the apostolic sources. No need for me to say that these very sources confirm us in our attachment to Peter and his successor, to whom we vow obedience when the occasion requires proof, even sometimes by shedding blood, in the various countries where eastern Catholics are an insignificant minority. With love and joy we who live near the beautiful Lake of Galilee where the Lord's words still resound: "Feed my lambs, feed my sheep", we make our act of obedience [to Peter].'

184. The Holy Office had deplored the participation of some Dominican fathers as authors in number 12 of *Esprit* (1961), and the [Order's] Vicar General S Gomez made this known to the Prior Provincial of France, J Kopf, on 17 June 1962: '*Reverende Pater, trasmitto ad P T hanc communicationem quam accepi a Suprema Sacra Congr. Sancti Officii. Ephemerides* Esprit *n 12 (December 1961) seriem scriptorium de futuro Concilio Oecumenico publici juris fecerunt; inter auctores nomina P P Chenu, Congar, et Liégé istius ordinis inveniuntur. Cum*

Tuesday, December 4

Brilliant conversation with a Polish Catholic intellectual <J. Turowicz> who recently took part in the Study Week for Catholic Intellectuals in Paris on 'Work and Contemplation.' He's from the group Znak. Editor of the journal <*Tygodnik Powszechny*> linked to this group (50,000 readers). See my notes.[185]

At noon, I ate with two Brazilian bishops, who confirmed the episode {at the assembly}. At the end of the famous session where Ottaviani's schema was rejected, Cardinal Ruffini who, like many Brazilian bishops, resides at the *Domus Mariae*, announced to the thirty or so bishops around him, 'We have just opened the door to Luther, to rationalism, and to Modernism.'[186]

Ruffini and Urbani, living at the *Domus Mariae*, eat by themselves and don't mix with the other bishops. By contrast, Lercaro takes his meals with them and chats.

One of the two Brazilian bishops tells us the following, saying that it comes from the ecclesiastical counselor for the German Embassy to the Vatican (and so coming from Cardinal Doepfner?): <with Mgr Dell'Acqua as its source>. The pope's upset with the attitude of Ottaviani and Ruffini at the Council seems to have played a role in his attack of stomach illness. And he [Dell'Acqua] supposedly said, 'I want the Council to know about it.'[187]

---

ephemerides hujus moderatores haud semel doctrinas periculosas in ipsa defendere minime erubuerunt, haec Suprema Sacra Congregatio aegre fert, immo et improbat, Theologos alicuius cum praefata ephemeride, collaborare eique scriptis propriis valorem addere.' That same day Kopf decided to assign Chenu immediately from Rouen to the Priory of Saint Jacques in Paris *'in virtute Spiritus Sancti et sanctae obedientiae ac sub formali praecepto'*, see SChn, *Correspondance*, 1962.

185.This dossier has not been kept. Turowicz had been the editor in chief of the daily paper *Glos Narodu* in Krakow in 1939, and then of *Tygodnik Powszechny* from 1943 to 1953, then, after its suppression, again in 1957. See *Autobiografia del cattolicesimo polacco* (Bologna, 1979).

186.A number of missionary bishops resided at the Roman house called the *Domus Mariae*; that is where conferences organised for the Italian episcopate were held.

187.The counselor for the German embassy was Höfer, a member of the Secretariat for Unity; the repercussions of the views of Ruffini and Ottaviani on the Pope's illness are nowhere confirmed.

A humorous story coming from the same [Brazilian] bishop: Ottaviani and Ruffini get into a car and ask to go to the Council. The car drives along, but at the end of fifteen minutes, the cardinals are surprised that it's taking so long and ask the chauffeur, 'Where are you going? The Vatican isn't that far away.' And the chauffeur replies, 'Well, I'm taking you to the Council of Trent!'[188]

Wednesday, December 5 (and the session of Tuesday)

Important session. <On 4 December> Cardinal Suenens made a much discussed intervention in favor of a church that, after being so long turned *ad intra* {focused on itself}, will turn itself *ad extra* to face the great problems of humanity—an essential principle. He listed responsible reproduction, social justice, the Third World, the evangelisation of the poor, and war and peace. This position [29 r°] has nothing in common with Ruffini's proposition < taking up the idea of Lefebvre, CSSP> for a two–fold schema—one doctrinal, the other practical aimed at the Christian people. That is an intolerable dualism.[189]

Cardinal Suenens's intervention brings to the assembly the project of a new secretariat treating the world's great problems. It was supposed to be presented to the extraordinary commission of seven cardinals, and doubtless would have been agreed upon there. But that didn't happen. It is said that Cardinal S[uenens] will bring it up again tonight at a new meeting. Will it succeed? The big question that needs attention is the creation of a commission to *regulate the work* to be done between the two sessions. The majority of the fathers are afraid that the conciliar commissions are not permeated by the new spirit of the council and so will not carry its spirit into preparations for the next session. That would lead to a painful conflict.[190]

There was an intervention by Patriarch Maximos who critiqued, among other things, the 'imperial vocabulary' of the Curia's texts.[191]

---

188. The same joke is found in DTcc 9 November 1962.
189. The interventions of Suenens and Ruffini are in AS 1/4, 222–227 and 290–291.
190. This is the commission for coordination whose structure was decided by the Secretariat for Extraordinary Affairs on 30 November, minutes found in Lai, *Il papa non eletto*, 355; see Alberigo, 'Concilio acefalo', 204–212.
191. AS 1/4, 295–298.

The severe criticism of the schema *De Ecclesia* was vigorously repeated. In particular: the {papal} primacy presented outside the context of episcopal collegiality which is its foundation and which is only mentioned marginally; constant recourse to recent texts of the magisterium, while citations of the Fathers, which would have brought the inspiration of treating the church as mystery, were rare.

On Wednesday, Cardinal Montini, up till now silent and mysterious, spoke up. He clearly endorsed, if discreetly [29 v°], the position (now explicit) of the church as both the presence of the {divine} mystery and not just a visible authoritative society, on the one hand, and as a presence to the world, on the other. It is said that his intervention will free up the consciences of many Italian bishops who are dominated by Cardinal Siri.[192]

Another position already taken by Cardinal Liénart: Don't identify the Mystical Body with the visible church—the Roman Church.[193]

Thursday, December 6

A bulletin from the Cardinal Secretary of State in the name of the Pope. It is an official document looking forward to the period between sessions. The fathers are pleased. A ratification of the Council's orientation—cf the text in my dossiers.[194]

At lunch at La Salette, a dozen French bishops are present—euphoria. Even those who are known to be more 'conservative' are taken in by the new spirit. My conversation was with Mgr Maziers (S[ain]t-Étienne).[195]

La Croix's headline (for 6 December): 'For a Church in Dialogue with the World'; and yesterday: 'The Church Must Be In Touch with People Today.'

A huge amount of work needs to be done to prepare the second session.

---

192. AS 1/4, 291–294.
193. AS 1/4, 126–127.
194. AS 1/4, 330 for the text.
195. On November 21, 1962 he had been elected by the French bishops to the *Comité de réunion* for the episcopal conference; see Perrin, 'Approches...', 132.

[30 r°] September 29–December 4, 1963, 2nd Session

October 1

I've been here since Thursday, September 26. The opening ceremony was Sunday, the 29th.[196] Monday, the 30th. Back to work. Peaceful, indeed a bit colorless.

Tuesday, the 1st. More substantial interventions. Repeated affirmations for a chapter *'De Populo Dei'* immediately following the chap[ter] on the Church as mystery, and before the chap[ter] on the hierarchical constitution. Very significant arrangement.

Mgr Rolland and Fr Dutil enthusiastically approved Mgr Elchinger's intervention; that of Mgr Garron[e] as well.[197]

---

196. AS 2/1, 179–201. See ST 29 September 1963: 'Today was the opening of the second session of the Council. This morning someone told me on the telephone that Mgr Volk got me an entry pass for St Peter's. So I went. There was a terrible crowd and as a result I couldn't see much. I could only see just the assembly of bishops. I waited until the Pope came in. Then I returned home to watch some parts on the television screen where it's possible to see much better. Unfortunately I couldn't hear the Pope's address. It must have been very significant and well done. I will read it tomorrow.' *'Heute war die Eröffnung der zweiten Sitzungsperiode des Konzils. Morgens bekam ich einen Anruf, daß Bischof Volk mir eine Eintrittskarte für St. Peter besorgt habe. So ging ich den hin. Es war ein fürchterliches Gedränge und dadurch nicht allzu viel zu sehen. Immerhin bekam ich eine Eindruck von der Bischofversammlung. Ich wartete, bisher Papst eingezogen war. Dann ging ich wieder nach Haus, um noch einige am Fernsehschirm anzuschauen, wo man das Ganze ja viel besser sehen kann. Leider habe ich die Ansprache des Papstes nich mehr gehört. Sie soll sehr bedeutsam und gut gewesen sein. Ich werde sie morgen lessen.'*

197. AS 2/1, 374–376; same impressions in ST 1 October 1963: 'The new schema *De Ecclesia* was accepted *in genere* with a crushing majority in the general congregation today. This is a heartening opening. Effectively the schema as it is now is on the whole good, even if it needs some corrections. These can be added in the debates on each of the chapters. So the news is false that the Italian bishops were very much against the schema and that they wanted it 'cut to pieces'. They almost all voted for it.' *'Das neue Schema De Ecclesia ist in der heutigen Generalkongregation mit überwältigender Mehrheit in genere angenommen worden. Das ist ein freulicher Auftakt. Dann das Schema, wie es jetzt ist, ist im ganzen eine gute Sache, wenn es auch einiger Korrekturen bedarf. Die werden dann bei der Spezialdebatte zu den einzelnen Kapiteln eingefügt warden können. Es zeigt sich damit auch, daß die Meldung, die italienischen Bischöfe seien sehr gegen das Schema, sie hätten es 'in der Luft zerrissen', falsch war. Denn sie haben ja jetzt fast alle dafür gestimmt.'*

This evening Fr Biot tells me as certain the news that the vicariate of Rome has forbidden the sale of works by (or about) Teilhard de Chardin—by Küng—and by two other theologians.[198]

We share our impressions of Ruffini's intervention in which he criticised the schema's proposition that says 'Peter and the Apostles are the foundations of the Church'. For him, only Peter is the foundation; and then concerning the proposition that calls the church *sacramentum*: 'there are only seven sacraments,' he says.[199]

October 3

A visit from Mayor (editor of ICI)[200] who has good relations with Fr Tucci, the director of *Civiltà cattolica*. Fr Tucci [30 vº] told him: 'Why was there no layman at the first session of the Council?' (That was something that was thought to have been agreed on by the Curia after long consideration.[201] To which Mgr Guerry had replied: 'But yes, you *were* present through your bishops, through your problems, you were present through… through… etc.')

---

198. Some variants in ST 1 October 1963: 'The Roman vicariate has ordered that the books of Küng and of two other authors may not be sold in Roman bookstores. These narrow methods are still being used here. It seems to me from another point of view that this is a sign of progress: before there would have been the danger of being put on the Index either automatically or explicitly. Today a book that is felt to be intolerable even in Rome by the Italians can avoid being put on the Index or remain without universal measures being taken by the Holy Office.' *'Das römisch Vikariat hat verfügt, daß die Bücher von Küng und noch zwei anderen Autoren in den römischen Buchhandlungen nicht verkauft warden dürfen. Hier also geht man immer noch mit diesen engen Methoden voran. Immerhin zeigt das doch wohl die Gefahr einer Indizierung oder die faktische Indizierung verbunden gewesen. Huete kann also doch ein Buch, das zwar hier in Rom selbt, von den Italienern, als untragbar empfunden wird, ohn Indizierung oder algemeine Maßnahmen vom Sacrum Officium her bleiben. Ich meine, das sei bedeutsam.'*

199. AS 2/1, 391–394: Ruffini had objected to the affirmation that says: *'Christum aedificasse Ecclesiam 'super Petrum et apostolos.' Haec Petri et apostolorum consociatio in fundamento Ecclesiae sine ullo discrimine, quae pluries invenitur in schemate, nullo testimonio biblico fulcitur et in errorem induci potest. [...] Quater in capite de quo agimus, Ecclesia vocatur 'sacramentum'. Quod nomen, ut omnes sciunt, iam dudum catechesi christianae septem sacramentis proprie dictis reservatur; idcirco ab indole Concilii pastorali omnini dissonum est,'*

200. See J Grootaers, 'Information religieuse', 218–21.

201. This is a problem also brought up in Fr Chenu's letter to Ancel on 3 January 1963; see page 52 n 1 in my Introduction here.

The Commission on the Laity, long after it began its work, had unanimously asked to designate lay experts to assist it. Cardinal Cento, the president, not daring to ask John XXIII directly, sent him a letter and a report. And got no response.

Fr Tucci one day at the audience that the director of *Civiltà* has every six months[202] (once with the Secretary of State, once with the Pope) brought up this question with the Pope. The Pope told him: 'I never received anything, I haven't been informed. Write me a report and send it to me through my secretary, Mgr Capovilla.'

Fr Tucci sent the report on paper without a heading and without a signature. And then nothing.

One day he had an audience with Tardini, and he saw on Tardini's desk the letter from Cento and his own report. Tardini scolded him vehemently. No laymen at the Council. That's the Pope's wish. Etc.

The same quarrel with Mgr Felici whom he met meanwhile. (He would be the secretary of the coming Council.)

So the question of laypeople at the Council was never raised {with the pope-tr.}[203]

[31 rº] *October 5*

I received a visit from Fr B Wiltgen, SVD, (American) who came to hire me for his information and press agency.[204] He told me how

---

202.In fact Fr Tucci's audiences were much more frequent than Fr Chenu thought.

203.See G Turbanti, 'I laici nella chiesa e nel mondo'; Tromp took note of the problem on 25 April 1961 during a meeting of the secretaries of the commissions with Felici: '*Hora 11* commissio Secretariorum *apud mons. Felici. […] 8) Dixerunt Cardinal Frings et Döpfner laicos nullius agere de suo collaboratione in Concilio. Res agitur in Austria (Cardinal Viennensis, et Nederlandiae et alibi). Papa haec in re manifestavit ideam suam Cardinalibus Germaniae et Exc.mo Felici: a) bonum est si laici interesse habeant pro futuro Concilio; orent, etc., etc.?; b) Sed Concilium est res Ecclesiae docentis non discentis; c) Laici non debent esse membra vel consultores commissionum. Multum magis justum esse rogare Moderatrices Magnorum Ordinum religiosarum, etc.; d) Laici possunt propagare sua vota, sed hoc faciant pro Episcopis; e) Possunt rogari pro voto: maxim. in Comm. pro laicis et Commissione pro stampa et spectaculis*' (DTrm 113). At its meeting of 23 November 1962 the Secretariat for Extraordinary Affairs had discussed the problem, taking note that if the 'heterodox' were admitted to conciliar work, one could also admit 'a small qualified representation' of lay Catholics; see Lai, *Il papa non eletto*, 354.

204.See Grootaers, *Information…*, 213; this American who visited Fr Chenu later the project for a secretariat for non–Christian religions got started, with himself as a liaison. [He had] a conversation with Mgr Thyssen [sic], SVD, a bishop in Indonesia, who spoke about it to the Chinese Cardinal Tien, SVD, who approved of the idea but who said, 'As a cardinal, I can't take an initiative on this, but you bishops should talk it up, and I will support you.' And that's what happened.[205]

During the conclave and the papal enthronement,[206] Fr W. had conversations with several cardinals: Liénart, Frings, Bea, etc. Also König who, as a specialist in the history of religions,[207] was able to get directly involved.

They asked Cardinal Tien to bring the question to Paul VI. He said: 'Let's do this the Chinese way; it would be difficult for me to do it directly. You, Fr Wiltgen, send me a report; then I will send it on to the Pope with a note from me.' That's what happened. (The detailed report included the strong approval of the cardinals.)

Tonight a reception given by the editor of Desclée de Brouwer to present J Guitton's book *L'Église et les Laïcs*.[208] I met M. Turowicz, president of the group Znak in Poland with whom I had an excellent conversation last year. While talking with him, I ventured to say that I find Cardinal Wyschinski [sic] hard, closed, and almost obsessed with persecution, something real for him. T[urowicz] answered me with wisdom and moderation. There is [31 vᵒ] of course an opposition between the government and the church, but we have to look for ways to coexist since neither one can boot the other out.

To point out the cardinal's situation he added: 'The cardinal said that Poland as a great Catholic nation used to have a first class nunciature, and he can't accept the fact that today it has only a consulate' (an allusion to the Secretary of State's proposal under John XXIII to put a 'consul' in socialist countries).[209]

---

published RM Wiltgen, *The Rhine Flows into the Tiber: The Unknown Council* (New York, 1967).

205. More exactly Antoine Thijssen, who was bishop of Larantuka.

206. This took place on 18 June 1963; about the transition of pontificates, see A Riccardi, *Il potere del papa da Pio XII a Giovanni Paolo II* (Rome–Bari, 1993).

207. See *Christus und die Religionen der Erde: Handbuch der Religionsgeschichte*, 3. vol, edited by F König (Vienna, 1951).

208. Caprile says nothing about this work of Guitton.

209. See A Riccardi, 'La Diplomatie pontificale en Europe orientale de la Révolution bolchevique à la coexistence pacifique (1917–1978)', in *Le Vatican et la politique*

Quaestitalia, July 1963:[210]

> Rome, July. Paul VI discussed at length with Cardinal Stefan Wyszynski the problem of resuming relations between the Church and State in Poland in order to address questions concerning the nomination of the respective consular or diplomatic representatives between the governments of Warsaw and the Holy See.
>
> The Pope said he was open to the possibility of sending a permanent observer {from the Holy See} to Poland. As to the formula to use for the Vatican's representation in Warsaw, we know that the Vatican has always been rather inclined to naming a consul. This idea, however, is hardly welcomed either by the government or by Cardinal Wyszynski. The cardinal thinks that Poland has always historically had a nuncio chosen from among the Vatican's best diplomats.
>
> If the present state of relations between Church and State in Poland does not permit naming a nuncio, Cardinal Wyszynski suggests as a transitional solution nominating an Apostolic Delegate accredited to the Polish episcopate. By contrast, the Polish government thinks that a nunciature should be opened without delay, beginning perhaps with a Pro–Nuncio so as to provide a certain political character to the new relations between Poland and the Vatican. Paul VI commissioned Cardinal Wyszynski to pursue the matter with the government so as to resolve, before opening diplomatic relations, the still enduring problems between Church and State, particularly with respect to the religious instruction of the young. Then, in order to arrive at the best formula for resuming diplomatic relations, the

européenne (Paris, 1994), 68–76.

210. Concerning this journal, see A Melloni, 'Lo spettatore influente' in *Il Vaticano II fra attese e celebrazione*; on the Polish attitude about this, see Ph Levillain, 'Les Épiscopats de l'Europe de l'Est à Vatican II', in *Documentation sur l'Europe centrale*, 11 (Louvain, 1973), 81–98.

Holy See is thinking of sending to Poland an apostolic
visitor who will discuss the matter directly with the
Polish authorities and with some representatives of the
local episcopate.'[211]

October 6

Had supper with Mgr Bazin, the Archbishop of Rangoon. With deep
feeling, he told Fr Biot and me how astonished he was by the first
session of the Council. He saw a church extracting itself from its routine
perspectives and becoming aware of the problems of the world.[212] He
was a bit scandalised and surprised at first to see the freedom with
which people spoke up—Maximos IV, for example—whereas he was
used to a docile passivity out of unconditional reverence for the Pope.
He can't wait to pass on this experience to all his people back home,
despite the hesitancy they will have in hearing it.

211.*Roma, 1uglio. Paolo VI ha discusso a lungo col cardinale Stefano Wiszynski i
problemi della ripresa dei contatti tra la Chiesa e lo Stato in Polonia, per giungere
alla regolamentazione di alcune questioni e successivamente alla nomina dei
respettivi rappresentanti consolari o diplomatici tra il governo di Varsavia e la
Santa Sede. Il Papa si è pronunciato favorevolmente sulla possibilità di inviare un
suo osservatore permante in Polonia. Per quanto riguarda la formula da dare alla
rappresentanza Vaticana a Varsavia, risulta che il Vaticano è tuttora orientato
verso la nomina di un console, ma che tale idea non è molto ben vista, né dal
governo, né dallo stesso cardinale Wiszynski. Il cardinale sostiene che la Polonia ha
avuto sempre nella sua storia un Nunzio, che era scelto tra i migliori diplomatici
vaticani. Nel caso che l'attuale stato delle relazioni tra la Chiesa e lo Stato in Polonia
non consigli la nomina di un Nunzio, il cardinale Wiszynski suggerisce in fase
transitoria la nomina di un Delegato Apostolica, che dovrebbe essere accreditato
presso lo stesso Episcopato polacco. Il governo polacco è invece del parere che si
dovrebbe procedere senz'altro all'apertura di un Nonziatura, retta inizialmente
magari da un Pronunzio, in modo da dare anche un certo livello politico ai nuovi
rapporti tra la Polonia et il Vaticano. Paolo VI ha incaricato il cardinale Wiszynski
di proseguire i contatti col governo, per risolvere, prima dell'inizio dei rapporti
diplomatici, i problemi ancora in sospeso tra la Chiesa e lo Stato, specialmente per
quanto riguarda il problema dell'insegnamento religioso ai giovani. Per definire
successivamente la formula più adatta alla ripresa delle relazioni diplomatiche la
Santa Sede si orienta verso l'invio in Polonia di un Visitatore Apostolico, il quale
sudierà la questione direttamente con le autorità polacche e con vari esponenti
dell'episcopato locale.'*

212.Mgr Bazin represented the Asian episcopacy at the 'interconference' which
Perrin describes in *Approches...*, 126.

[32 rº] *October 8*

Il Quotidiano for October 8, a Catholic magazine, summarises the debate on episcopal collegiality under this heading:

> Bringing up this truth [collegiality], said Cardinal Siri in his intervention, signifies: being in favor of unity and collaboration among the bishops and of promoting feelings of obedience among the faithful toward their pastors. The interventions have been made with the authority of the eight cardinals and the sixteen bishops {of the Commission} on this second chapter of the schema *De Ecclesia.*[213]

So nothing here about the ideas of the seven or eight cardinals who gave a completely different meaning to collegiality. As to Cardinal Siri's idea, surely more nuanced in his text, see how it looked to an ordinary listener.[214]

October 9

A visit from Fr Balducci, who is inviting me to take part in the presentation to the public of his recent book, *Cristianesimo e*

---

213. *'Rilevari questa verità, ha detto nel suo intervento il Cardinale Siri, significa: favorire la unità e la collaborazione tra i vescovi e promuovere tra i fideli sentimenti d'obbedienza ai propri pastori. Gli autorevoli interventi di otto porporati e di sedici presuli sul secondo cap. dello schema De Ecclesia.'*

214. See Semmelsroth in ST for 7 October 1963: 'Today in the aula of the Council Cardinal Ruffini, who had spoken in recent days against the collegiality of bishops, was repudiated by an impressive series of eight cardinals, by the Patriarch Maximos, and by several bishops. This began with Cardinal Siri, from whom one would hardly have expected it. He spoke a lot in favor of collegiality. And all the others, except for a Yugoslav who wasn't very clear, spoke in favor. This theme will therefore be maintained and possibly—one can hope—solidly anchored.' *'In der Konzilsaula wurde heute durch eine stattliche Reihe von acht Kardinäle, Patriarch Maximos und mehreren Bischöfen Kardinal Ruffini, der dieser Tage so gegen das Kollegium der Bischöfe gesprochen hatte, sehr desavouiert. Am Anfang stand Kardinal Siri, von dem man das kaum erwartet hatte. Er sprach sehr für die Kollegialität. Und alle anderen außereinem Jugoslawen mit unklaren Ausführung haben dafür gesprochen. Dieses Thema wird also doch wohl erhalten bleiben und höchstens zum Vorteil —so kann man doch hoffen—verankert warden.'*

Cristianità. He told me that he has been exiled from Florence for the past four years by a decision of the Holy Office and that he now lives in Rome, going to Florence only for brief trips.

Last March he got a phone call from the Holy Office saying: 'During the Council's session, did you meet with Fr Congar and Fr de Lubac?—Yes.—It would be better for you to stay away from them; they are dangerous persons.'[215]

[32 vº] *October 11*

With respect to the wily and shady tricks carried off in managing texts in the commissions, I am copying here a note written by M Martimort for the use of the French bishops about the liturgy.

> Both in the theological sub–commission and in the sub–commission on the sacraments and also in the plenary Liturgical Commission, we have always kept to the original formula: '*sacramentum quod communiter extrema unctio nuncupatur, deinceps unctio infirmorum vocabitur*' {the sacrament that is commonly called extreme unction will henceforth be known as anointing of the sick}; we thought the objections posed in the Aula by only two fathers, Cardinal Browne and Mgr Savoia Boudeiro, bishop of Palmes (Brazil), negligible. But at the moment for a final vote of the commission, the text was found to be changed without any discussion and perhaps without some of those voting having noticed: '*Extrema unctio, quae etiam unctio infirmorum vocatur*' {Extreme unction, which is also called anointing of the sick}. This is no longer the invitation to improve catechesis; we are far from the perspective proposed 50 years ago by Cardinal Mercier, far from the liturgical movement and far from the Eastern practice.
>
> (Then with regard to religious profession that, in the original text, can be made during Mass):

215.See E Balducci, *Il cerchio si chiude: Intervista autobiografica con L Martini* (Genoa, 1986), 75.

The last point seemed insufficient to several conciliar fathers who wanted a more forceful phrasing such as *'fiat'* [is made] or *'regulariter fiat'* {usually is made} (proposal of the Chilean episcopate). Our sub–commission on the sacraments [33 r°] pronounced itself in agreement with that. However without any discussion the definitive text that was voted on changes the perspective into an opposite meaning: *'Conficiatur ritus... ab iis qui professionem vel votorum renovationem intra missam peragunt assumendus'* {The rite may be done... by those who chose to make profession or renewal of vows within Mass}. Extravagances will continue where ceremonies are performed outside Mass, and the *ideal* of profession *intra missam* disappears. (With regard to reserved blessings): No remarks were made at the Council, no modification was proposed by our sub–commission *De sacramentis*. However the text put forward for the final vote was completely changed by introducing a single word: *'in favorem tantum episcoporum* vel ordinariorum', which destroys the whole meaning and goes against the wishes expressed by the great majority of the bishops before the Council, because erections of stations of the Cross, blessing of scapulars, and what else besides, can become the prerogative of Provincials. (*Études et documents*, General Secretariate of the French Episcopacy, Sept 2, 1963, n 19: 'What is the state of the schema *De sacra liturgia*?')

At the general assembly this morning, an intervention by the new auxiliary bishop of Bologna, very recently consecrated. Surely Cardinal Lercaro was not unhappy to put him in front of the Council. A brilliant, clear, open intervention. He charmed the listeners who applauded, even though Cardinal Lercaro had requested at the beginning of the session not to applaud. [33 v°] He rejected the positions of Ruffini and Siri that he characterised (what a put-down!) as *novatores* {innovators}.[216] From the peritis' tribune, Fr Kéramé observed Siri react with shock.

216.Luigi Bettazzi, auxiliary bishop of Bologna; his intervention at AS 2/2, 484–487 ('too quick a treatment' according to DCcl IV, 11 October 1963) brought up authors who supported the direct communication of universal jurisdiction to the bishops, and he concluded: *'hunc haud interruptum et cohaerentem processum historicum amplissime probare possem: nunc parco. Satis tamen sint ea quae per pauca nunc dicere potui ut confirmetur hanc doctrinam, quam defendimus, novatricem non esse, sed Sacram Scripturam et traditionem primitivam ac sequentem fideliter repetere, ita ut novatores dici possent qui contraria affirmarent.'* The intervention picked up on a note by G Alberigo and G Dossetti that Cardinal Lercaro had not held on to as a rough draft of the intervention; see DAna 12 October 1963: 'We were waiting for an intervention from Lercaro on collegiality that was supposed to develop the note of Pino [Alberigo], later enlarged and rewritten with ideas from Pippo [Dossetti] on Bolgeni. The speech was ready Wednesday night [9], but the cardinal was having a difficult time, following very unhappy events touching the liturgy schema [...]. Also Pippo asked Bettazzi to come to the Chiesa Nuova, and he agreed on the afternoon of Thursday [10] to make the speech the next day. On Friday [11] morning, Lercaro was the moderator, and the youngest bishop at the Council spoke for exactly 9 minutes. "*Juniori et italici*", he said, "are speaking in favor of collegiality". Unquestionably he won over the Council because, although the fathers first put down their papers, little by little the assembly began to pay great attention to him. At the end he was applauded— the only applause at this point during this session. This morning [Saturday 12] *L'Avvenire* appeared with a headline that was too triumphal ['Applause at the Council during the session for the youngest Italian bishop']; let's hope that the fathers who now get everything through the services of the Secretary of State (I believe Don Angelo [Dell'Acqua]), will interpret it only as a kind of parochialism – otherwise that could be annoying. Pippo is beginning to be a bit worried by the exaggeration of this success and he says, 'they will make us pay for it...'. *'Si prevedeva l'intervento di Lercaro sulla collegialità che doveva avvenire sull'appunto di Pino [Alberigo] che è poi allargamento e ulteriore elaborazione delle tesi di Pippo [Dossetti] su Bolgeni. Il discorso era pronto mercoledi sera [9], ma il cardinale stave attraversando un brutto momento a seguito delle abbastanza insoddisfacenti vicende dello schema liturgico [...]. Così Pippo aveva convocato a Chiesa Nuova Bettazzi che aveva accettato nel pomeriggio di giovedi [10] di intervenire il giorno dopo. Venerdi [11] mattina, moderator Lercaro, per ultimo ha parlato 9 minuti esatti il più giovane vescovo del concilio. 'Juniori et italici ha detto parlo a favore delle collegialità.' E indubbiamente ha conquistato il concilio perchè mentre i padre all'inizio già riponevano i loro fogli, a poco a poco si è fatta in assemblea una grande attenzione. E alla fine è stato applaudito: unico applauso fino ad ora di questa sessione. Stamattina [sabato 12] L'Avvenire è uscito con un titolo anche troppo esultante ['Applausi in concilio a scena aperta per il più giovane vescovo italiano'], speriamo che i padre, che ora lo ricevono tutti per disposizione della Segreteria di stato (credo don Angelo [Dell'Acqua]), lo interpretino solo come campanilismo, se no si potrebbero seccare. Pippo infatti è tornato [12] un pò preoccupato dall'eccesso del successo dicendo 'ce lo faranno pagare...'.*

Metropolitan Slipyj, set free several months ago, spoke for the first time. The announcement of his speech provoked several moments of warm interest. But his speech was very disappointing (papal triumphalism, refusal of collegiality, and a naïve glorification of the Ukrainians role in the past...) and in the end it got a chilly reception.[217]

A visit tonight from Fr Kéramé who invited me to dine tomorrow with the Patriarch Maximos. He is, as always, lively, straightforward, and charming. He told me that the French Jesuits, after being under the rule of a Belgian Jesuit 'visitator', said: 'He left us in the same condition that the Belgians left the Congo.'[218]

October 13

I had lunch next to Fr Pegon, SJ, who is going to preach the retreat for the young priests of La Salette. Among his anecdotes, he told me this story about Fr Lieber, SJ, one of the closest confidants of Pius XII! 'When Pius XII dies, Mother Pasqualina and I will have to pack our bags. Mother Pasqualina will have twenty–four hours. But me?...'

[34 r°] November 5

October 30 was a 'historic' day, the day of the vote on the five questions {touching collegiality}.

Dr Montisanti, coming from Don Dossetti, the secretary and confidant of Cardinal Lercaro (one of the four moderators—harassed by the integrists), told me that the moderators (three of them, not Agagagianian [sic]) went to give a report to Paul VI on the session. The Pope got up to greet them and said, 'Well, we won!'[219]

---

217. AS 2/2, 442–447.

218. The visitator of the French provinces in 1957–1958 had been Fr Étienne Plaquet, ironically known as 'slow speed' [*petite vitesse*]; he was from the South Belgian Province—that of Janssens [the Jesuit General]. He was the reason for sidelining Fr Lucien Fraisse, who was at the time the chaplain for the [elite] Lycée du Parc in Lyons. In 1949, before *Humani generis*, Fr Édouard Dhanis had visited the Jesuit scholastics and brought about—according to de Lubac—the troubles that Fourvière had in 1950.

219. *Vaincu!*, rather than *vaincus!* as in the manuscript. See Lercaro's letter for November 4 1963 in *Lettere dal concilio*, 200–201: 'The Holy Father, receiving us during the regular audience began in this way: 'Today [October 30] was a great

[34 v°] *November 12*

A visit from Fr Féret.[220] He told me yesterday that H Küng went to dine with him and the French bishops living on Viale Romania.[221] He had prepared a paper to give give to Maximos about the paralysis of the Council caused by the commissions, particularly Ottaviani's commission. In conversation they agreed to adjust and improve the paper. Fr Féret and Küng got together to do that. Küng took the new draft to Maximos who, that night, at 7 pm had an audience with the Pope.

The paper was given just like that directly to the Pope.

Further, I learned that Maximos had been very pleased with this audience—first, he himself, and then his bishops as well.[222]

[35 r°]

I've come to a standstill.[223]

---

day.' Chenu learned this news from a person who—if he is actually so named—wasn't particularly well known in the circle of Italian intellectuals and who is not really identifiable. See DAna 30 October 1963: 'Finally the vote on the 5 points arrived and it was approved by a very large majority; tonight we telephoned Dossetti in Rome. At the audience for the Moderators with the Pope, he greeted them saying, "We won".'

220. A Dominican of Saint–Jacques Priory in Paris: see his letters in the archives of Le Saulchoir.

221. The *Peregrinatio Romana* had published a listing of residences with the addresses and phone numbers of all the council fathers.

222. Actually the audience for the Melkite episcopate took place in a very special way, see SEdb November 11 1963: 'This evening at 5 pm our episcopate was received by the Holy Father. The Patriarch went in alone first and met with His Holiness for about fifteen minutes.'

223. The expression *'en panne'* is most often used for an automobile malfunction: the car won't start, it's out of petrol, it's had an accident, etc. Chenu is using the expression metaphorically here to mean, I think, that his interest (or energy) in keeping up this journal has come to an end (*translator's note*).

Index